PRAISE FOR MARK ORWOLL'S JUST ONE LITTLE HITCH

I've long enjoyed Mark Orwoll's travel writing, and was delighted to discover the genesis of his storytelling in this hilarious and revealing memoir. So fun!

—**Samantha Brown, PBS host,**
Samantha Brown's Places To Love

A charming romp of a travel memoir that weaves together the author's adventures on the road in Europe in the '70s with the history, oddities, and zeitgeist of the places he visits. Along the way, Orwoll picks up traveling companions, drops acid, and learns that travel will not just be a passing fancy for him. A terrific read for those with wandering souls (and soles).

—**Pauline Frommer, co-president of Frommer Media, host of** *The Frommer Travel Show*

Funny, touching, inspiring. An ode to the transformative power of hitting the road with no plan, and a marvelous look back at a forgotten golden age of travel, the 1970s.

—**Tony Perrottet, author of** *¡Cuba Libre!*

With a sprinkling of the humor of David Sedaris, the storytelling wit of Bill Bryson, and an ounce of Anthony Bourdain's snark, Mark Orwoll's *Just One Little Hitch* is a fun, hard-to-put-down voyage

through bohemian Europe at a time when mass travel was still in its infancy. This is a must-read for anyone who either wants to refresh memories of their own travels or to know what it was like to travel before the digital revolution.
—**David Farley, author of** *An Irreverent Curiosity*

Just One Little Hitch is the *Innocents Abroad* of hitchhiking memoirs. Mark Orwoll, escaping 1970s-beige California suburbs, uses his scholarship money to ditch school and finance a spontaneous overseas education, living in a fabled Parisian bookstore, adventuring through Morocco with a pair of Aussies, and thumbing rides from Pamplona to Stonehenge. His writing is so thoroughly entertaining, and his memories are so vivid, you'll be reminded both of the poignant uncertainty of your not-quite-adult years and the thrill of discovering that the world is a wondrous place.
—**Kim Brown Seely, author of** *Uncharted*

There once was a young man who, during the Bicentennial of American independence, ventured out to plumb his own. It was an era of high fuel prices but warm acceptance of international exchange, when a randy American backpacker could introduce himself to new lands with few resources other than eagerness, raw wit, and an outstretched thumb. His life was an open book waiting to be written, and this is it. Like many entertaining travel memoirs are, *Hitch* is a carnival of misadventures that, in a comic accumulation, actually point the way to the clarity of self-discovery. It's the story of how the passing connections we have when we travel can often feel inconsequential at the time, but can still shape us for life. Orwoll's affection for the simple pleasures of travel shines, and his knack for finely observed cultural detail is superseded only perhaps by his uncanny ability to recall the bygone prices of cheap beer. His shoestring odyssey down the road to his destiny makes for a breezy chronicle of many pints, late nights, and some indispensable advice about camels.

—Jason Cochran, author of *Here Lies America*, editor-in-chief of Frommers.com

In 1976, hippies still roamed the earth via thumb. Luckily, this veteran travel writer lived it and nails it by resuscitating the Golden Age of globetrotting-backpacker travel before the social-media–driven look-at-me tourist apocalypse.

—Bruce Northam, author of *The Directions to Happiness*

A raucous road trip through scruffy, bohemian 1970s Paris, London, Marrakech, and beyond, Mark Orwoll's coming-of-age travelogue is written with warm nostalgia for life's misadventures, wrong turns, and calamities. Pure fun!

—Luke Barr, author of *Provence, 1970* and *Ritz & Escoffier*

Mark Orwoll's rollicking account of his travels brings vividly to life a time when the highways of Europe brimmed with youthful foreign hitchhikers blessed with nonchalant confidence, just enough money, and a willingness to try anything once. In describing the informal education of a young American on and off the road, *Just One Little Hitch* revels in the goodwill, kindness, and humor he found from Wales to Morocco—except among camels, that is.

—Mark Abley, author of *Strange Bewildering Time: Istanbul to Kathmandu in the Last Year of the Hippie Trail*

My train was called the Paris Express, possibly the coolest name for any rolling stock that ever chugged out of any station on earth. This line leapt out at me soon after I started Mark Orwoll's *Just One Little Hitch*. It's indicative of the charm, detail, and quirkiness of this fascinating memoir. We are regaled with the tale of how a curious young man evolves into an all-seeing traveler. Orwoll shares his naïveté with us. He shares his discoveries with us. He shares his mistakes. And he invites us to ride along with him. He patches together a parade of fascinating, shocking, side-splitting, surprising, odd, humiliating, and eye-opening anecdotes, and fashions them into a travelogue that is somehow both innocent and sophisticated at the same time. It's a super journey.

—**Geoffrey Weill, author of**
All Abroad: A Memoir of Travel and Obsession

Also by Mark Orwoll

Cross Purposes
John Wayne Speaks
Teach Yourself e-Travel Today

Just One Little Hitch

Curious Companions, Debatable Choices, and
Life-Changing Revelations on the
Hitchhikers' Road Through Europe and Morocco

Mark Orwoll

PRESS

PLEASANT VILLAIN PRESS

PVL NY USA

First published in the United States by Pleasant Villain Press.

JUST ONE LITTLE HITCH. Copyright © 2024 by Mark Orwoll
All rights reserved. Printed in the United States of America.

www.markorwoll.com

ISBN 979-8-9887942-2-6

First edition: 2024

10 9 8 7 6 5 4 3 2 1

FOR CAITLIN, GILLIAN, AND RORY

Fearless. Adventurous. Pretty good at Jeopardy

Just One Little Hitch

Contents

Author's Note

"I too was young once." Those were the plaintive words of a middle-aged hotel desk clerk on the overnight shift in Madrid who looked at me wistfully as I escorted two young Welsh women to our shared guestroom.

Now I'm older than that desk clerk was at the time. And this book is my way of saying, "I too was young once."

Just One Little Hitch is a work of creative nonfiction based on a detailed journal that I kept during those weeks and months abroad almost fifty years ago. The names of some characters have been changed for reasons of privacy. Also, so they won't track me down and beat me up.

Mark Orwoll
Pleasantville, New York

Introduction:

An Idiot Abroad

I was hitchhiking the other day and a hearse stopped. I said, "No thanks, I'm not going that far."
—Steven Wright

I grew up halfway between Hollywood and Disneyland.

If you wanted a safe, attractive, postwar suburb—one with handsome ranch homes, parks and playgrounds, good schools, and a modern library with after-school programs—La Mirada was just the place.

I hated it.

The years have softened my feelings, as years tend to do, and I would come to love it. But at the age of twenty-two, I wanted nothing more than to leave. Stultifying. Staid. Stifling. Choose your sibilant adjective.

The fact that I was at a personal crossroads exacerbated my feelings. You've heard of the five-year plan for college? Ha! The way I was heading, that would have been a shortcut. I had already spent a year and a half at Cerritos J.C., the nearby community college, followed by a year at the College of Marin north of San Francisco, where I'd earned an associate's degree. Then I enrolled as a junior in the Creative Writing program at San Diego State. The curriculum was strong, but I had absolutely no idea where it would lead or how to make a living with such a diploma.

"Will write short stories for food."

When I received a small scholarship to pay for the spring semester in 1976, I asked for a temporary academic leave, which the registrar granted—a little too willingly, come to think of it. I'd decided to spend the next several months in Europe, funded by the scholarship money.

The reason for the choice of destination had something to do with a post-WWII travel book I owned, *Europe: A Journey with Pictures* (which still occupies a cherished space on my bookshelf after fifty years). Published so soon after the war, the black-and-white photos of France, Germany, and England were artfully staged to avoid the remaining piles of rubble and half-destroyed houses from the conflict's bombs and artillery fire. Its chief aim, though, was to celebrate the continent's cultural and architectural wonders.

It worked. What's the travel equivalent of blue balls? Yeah, I'm not sure either, but I *ached* to be in Europe with an epididymal hypertensive arousal that would not be denied. "Not tonight, Mark," was not going to put me off this time, Europe.

In my mind, Europe was a mixture of Brothers Grimm cottages, imposing stone castles, Sherlock Holmes, American expatriates at Paris cafés, hot chocolate on the snowy decks of Swiss ski chalets, and, possibly, bosomy Bavarian barmaids proffering liters of strong Swabian beer on a silver tray. A pretty picture. And yes, feel free to write in the margins, "What an idiot" as you see fit. I probably would if I were you.

At last, only weeks before leaving, I buckled down and boned up on my Baedeker, prepped my clothing and gear, and made potential itineraries with enough latitude for kismet to sprinkle stardust in my path and guide me where it might. I already had a sturdy backpack, sleeping bag, and pup tent for the nights I would camp to save money on hostels and one-star hotels. I still had to get my International Youth Hostel Association identification card, without which I couldn't stay in the two-dollar-a-night bunkhouses listed in my IYHA guidebook. I had yet to buy my air ticket, which turned out to be for a charter flight on some long-forgotten and little-lamented airline called Condor, no changes allowed. I bit the bullet and paid the $450 fare. I spent time with my on-and-off girlfriend to reassure her that I would be faithful and would come back to her and everything would be all right and, dammit, no bosomy Bavarian barmaids could ever come between us. No matter how hard they tried.

Nothing left to do now but go.

1

The Stumbling

Arrival

*Hey, nice tie! - The first of many who take pity on me -
What's a hostel? - Superior scissors - Bring out the thumb
- Udo - Unhorsed by schnapps - Excuse me, have you seen
my jacket? - First lesson learned*

A jerk. I looked like a freaking jerk.

Back then I thought you were supposed to dress up
for an airplane flight. My Mom and my Grandma both
asked the same question at different times: "What are you
wearing on the airplane?" Some hippie I was, engaging in
couture conversations with Moms and Nana.

In those days, flying was considered a privilege, a luxury acknowledged by dressing up. Women would buy a
new outfit "for the plane ride." Men wore suits. Unfortunately for fashion history and, in retrospect, my sense of
self-worth, I chose to wear a white linen tie from the discount rack at J.J. Newberry that was about seven inches
wide and poorly knotted around the neck of a casual plaid
shirt. That tie was so wide it probably could have flown

me to Europe without the plane. With my long bushy hair, attempted mustache, and that goddam tie, I was a bloody style icon. Watch out, Europe! Here I come.

But nobody seemed to care one way or the other when I landed in Frankfurt fifteen hours later. And honestly, why would they? Germany was a country that had been defeated in a world war just thirty years earlier, then carved into East and West, one Communist, one democratic. Unemployment and inflation were ravaging the economy in the mid-Seventies. The Baader-Meinhof Gang, a terrorist group, blithely assassinated, kidnapped, bombed, and possibly shoplifted their way from Cologne to Munich in their fight against "global capitalism." To top it off, Frankfurt was the gangster capital of Western Europe.

The Germans had bigger fish to fry than the egregious width of my blazing-white tie.

I figured out how to take a bus from the airport to the city center, where a Filipino backpacker told me to go to the main train station. There, he said, I could get transportation to wherever I wanted.

"Whenever you get to a new city," he advised, "always go to the train station first. They usually have a tourist office there. You can get brochures, maps, advice about the nearest hostels, and recommendations of cheap things to do."

Once at the tourist office, I plucked a map of Frankfurt and a bus schedule from the racks of complimentary brochures. Both were in German, of course, so I couldn't understand anything. Not that that stopped me from looking at them, probably upside down, and nodding sagely in case anyone was watching.

Despite any bravado I might have shown when I kissed my weeping mother goodbye at LAX, I was anxious about being alone in a big new city, unsure of exactly where I was going or how to get there. I stood on the street in front of the train station, looking like a dope. A passing young American woman who seemed to know the ropes, able to spot a dysfunctional landsman in distress, took pity on me. She introduced herself, literally took me by the hand, and led me away from the train station. We walked a short distance to a set of tracks on a street called Am Hauptbahnhof. Soon the right tram came along that would take me to the youth hostel where I had hoped to stay for a few nights.

"Just get off at the Konstablerwache stop," she said, soothingly. "You'll be fine."

"The Gonchachavodka stop," I said as I boarded, my confidence returning. "Got it. Thanks."

I waved to her through the window and saw that she was frantically shaking her head and saying something. Oh well. On to the hostel.

She and the Filipino hitchhiker were the first in a long line of Florence and Frank Nightingales who would come to my rescue over the next several months.

THE EUROPEAN YOUTH-hostel movement began in Germany before World War I. The system was designed to encourage young Germans to get outdoors and learn self-reliance by providing them with safe, inexpensive bunks, communal kitchens to cook their dinners, chaperoned social settings to meet other young people, and handy tips on how to invade and conquer vast swaths of Eastern Europe. One imagines hordes of apple-cheeked, blond *Jugend* in lederhosen hiking vigorously up the Bavarian Alps and boldly singing the Horst-Wessel-Lied in chorus as they march into the hostel. Health! Camaraderie! The Sudetenland! You think I'm joking, but the moment the Nazis finished burning the Reichstag and adjusting the seat cushions on their shiny new dictatorship in 1933, they merged the German Youth Hostel Association with the Hitler Youth.

The movement (hostels, not Nazism) spread to England in the 1920s and '30s. The sleeping accommodations were usually bunkhouse-style with communal bathrooms, one for the men and one for the women. Youths (twenty-five was often the cut-off age) could stay for a maximum of three nights, and while in residence were obliged to perform basic chores, such as sweeping the floor, emptying garbage, and washing dishes, at the direction of a hostel's "warden."

To stay at the hostels, one had to be a member of a recognized international hostel association. The bar for acceptance was low, the two main criteria being if you were breathing and could pay the ten-dollar fee—and I'm not sure about the breathing part. The association issued members a laminated photo I.D. card that was sadistically designed to be too large to fit conveniently into normal pants or shirt pockets. This was to be handed to the warden on arrival, along with the overnight fee. Guests retrieved their I.D. cards on departure, assuming they had completed their assigned chores.

My room in the Frankfurt hostel held four bunk beds. Each had a mattress but no sheets or pillows, which were the responsibility of the hostelers themselves. I planned to use my sleeping bag on the mattress and roll up my Levi's in a ball for a pillow. I still have a callus on my lower left ear as a memento.

I slept soundly that first night. Breakfast the next morning in the hostel's common room was just ersatz coffee and some buttered rolls, included in the rate. At my table were Peta, a quiet girl from Australia, and Mahboob, a Pakistani traveling scissors salesman who seemed amused that I smiled every time I said his name. Mahboob was excited to be in Germany, which he considered a ripe market for his company's scissors.

"You see, Mark," he explained, in precise English, "the Germans appreciate fine quality like no one else. No one! And my company's scissors are superior, I tell you. Superior!"

"They're very good, actually," said Peta. "Mahboob showed me some. I would buy a pair if I could find them in Perth. I like the cuticle scissors, Mahboob."

Mahboob slammed the table with his open palm and made an expression of frustration and self-loathing.

"We have not yet been able to crack the Australian market," he said, almost woefully, as if it was a matter of no small personal disgrace. "But we shall." He turned to me, defiantly. "We shall, Mark. Count on it."

He waited for my response.

"I guess if you do well in Germany," I said, having no clue, "the Australians couldn't help but notice. Success breeds success. Building blocks, Mahboob. First Germany, then the world. I think Himmler said that."

Mahboob brought out a notepad from the breast pocket of his white short-sleeve business shirt and began writing.

"This is very wise, Mark," he said, placing his tongue in the corner of his mouth as he scribbled. "Success breeds success. That's superior logic, Mark. Superior."

DESPITE THE NOVELTY of everything (Hey look, that's a German supermarket! Wow, there's a German plumbing and heating truck!), Frankfurt lost my interest after a few days. I rolled up my bedding, strapped on my backpack, and walked toward the nearest autobahn entrance, where I planned to hitchhike. At the onramp, I stuck out my thumb and hoped for a ride. I had hitchhiked up and down the California coast, but this was Europe; I had no idea what to expect. Almost immediately a Hungarian man stopped for me, apparently for the express purpose of confiding that he had flown planes for the American CIA.

"I thought if you worked for the CIA you weren't supposed to talk about it," I replied as we sped down the expressway.

That pretty much killed the conversation, and I decided not to be so harsh with the next person who bared his life story. The Hungarian, after all, had been kind enough to stop for me.

Two more rides followed from drivers who spoke only German. In the States, I'd been assured by numerous know-it-alls that I shouldn't worry about language. "Everyone speaks English," they said. Not true. One of the drivers sneezed, I said *Gesundheit,* and he laughed, amused by my use of the German word. That was the extent of our conversation. The next driver, trying to be helpful, pointed at things along the road and told me their German names.

"Die Kuh. Die Scheune. Das Flugzeug."
The cow. The barn. The airplane.

I doubted I would ever need any of those words, but I wanted to be polite. I smiled and repeated everything he said, trying my darnedest to sound enthusiastic. He wanted to be helpful. And I've always been a people-pleaser. It went on that way for half an hour before he dropped me off. *Gott sei Dank,* I thought.

I found myself at an onramp to the No. 66 autobahn for about two hours, waiting patiently for a ride while being pelted by a steady, heavy rain when a young lieutenant in the German army stopped for me. The idea of being picked up by a German army lieutenant was about as repulsive as if Hermann Göring had pulled over in his swastika-flagged staff car and said, "Hey man, how far ya going?"

But Udo Kortz seemed so...*normal.* He was a good-looking young man, perhaps twenty-two years old, about my age. His English was excellent. When he learned that I was on my first visit to his country, he decided to take me on a more scenic route, away from the autobahn. Soon we were driving down a two-lane country road paralleling the Rhine. Udo pointed out hilltop castle after hilltop castle. He invited me to his house to meet his roommate and fellow soldier, Klaus. The three of us talked for several hours, drinking vodka and schnapps and listening to the rainstorm. And I managed not to make a single Nazi joke. My self-restraint was award-worthy.

"When a man is twenty and not a Communist," said Udo, completely out of the thin air, carefully pouring three more shots of schnapps, "he has no heart. When a man is fifty and *still* a Communist, he has no intelligence."

Klaus and Udo were a jovial pair and insisted on driving me to my next youth hostel, which was housed in the foreboding Festung Ehrenbreitstein, a former nineteenth-century Prussian fortress high above the lively town of Koblenz at the confluence of the Rhine and Mosel rivers. Merely gazing at the stern crestline castle caused lightning to shimmer and thunder to rumble as a foreshadow of disaster. Its joyless bare-dirt courtyard looked like the sort of place where SS *Sturmbannführers* with Heidelberg dueling scars dragged deserters and spies for pistol-to-the-head executions.

Willkommen, campers!

After I reluctantly checked in and dropped off my things, Udo, Klaus, and I went to dinner at El Toro Pizzeria, whose clash-of-cultures name puzzles me to this day. Only after our meal, when the two jolly soldiers had dropped me off at Count Dracula's hostel and we'd said our goodbyes, did I realize I must have left my jacket at the restaurant.

I awoke in the morning with a slight schnapps

hangover, but I didn't have time to waste. The most important thing on my agenda was to find my missing jacket. Winter hadn't gone completely away; the weather was still chilly. I was traveling light, and because I had limited funds, I wasn't in a position to lose and replace any of the clothes I'd brought with me. El Toro Pizzeria, when I got there, hadn't yet opened, but an early-arriving waiter answered my insistent knocking and let me in. I headed straight to our table from the previous evening. No jacket. The waiter searched the closet, the backroom, the kitchen. No jacket anywhere.

I had no option but to carry on. *Maybe I left it in Udo's car,* I thought. That would be fine, because the previous night I had promised Udo that I would meet him for lunch that day at twelve-thirty. Our meeting point was the Deutsches Eck, an arrowhead-shaped plaza that juts dramatically into the Rhine where it joins with the Mosel. I waited and waited, looked at the tourists and local strollers, and wondered if I'd gotten the time wrong. Udo never showed up. But as good Cold War spies did, we'd planned a fallback meeting several weeks later, beneath the Arc de Triomphe in Paris, where Udo had planned a getaway. Meantime, I would have to do my best to get by without any protection against the early-spring cold. I didn't look forward to it.

At least I'd learned my first lesson on the road: Traveling light can be a virtue, but those who travel light may have more to lose than those who carry a lot.

2

A Magnet to
Dogs and Children

Sexier in Europe - Language problem solved - The fine art of dining without money - The U.S. Air Force supplies me with hash - Stalked by the Three Stooges

K oblenz was an extraordinarily beautiful small city, especially the *Aldstadt*, or old town. And the young women of Koblenz, *mein Gott!* They looked and acted so much more sophisticated, better dressed, more beautiful, and sexier than the girls back in La Mirada. They were chic. Cosmopolitan. Stunning to look at. And those plump red cheeks.... I must have fallen in love twelve times strolling around the Deutsches Eck.

By the end of my first full day in Koblenz, I felt as if I'd walked twenty miles. Unfortunately, the skimpy blue sneakers I wore did little to provide foot support. How a man planning a long trip during which he would be standing for hours and walking vast distances could have given so little thought to appropriate footwear is beyond me.

With each day, I grew more comfortable with my lack of German. Somehow, I was getting by. Thanks to my helpful, pocket-size idioticon, combined with some pidgin, me-Tarzan-you-Jane English and ridiculous mime gestures, I made myself understood. God bless the Germans.

A greater concern than language, though, was more existential: eating. Budgeting for meals was and would continue to be a constant worry. I quickly learned which foods were cheap and filling, whether in Germany (a wurst was always a safe bet for inexpensive sustenance) or, later, France (croque monsieur), Spain (*bocadillo de jamon*), England (cheese toastie), Morocco (couscous), and beyond. On that first full day in Koblenz, after missing connections with Udo, I ate bratwurst and pommes frites (oddly, the Germans had adopted the Gallic phrase for French fries) for both lunch *and* dinner.

I LEFT KOBLENZ without a jacket, though I still hoped Udo might have it in his car and would bring it with him when we rendezvoused in Paris. But the day was sunny, with a gas-fire blue sky and a high temperature of 65 degrees F., so for the moment I was fine.

Two young American Air Force technicians, Carl and Andy, pulled over for me, somehow sensing I was a fellow Yank. Not sure how. It may have been the upside-down American-flag T-shirt I wore. They had some Turkish green hash and Lebanese blonde and were more than generous in smoking it, even giving me some to take with me on the road. We got along so well that they invited me to stay at their off-base apartment in Bitburg. I told them I might accept their offer in a few days, but first I was eager to see nearby Trier and its well-preserved Roman ruins.

I'd never seen Roman ruins. I'd never seen *any* ruins,

for that matter, unless you count Mrs. Trine, my elderly second-grade teacher. Ruins were one of the main reasons I had come to Europe. I wanted *old*. I wanted to mount the ramparts of foreboding castles, meander along medieval streets lined with crumbling, overhung Tudor houses, scour ancient battlefields to find a dented war helmet somehow overlooked by the professional shovel-bums, and dine before a roaring fire in a countryside brasserie that had once fed Napoleon's soldiers (as long as croque monsieurs were on the menu)—the older, the better. You couldn't get much older than Roman ruins. At least, not in Germany.

THREE BOYS, TEN or twelve years old, shadowed me from a block away. We were in the riverside town of Cochem, which was as far as I'd traveled that day before the rides petered out. They had a mangy dog attached to them, a nothing, short-haired, black-and-brown mutt of dubious parentage. I wasn't surprised the kids were following me; children find me irresistible. I am utterly fascinating to anyone under the age of twelve. Babies in their mothers' arms stare at me in wonder in line at the bank; strange toddlers in department stores don't think twice about hugging my leg to maintain their balance; elementary-school kids on the street have even asked me if I was a teacher and could help them with a math problem. So I wasn't surprised in Cochem's old town to see that I had a tail. I decided to approach the boys directly and make their day.

"I'm Mark," I said after turning around abruptly and marching up to them. "I'm from the USA. What are your names?"

The dog hid behind the boys and, like Pete the Pup in an Our Gang comedy, peeked out at me from behind their knees. Jürgen, Martin, and Andreas, though, weren't frightened by me. They disclaimed any knowledge of the dog's name or ownership. They called the stray a *streu-nende hunde*. I made the mistake of giving the mongrel a small slice of prepackaged pepperoni from my day pack, which is seemingly how you adopt a rescue dog in Germany, because it wouldn't leave my side after that. All three boys knew some rudimentary English. (How many American fifth-graders have an introductory knowledge of German?) They seemed like good boys, too—a little rambunctious like boys should be, but polite and genuinely curious about the stranger in their midst. Where did I live, they asked? Where was my wife? What was my profession? I felt I needed to be honest with them.

"I live in Hollywood," I said. "My wife is an actress, busy starring in a new movie. I am a famous film director. Now, let's walk around town," I said. "I'm also a tourist."

I wanted them to think well of Americans, so I taught them to say *motherfucker* and *son of a bitch* with just the right amount of attitude. They in turn taught me to put my thumb between my index and middle fingers to indicate fornication and to say *leck mich am Arsch* (kiss my ass) and *scheisse* (shit). Their rudimentary English often lapsed into straight German, so I couldn't understand everything they said, but fully got it when they purposely walked me past the local whorehouse, where they stopped, giggled, pointed, and put their thumbs between their index and middle fingers.

I taught them how to play tic-tac-toe. I was stunned to learn they had never even *heard* of it. I'd simply assumed that such a basic game was known in virtually every country, every culture, so common was it in America. I like to think that I spawned a tic-tac-toe cult in Germany that continues to flourish to this day, one whose motto is "*Leck mich am Arsch*" and whose mascot is a mangy *streunende hunde*.

At a lively *bierhalle* that night, after checking into the

hostel, I ordered a dunkel lager with my budget-conscious supper of schnitzel, salad, and pommes frites. The place was jammed with young people, everyone singing and shouting and girls smiling as they passed by my table. No bosomy barmaids, perhaps, but my kind of place nonetheless. When I came outside, the dog was there and followed me back to the hostel, where I told it to get lost.

I FIGURED I'D spend a few days in Cochem, which I'd already grown to like. When I awoke the next morning, I decided to hike up to the old castle, the Reichsburg, and wander through the surrounding hills and vineyards overlooking the river. But first, I needed to do some carboloading with a chunk of good German bread.

Breakfast, included in the hostel rate, comprised two *brötchen*, margarine, marmalade, and a half-liter of ersatz coffee. The meal was similar to what I'd been served in Frankfurt and Koblenz, and was routine at Germany's hostels. The bare-bones meal was as German as it could be. When the Allies blockaded German ports in both world wars, food, and coffee in particular, was often hard to come by. To drink with their pathetic morning meals, the crafty Germans made a pseudo-coffee from roasted chicory roots, malt, barley, acorns, dust bunnies, and possibly mouse poop. The result was a hot beverage that had no caffeine and a rank taste. But ersatz had a downside too: It left you with bad breath. Thirty years after the war's end, the Germans still hadn't given up the devil's brew. Real coffee was viewed as a luxury reserved for Nazi *gauleiters* and munitions magnates, and certainly not in keeping with the youth-hostel ideal of bare-subsistence living. Thus, ersatz coffee was on the morning menu at nearly every German hostel.

That evening, after a day of hiking with the mangy *streunende hunde,* I returned to the same festive *bierhalle*

I'd stopped at the night before, and even got a nod or two of recognition from some of the other young people there. I ordered bratwurst and French fries for my supper, drank only one beer, and managed to save five Deutschmarks, or about two dollars, from my budgeted dinner allowance. In a few days, I would "tramp," as the Germans referred to hitchhiking, to the city of Trier and see what awaited.

What I found would prove to be the best, and the worst, of Americans in Europe.

3

Sort of Homeless in Paris

Trier - Tom Starr - Frisbee - Basically, Fresno in Germany - Paris, what the hell? - Too late for the hostel - Midnight picnic at Notre-Dame - How to hobo in the Latin Quarter

When the Romans invaded in 15 B.C. the Germans considered them uncouth arrivistes. Trier had already been inhabited for thirteen hundred years. That didn't stop the conquerors from making the city their own. They built a twenty-five-thousand-seat amphitheater, a four-mile-long city wall, temples, baths, palaces, massive city gates, and other evidence of hard-charging, in-your-face cultural imperialism. Emperor Constantine authorized the building of a cathedral, now the oldest Christian church in Germany, in 326. All that Roman activity set a precedent. Everyone in charge of Trier from then on felt compelled to leave *something* behind as an architectural legacy, if only to save face, resulting in grand market squares, statues, imposing civic structures, monasteries, and medieval mansions. Trier, Germany's oldest city, became an outdoor archaeological museum.

In the hostel at Trier, I met Tom Starr, a native Minnesotan who was then teaching English to Germans in West Berlin. He had ridden his motorcycle to Trier from East Germany, tense as a rabbit hiding from a hawk.

"You have to stick to the main highway the whole way," he said, not particularly happy with the memories. "If you get off the highway, the Stasi will grab you, confiscate everything you own, throw you in Berlin-Hohenschönhausen, and that's it, man. Your family'll never hear from you again."

The handsome, long-haired Starr and I hit it off right away, despite his being four or five years older than I. We roamed Trier together over several days. He was on holiday, and, like me, was in that city for the first time, so every turn at every corner brought another discovery to both of us. At the St. Paulin Church, we marveled at the ceiling fresco that was as beautiful as anything painted by Michelangelo, and the intricately carved altar of gold, forty feet high and wider even than that. We smoked most of the hash my Air Force friends had given me in between stops at the Roman amphitheater and the Kaiserthermen baths. We bought cheese, salami, liverwurst, a loaf of bread, and some beer, and ate and drank in a park called Palastgarten. Only after we finished our al fresco lunch did we find out that the park had once been the garden of the ornate sixteenth-century Electoral Palace and was now an afternoon hangout for the town's hippies.

Being Americans, Tom and I had grown up playing Frisbee, that most American of sports. So when one of those flying discs appeared among the crowd of young people, our eyes went wide and we joined in. Without wanting to sound like a braggart, and realizing that our average skills at Frisbee only *seemed* Olympian in comparison to the German newbies, we blew their minds. We caught the Frisbee behind our backs, on our fingertips, while leaping into the air, between our legs, and running full speed across the open field. Then we would whip the disc twenty-five yards across the grass at an angle that caused the Frisbee to fly right back into the hands of the thrower.

I *liked* being an American in Europe, and not just because of our nation's utter dominance on the world's Frisbee fields. I enjoyed people like Tom, who had the courage and ambition to leave everything behind, go to a foreign country, buy a cool motorcycle, and convince the local people that they should pay him to learn how to talk like he did. I admired Carl and Andy—not just for their choices in hash but because they had decided to serve their country, get paid for it, and live in distant lands on someone else's dime. A different sort of ambition from that of Tom Starr, true, but still...

Tom barreled back to Berlin on his motorcycle after a few days, his brief holiday having come to an end, but not before extending an invitation for me to visit.

I decided to set out for Bitburg AFB, about twenty miles north of Trier, to finally see my new friends Carl and Andy again. I left the hostel around nine a.m. and got a single ride to the base. (Hitchhikers, unlike airline passengers, rarely traveled nonstop, so I was lucky.) The driver dropped me off in front of the barracks, and I began walking until I got directions to the shopping area of the massive complex. I tried calling the number that Carl had given me, but no one answered the ring. I strolled around the uninteresting streets and buildings, cashed a travelers cheque at the bank, and was appalled at the Fords and Chevys and the Okie ladies complaining about sore feet and little kids screaming about candy. Shortly, I'd had enough. I had come to Europe to get away from all that.

And who in their right mind ships a Chevy Nova to the land of Mercedes-Benz?!

Forgoing a follow-up call to the boys, I made my way to the transportation center near the base after failing for thirty minutes to thumb a ride. There I caught the slowest bus that ever was. I ended up back in Trier, hoofed it across town to the *Hauptbahnhof,* and bought a one-way train ticket to Paris for sixteen dollars. I reluctantly did some math in my head and calculated that the train fare was approximately equal to the cost of a week's lodging at a hostel. While waiting for the departure, I bought two loaves of bread, a sausage, and a bottle of Mosel wine for the five-hour ride.

My train was called the *Paris Express,* possibly the coolest name for any rolling stock that ever chugged out of any station on earth. The conductor confirmed that we would arrive in Paris at about ten-thirty that night. He failed to mention that he was referring to German time. We pulled into the Gare de l'Est at eleven-thirty p.m., long after most shops and restaurants had closed for the night. I had planned to go to a youth hostel not far from the station, but according to the guide, it closed at eleven-thirty, and I couldn't have gotten there in time.

Don't ask me how it happened. I've examined this in the years since, without luck. Normally, a country to the west, like France, would have an earlier time zone than a country to the east, like Germany. But mix it up with WWII, the Vichy government, differences in daylight saving time, Adenauer and De Gaulle, and, well, hell, I got the time wrong somehow. I'll just blame it on Marshal Pétain and leave it at that.

The late arrival meant an unplanned stay at a hotel— probably an expensive hotel. A one- or two-star hotel at that time could indeed be had for less than five dollars a night, even in Paris, but my budget was based on spending just two or three dollars a night at a youth hostel.

Now I was in a fix. I couldn't research any cheap hotels, since the time was near midnight and the tourist office would be closed. I was tired and irritable. My
guidebook suggested that a newly arrived visitor would
do well to take the Metro to the area around Saint-Ger-
main-des-Prés or Place Saint-Michel and just look around
for a hotel. Randomly wander. Midnight had come and
gone by the time I finally found my way to that Left Bank
neighborhood. I went to more than a dozen hotels listed
in the guidebook without entering a single one: They all
had signs out front that said *Complet*. Only then did I remember that we were in the initial weeks leading up to
Easter vacation for people from throughout Europe. Silly
me. Udo Kortz had warned me that Paris would be
swarming with Germans for two or three weeks on either
side of the holiday.

The Left Bank, thanks to its colleges, restaurants, and
bars, was full of students having fun into the early morning hours; throngs of people were still milling about the
avenues and cobbled lanes of the ancient quarter when I
staggered out of the subway. I searched the guidebook for
another likely hotel, then moved on to the next address,
only to be disappointed again. Not long after that, the
Metro stations closed, and I estimated (I had no wristwatch) that it must be around one-thirty a.m.

Suddenly, all the people were gone. The boîtes, bistros,
brasseries, and beer joints went dark. I was completely
askew as to directions and desperate to lie down and
sleep. Then I turned a corner to confront a sight I will
never forget.

Cathédral Notre-Dame.

I almost couldn't believe I was looking at it, the most
famous church in the Western world, a building whose
towers had loomed over kings and revolutions, wars and

emperors, and at least one hunchback bell-ringer. The pages of history had played out on its front steps. And there it was! I began to giggle, then I laughed so hard I started to shake. *God damn!* Notre-Dame Cathedral! The majestic façade, the starry sky beyond the crowning spire, and the emotions that swelled up in me were exactly as I had known they would be. Everything was...*perfect.* Just right, exactly so.

I crossed the river to the island on which it stood and sat on some steps directly facing the church. I was the only waking person in sight, just me and Notre-Dame. From my rucksack, I retrieved what remained of the bread and wine that I'd purchased in Trier and had a picnic supper. True, the Metro was closed and I was stranded—but I was stranded *in Paris.* And yes, the air was cold, nearly freezing. The wind, though, was light, and I was sheltered by the buildings surrounding the plaza. I had nowhere to go—but I wanted to go nowhere more than exactly where I was. I was almost painfully happy. I didn't give a damn about my situation.

Except that the time was past two in the morning, and I was ready to nod off.

I would have to find *somewhere* to sleep. But where? I drained the rest of the Mosel wine and began again to search for a place to crash. Anywhere. I sure as hell didn't know where.

Back on the Left Bank, still in sight of the cathedral towers, I came to the Rue Saint-Julien le Pauvre, named for a small but ornate church one block off the Quai de Montebello. The churchyard, called Square René-Viviani, held a fountain at its center, the oldest tree in Paris (which I learned only later), and abundant foliage around its perimeter. The place seemed an ideal spot to spend the night—or at least the next four hours, until sunrise.

Unfortunately, the park grounds were locked and

surrounded by an iron fence made of spiked poles about five feet high. But once I had thrown my backpack over the barricade, I had no choice but to climb over. I was committed.

Managing not to impale myself, I hopped onto the other side with a thud, grabbed the backpack, and found a dry place well hidden between some hedges. The last thing I wanted was to have a policeman's torch and a boot to my back waking me up at four in the morning. I laid my plastic rain poncho (a last-minute gift from my mother) on the dirt to use as a ground cloth, then spread out my sleeping bag. With my backpack for a pillow, a goose-down sleeping bag to keep me warm, and the knowledge that I was in Paris, I knew I'd be all right.

I was in Paris.

4

Vestiges of Bohemia

Baby steps in Paris - Daniela - A bidet, and how to use it - The rendezvous with Udo - The old bookseller - Self-immolation in Place Contrescarpe

The chiming of church bells woke me just past sunrise, but the open air was still so cold I lingered in the warmth of the sleeping bag. Oddly, when I finally braved the chill and stood up, I wasn't stiff from having slept on the hard dirt among the bushes of the park, but I was hungry and ready for some hot water and a washup.

The gates to the park hadn't yet been unlocked, so I had to (carefully, carefully, wanting to father children one day) clamber over the spiked fence once again, onto the Rue Saint-Julien le Pauvre. As I dropped down onto the sidewalk with a loud *oof!*, a middle-aged woman with bright red hair and a black shawl across her shoulders crossed to the other side of the street when she saw me. Strange, wild-maned vagabonds leaping less-than-deftly out of the bushes have that effect on people, for some reason.

I stopped at a simple *tabac-café* just outside the park and ordered a coffee and croissant with butter. I took the

Metro to the main tourist office on the Champs-Élysées to see if they could find me a place to sleep. I waited in line for an hour and managed to reserve a room for that night at Daniela's Hotel. Not the Hotel du Daniela or something appropriately Gallic, but Daniela's Hotel.

The establishment was situated a block from the Arc de Triomphe, but make no mistake: Daniela's was anything but recherché. I'm grappling with a category into which it might fit in a guidebook; possibly "last-chance lodgings" or "hostile hostelries." When you entered the hotel, a Max Steiner-led orchestra played an ominous minor chord.

Daniela herself, olive-complected, thick-shouldered, and spying me doubtfully from under her heavy eyebrows, was hunched on a stool at the front desk in the minuscule lobby, knitting and watching a program on a portable TV set. She was perhaps fifty, with short dark hair cut into bangs. She looked at me as if I were a bill collector. When I asked for a single room and presented my passport, she pointed to the desktop, as if she didn't want to accidentally touch my outstretched hand by accepting the I.D.

"How long?" She didn't look at me when she spoke.

"I'm not sure," I said. I knew already I'd like to leave this uninviting flophouse the moment I could find an alternative. "A few nights."

You'd have thought I'd just said, "And then I'll steal the bed linens and towels and break a window on my way out." She scowled at me. Nonetheless, she removed a key from a set on the wall and dropped it on the counter, again as if she was determined to avoid accidentally touching me.

The room Daniela had personally selected was not much more than ten feet square, with a panoramic view of an alleyway and brick wall out the lone window. At least the bed was soft and sturdy. Opposite the footboard was a creaky oak dresser next to a full-length beveled mirror. A small writing desk was a useful touch, and a Persian rug added a degree of hominess. The bathroom was down the hall, but my room had a wash basin and a bidet.

I had never seen a bidet before. I had no idea what its use could be. Was it a sort of tiny bathtub, for washing up? Was it a urinal, so guests weren't obliged to rush down the chilled and darkened corridors in the middle of the night to pee? Erring on the side of caution, I went with urinal, and used the bidet accordingly.

By the time I'd settled in, the time was nearly three in the afternoon, and I still hadn't taken in much of the great city around me.

My passion for the American expatriates of the 1920s eventually led me to the corner of Boulevards Montparnasse and Raspail, the heart of the literary quarter for such folks as Ernest Hemingway, Harold Stearns, Ezra Pound, Malcolm Cowley, F. Scott Fitzgerald, Kay Boyle, Robert McAlmon, and so many others who went on to achieve literary heights and bohemian myth.

I carried on down Boulevard Montparnasse toward Boulevard Saint-Michel, the Boul'Mich, and unexpectedly found myself in front of Hemingway's favorite drinking and writing spot, the Closerie des Lilas, next to the statue of Marshal Ney. Hemingway had written much of *The Sun Also Rises* at these tables, rising once in a while to stretch and stand before Ney, Napoleon's "bravest of the brave," hoping for inspiration or at least the fortitude to go on writing. The moment, for me, a sincere acolyte of Hemingway's writing, was profound. Was it also stupid, this…this *idolatry*? I didn't care. I don't care now. We learn from those who excel, we take encouragement, and we sometimes feel a connection that helps spur us on in our own work. Who can say that's wrong? Seeing *his* café was important to me, meaningful. But even that was nothing compared to what I would see in the days ahead.

THE NEXT NIGHT was the planned (and much hoped-for) rendezvous with Udo Kortz, the German lieutenant who had kindly shown me the Rhine and paid for my pizza in Koblenz. I was eager to see a friendly face, but even more eager to retrieve my jacket, assuming that he had it.

I left Daniela's on the short walk to the Arc de Triomphe to meet Udo at seven, the appointed place and hour. Walking down the Champs-Élysées, I felt as if everybody in Paris was out strolling, so crowded were the walkways. The scene was a giddy promenade of *la tout Paris*! But Udo wasn't there below the arch as planned. I waited, walked around the monument, and circled it again in the opposite direction. I stayed there until eight. No Udo.

Soon enough I found myself at the base of the Pont Neuf on the Seine, where the Île de la Cite pointed into the river like the prow of a boat. The weather was calm and warm. The river water, stirred by a passing barge, slapped against the concrete banks. Along the quays were pairs of lovers. I could hear faint singing echoing among the massive stone buildings around me. On the opposite bank, everything seemed restful, dusky, easy, and relaxed.

Again I walked over to Notre-Dame. The plaza in front of the church turned out to be a popular hang-out, and I immediately felt like I'd struck gold. Music was everywhere. People played bongos, sang songs without accompaniment, strummed acoustic guitars, clapped their hands, and laughed. The smell of pot was thick, and wine bottles seemed to be everywhere. I saw no one over the age of thirty, nor anyone without a smile. A sightseeing boat sailed past, traffic hummed on the distant boulevards, and somehow, we seemed to be in a cocoon of youth and joy, with no one to interrupt us.

I stopped for a beer at a bistro off the Place Saint-Michel, and stretched it out for as long as was seemly, then found my way back to the park where I had slept the first night in Paris, drawn there as if by a homing beacon. Across the street was a bookstore called Shakespeare and Company. I was surprised by the name because there had long been another Shakespeare and Company bookstore in the 1920s and '30s founded by an American woman, Sylvia Beach. Beach was an important figure among the American literary expatriates of that era. Her shop was a gathering spot for writers like Hemingway, Gertrude Stein, and James Joyce, composer George Antheil, photo-artist Man Ray, the poet Ezra Pound, and many others who subscribed to her lending library and sometimes used the store as a temporary mailing address. Beach even published, at her own expense, the first edition of Joyce's *Ulysses*. Beach closed the shop in 1941, after the Nazis occupied Paris in World War II, and never reopened it before she died in 1962.

This new shop with the old name made me curious.

Inside was the kookiest bookstore I'd ever seen, like something from Balzac, with tiny rooms here and there, long corridors, dangerously leaning shelves, and volumes on upper racks utterly out of reach of any client. Some twenty or so customers browsed among the cramped spaces. One of them, when I asked, pointed out the owner to me.

George Whitman, the proprietor, was just sixty-two at the time but seemed much older. With his mustache and Van Dyke beard, he somewhat resembled Ezra Pound, and had a distracted air, as if he were eager to return to a chess match he'd reluctantly and abruptly been forced to leave. I knew I would revisit the bookstore soon, but for the moment I was content with buying a copy of Hemingway's Paris memoir, *A Moveable Feast*. After I paid, Whitman opened the book and, on the blank page opposite the title page, inked it with a rubber stamp: *Shakespeare and Company, Kilometer Zero, Paris.*

As pleased as I was by the book purchase and the discovery of the shop itself, all I could think about as I walked outside was that I had just spent eight francs, about U.S. $1.75, an amount that might have paid for a night's lodging at a decent hostel.

At the Café Lutèce around the corner from Shakespeare and Company, I watched as four waiters fought a drunken patron on the terrace. The drunk nearly won before he was thrown into the street. Another inebriated man, this one in the Place Contrescarpe, was attracting an amused crowd by spitting alcohol across a flaming torch to create a jet of fire. That was it, the whole show, nothing more. Somehow, he managed to get an audience, and many people tossed coins at him as he smiled, spat more alcohol, and gurgled out a maniacal laugh. Then he set himself on fire accidentally, his right arm and chest blazing away. He began to beat his torso with his open palms and turn in tight circles. The people in the crowd stared, horrified, unsure whether this was part of the man's busking routine. When he began to moan and wobble, some audience members more astute than I rushed to him and began smothering the flames with their scarves and jackets.

Unable to speak French or administer first aid, I backed out onto the street and returned to my hotel, wondering if Paris was a funhouse—or a madhouse.

5

Shakespeare & Co.

Down, then up - Goodbye, Daniela, and fuck you very much - George Whitman - Employed - Ted Joans, the coolest man on earth - I am assigned the Famous Writers Bed - A bookstore is an aphrodisiac, apparently - An odd connection - Adieu, Paris

Did you ever have a day with a beginning and end that were polar opposites? You wake up in the morning depressed, hungover, and concerned about that new mole on your neck, but by dinnertime, you've somehow found an envelope on the sidewalk with fifteen thousand dollars in well-used tens and a lifetime pass to four third-base box seats for every Dodgers home game until the Second Coming of Don Drysdale. Also, the envelope has a get-out-of-guilt-free note: "Dear Finder, It's yours. Keep it. I don't want it."

That sort of day.

No, neither have I. But this one came close.

I climbed out of bed at about one p.m., an oh-so rock 'n' roll wake-up hour but not conducive to finding breakfast on anyone's menu. I was famished but had spent more money on food and drink the previous day than I'd planned, so I needed to economize. I'd decided to leave Daniela's House of Detention because of the inordinate expense of three dollars a day and search for a hostel or some other sort of affordable student accommodation.

I'd already stayed past the eleven a.m. check-out time, so I wouldn't be able to leave the place until the next morning. At the tourist bureau, a young woman with good English said I couldn't reserve a student room in advance, only on the day of arrival. That was a waste of an hour.

Because I'd been rationing my money severely, owing to the unexpected hotel stay in Paris instead of a cheaper hostel bed, I had only nine francs with which to feed and amuse myself all day. A franc was worth about twenty-two cents U.S. in those days; cue the sad violins. I needed a place to cogitate about how I would apportion my wealth, so I stopped at an Arab-owned bar on Rue des Acacias, where I paid one and a half francs for a beer. At a bakery next door, I bought a loaf of bread for another franc and a half, then walked to the Bois de Boulogne to eat it. I now had only six francs left for the day.

I sat on a bench.

I stuffed bread in my mouth.

I felt sorry for myself.

Who wouldn't?

An attack of wistfulness washed over me. The only time I could remember feeling so homesick and out of place was when I was ten and my parents sent me to spend the summer with my aunt and uncle on their chicken ranch in Grand Junction, Colorado. Well, *ranch* may be going overboard; they had a chicken coop out back. I had to catch chickens by their legs with a hooked metal stick. The smell of chicken shit was revolting. I hated picking up the slimy eggs from the nests. I was bored, unhappy. Even having a cousin there my own age wasn't enough to overcome my desire to go back to La Mirada.

Homesickness, a ruthless mistress, can transform Paris into a Colorado chicken ranch.

I went back to Daniela's Dungeon of the Doomed, where the madame herself, as usual, ruled the roost in the lobby, smoking up a storm, knitting, and watching her shows on her tiny desktop TV.

"Hey, Daniela," I said, with a wave.

She eyed me as if I were trying to steal her watch.

In my room, I closed the curtains and lay on the bed. But just as ennui and sulkiness had come over me so suddenly, so too did a newfound sense of purpose. I don't know why; it just did. Imagine Paul on the road to Damascus. Archimedes in his bathtub. Scrooge awaking on Christmas morning. OK, my spiritual renewal was nothing like those things, but still pretty darn uplifting. I knew that I was a visitor in one of the greatest cities on earth, home to one of the most important cultures of Western civilization, all of it available to anyone willing to seek it out. Who cared that I had only $1.98 to spend (well, $1.32 after the beer and the bread)? And what was I doing? Lying on a creaky bed in a dark room in a cheap hotel, feeling sorry for myself.

I stood up, tore open the curtains (they were so sun-dried and old that they actually tore), flicked on the overhead light, removed my clothes, gave myself a sponge bath, washed my hair in the sink, pissed in the bidet, shaved, and brushed my teeth. I pulled a fresh change of clothes, including clean socks and underwear, from the dresser drawer where I stored them. To my delight—and this just goes to prove that a positive mental attitude pays off—I found three francs, fifty centimes in the pocket of my fresh blue corduroys. More than enough for a couple of beers, plus what I already had in my pockets! I must have overlooked the money when I washed my clothes in the sink a few days earlier. I fished my beret out of my pack and put it on at just the right angle, appraising my-self in the mirror above the basin. Merriam-Webster had only one word for how I looked and felt: *jaunty*. I was clean and fresh and energized. *Take your francs and go outside. Enjoy!*

In the lobby, which was barely bigger than my skimpy room, I walked up to the counter, reached across it, and took Daniela's hand.

"Tomorrow, I flee, Daniela," I said, then kissed her rough, gnarled knuckles.

Daniela withdrew her hand in disgust, as if I'd just laid a turd in it, and crimped up her face in revulsion while I waltzed out the door.

Over to the Quai du Louvre I went, from where I could see that most charming of small Parisian parks, the Square du Vert-Galant, sitting prow-like at the western end of the Île de la Cité. I crossed the Pont Neuf and skipped down a flight of stairs to the edge of the park. Lovers dangled their legs over the edge of the embank-ment and listened to a busker strumming a guitar and singing something romantic in French. Elderly people, standing, hands held behind their backs, still dressed for winter, gazed serenely at the river. The setting sun was now deep orange with a square of bright, bright yellow near the top, leaving a reflection on the water that passed below seven bridges before ending at my poor pair of blue canvas sneakers. The green and spreading chestnut trees sent out clean, rich aromas. Had it been a scene from a 1930s Merrie Melodies cartoon, the flowers would have begun to sing falsetto and dance. I thought I would ex-plode with wonder.

All of Paris was on the streets, as if for some festival; a celebratory mood was rife in the air. In the course of an hour, I passed the same people on different streets two, three, four times. They appeared to have as little purpose in their strolling as I had, other than just *to be in Paris.* I bought a beer at the Café Melody off the Place Saint-Michel. The bar was warm, and I enjoyed the simple act of standing at the zinc counter, sipping my bock, and watching through the window as the happy people streamed by.

Before I returned to Daniela's Hotel du Hell, I decided to stop again at Shakespeare and Company, the bookstore, intending to speak with the owner, if only to say later that I had. The store wasn't nearly as jammed with customers as it had been the first time I was there. George Whitman was standing at a tall bookshelf, meticulously rearranging its contents. So intent was he that I hesitated to interrupt him.

"Uh, hullo? Um, excuse me? Er, sir?" I stammered.

He stopped what he was doing and turned to me. He was wearing a wrinkled, not particularly clean, brown corduroy suit with a white shirt and black knit tie. His hair was mussed, and what I could see of his mouth, hidden beneath his mustache and goatee, formed into a soft smile with few teeth.

"Please, no," he said, in a New England accent. "Call me comrade."

He was thin, with pale red hair, what the Brits would call a ginger.

"I was wondering…" I tried to continue, but he cut me off.

"Well, it's a bad habit," he said, turning back to the books he was shelving, but continuing to talk to me. "You're still young yet. There's time to quit."

"You're funny," I said, less nervous now.

"No," he replied. "I've lost all sense of humor after twenty-five years in this business. Now, let me finish this and we'll talk." He nodded over his shoulder. "Hand me a few of those books over there."

For the next fifteen minutes I was like an O.R. nurse passing scalpels and retractors to a surgeon, except that I was handing off books to a legendary bookseller. We didn't speak as he finished reorganizing the shelf. In the meanwhile, I stared around the place. What a cock-eyed crazy shop. The wonder was that the shelves weren't toppling over onto the heads of the handful of Vassar poetesses, budding Fitzgeralds, and other customers who studiously scrutinized the volumes. The walls were out of plumb, and the ceilings seemed to be different heights from room to room. And everywhere were upholstered chairs and settees, coffee tables, end tables, shaded table lamps, and other accouterments of hominess.

"There!" he said at last, patting the spine of a book and nudging it into place with his fingertips. "Come with me. Mustn't leave the exchequer unmanned."

I followed him to the shop's cash register. He took a seat on the kind of high stool I imagined Bob Cratchit once sat on. I stood on the opposite side of the sales counter. Barely before he could get comfortable, questions came blurting out of my mouth. Was there a relation to Sylvia Beach, owner of the original Shakespeare and Company? What motivated him to set up the shop? How was business? Were his customers mostly British and Americans? Did he have poetry readings? Did authors ever stop by?

I was making an idiot of myself.

"Do you always talk so fast?" he asked before answering some of my questions.

George Whitman and Sylvia Beach had no business relationship, he told me, but she was aware of his store's existence. Whitman opened his shop in Paris in 1951 with money acquired from a small inheritance. He named that shop Mistral Books, after the strong, dry northerly winds of southern France. Sylvia Beach lived around the corner from Mistral Books in those days, well after she had closed her own shop during the Nazi occupation. While she never returned to the book business, she joined the growing ranks of Whitman's famous, and famously motley, clientele.

"She told me," George recounted, "that she considered my bookshop the spiritual successor to her own Shakespeare and Company."

He later named his daughter, born in 1981, Sylvia, after his literary kinsman.

In 1964, on the three-hundredth birthday of William Shakespeare, Whitman renamed his shop Shakespeare and Company. Beach had died a year and a half earlier, so no one can say for certain what she would have thought of the name change, but for her to have objected seemed implausible to me, then and now.

The shop was empty of customers at that moment, so George asked if I'd like to see the private "By Invitation Only" library upstairs. Up we went, and I examined his magpie collection of first editions, curiosities, and signed copies, and marveled at the vast numbers of books in that wonderful, Dickensian shop. A sign on the wall read, "Be not inhospitable to strangers, lest they be angels in disguise." Another, above a book-crammed alcove, proclaimed the space to be "The Rag and Bone Shop of the Heart." George returned to the cash register, the "exchequer," while I continued browsing.

An athletic man, clean-cut, perhaps in his late twenties, entered the private library.

"Hey, how's it going?" he said, as if we'd known each other for years. "Brad," he said, sticking out his right hand.

I introduced myself and we chatted. Brad had been living in the library, he said, for the past three days. I looked around and saw no couch that could be used as a bed, and wondered if I had misheard him. But before I could ask about it, a hawk-nosed Cockney entered the room as if it were his own and claimed he was "politically aware, you understand?"

No, I didn't understand, but I understood when he said, "Pints on me," and led us around the corner to an unassuming café where we drank several beers each.

When we returned to Shakespeare and Company, Brad grabbed a push broom, unbidden, and began to clean the floors. The Cockney, whose name I didn't get (was it Mortimer? Murgatroyd?) because I could barely understand him, walked around the rooms and began shutting off the lights and ensuring the windows were latched. Did they *work* here, I wondered?

Clearly, the night had ended for the bookstore. I walked to the front of the shop to say my goodbyes to the owner.

"Thanks for letting me hang out," I said. "I love your shop, George."

Comrade George looked up from his account book in the little nook by the cash register, a quizzical look on his face.

"You're not leaving, are you?" George asked, as if I'd hurt his feelings. "We have beds, if you need a place to stay. I'd sort of taken to you."

Brad, who had overheard this, stopped sweeping.

"Look at this," he called to me. He reached into a corner of one of the bookcases and swung the shelves open to reveal a Murphy bed. He smiled as if he'd just discovered it himself. "They're all over this place."

"You'll have to work for your keep," George continued. "Sweep up, man the cash register, run some errands, organize books, that sort of thing."

I had no idea how to react. The offer had come so unexpectedly. I looked back at George, who stared at me questioningly. I didn't have to think long.

"I'm at a cheap hotel on the Right Bank," I said. "I hate it and I can't afford it. I'll be back here tomorrow."

"Good," Whitman said, again scanning his accounts book as if I weren't there. "It's a deal. See you then."

GEORGE WHITMAN TURNED out to be as I had expected from our first meeting: a fascinating, crotchety, scatter-brained, intelligent, and friendly man. There would be times when I thought he might bite me angrily if I didn't jump fast enough at one of his orders. But when he was relaxed and talkative, he was kind, chivalrous, and charming. Despite his age, he was active and ambitious, with distant hopes of expanding the bookstore and opening part of it as a literary café serving hearty home-style dishes. (His goal eventually came to pass.)

I had already been "on the job," if you could call my less-than-taxing duties a job, for a full day. The previous night I had swept the floors at closing time, checked that the windows were all locked, and made my way to the guest room to which I'd been assigned. Just as Brad had shown me earlier, one of the bookshelves could be pulled outward on a hinge to reveal a fold-down bed buried in the wall behind it. A pillow, but no bed linens, lay across the mattress, so I unrolled my sleeping bag and hit the sack.

The next morning (after using the primitive bathroom, with its enameled "Turkish toilet" embedded in the floor) I was assigned to the cash register. I was as nervous as a junior seaman ordered to man the helm, but grew more comfortable after the first sale. There I enjoyed flirting with a never-ending stream of young American women who flocked to the store. Shakespeare and Company seemed to be a site of pilgrimage for these literary-minded girls. Three freshman co-eds from the University of Virginia treated me as if I had been running the cash register there for years; they giggled and smiled bashfully whenever I made some stupid crack.

"Say, listen, I work until five," I said to the prettiest. "Let me show you my favorite café. It's where Kay Boyle first met Robert McAlmon."

Boom! I had a date. I vowed to open a bookstore once I got back to California.

I was impressed to meet an attractive young author, Linsey Lee, who had recently published her first book, *Edible Wild Plants of Martha's Vineyard.* A published author, and not yet twenty-five years old! So modest was she that, again, I fell in love. She had long hair, well past her shoulders, brown with blonde highlights. Her round face was intelligent, intellectual, but approachable. She was two years older than me, though, which, when you're twenty-two, can seem an insurmountable challenge to romance. She went on to become the curator of the Vineyard Oral History Center at the Martha's Vineyard Historical Society, as well as the author of another book, *Vineyard Voices.*

Among the visitors were a few serious writers and poets, none of whom acted as if they were anything other than regular folks. One morning I was in one of the reading rooms (a sign above the door proclaimed it the "Writers Guest House") when in walked an exceptionally cool middle-aged Black man with a gray-streaked, well-trimmed beard and a blue beret. I knew him immediately: Ted Joans, the Beat poet, painter, and jazz trumpeter who was a veritable Zelig of the post-war international art world.

Joans had moved from the Midwest to New York City in 1951, where he shared a room for a time with bebop sax god Charlie Parker. As both a painter and a poet he was enamored of Surrealism, and became friends with Salvador Dali (he named one of his daughters Daline, in tribute) and André Breton, the father of Surrealism. He counted among his downtown friends in New York the likes of Jack Kerouac, Allen Ginsberg, Amiri Baraka (the former LeRoi Jones), and Gregory Corso. One of his paintings, *Bird Lives*, was in San Francisco's De Young Museum. A true citizen of the world, he had lived in Tangier, Timbuktu (seriously), Paris, Berlin, and Greenwich Village. Joans would go on later in his career to win the Lifetime Achievement accolade from the American Book Awards.

I had learned early not to be intimidated by people (at least, not outwardly), so I hesitated only a second or two before walking over to the distinguished-looking hipster, who had by now taken a book off the shelf and was sitting by a window overlooking the river and Notre-Dame.

"Excuse me," I said. "I hate to interrupt, but I thought I recognized you. Are you Ted Joans, the poet?"

I could have said "Ted Joans, the painter" or "Ted Joans, the jazz trumpeter," or "Ted Joans, who well may be the coolest guy on the planet," but he seemed pleased with the designation of poet, because he stood and smiled.

"Just digging Paris for a while," he answered when I asked what he was up to these days. "I usually have a place here but I'm traveling now. I was here for George's poetry reading last week. I always get a kick out of those when I'm in town."

He was getting ready to leave Paris again for a trip back to the States, where he had some poetry readings scheduled as part of the American Bicentennial celebrations that summer. He also planned to visit Lawrence Ferlinghetti at City Lights, the San Francisco bookstore, which I knew well from when I lived in nearby Marin County.

"I know the cat from seeing him in New York," he said of Ferlinghetti, "but I've never actually been to San Francisco. Crazy, right?"

"You've got to go to Specs Simmons' bar, right around the corner from City Lights," I said eagerly. "The hippest bar you've ever seen."

"Yeah, I know all about it," he said, two steps ahead of me. "And Vesuvio and Tosca and the rest. What is it with you Bay Area cats? All you do is drink!"

Ted Joans, the man himself, had just dubbed me a "Bay Area cat." My bohemian credentials had been poured in concrete.

After some more chit-chat, we shook hands, and Joans split. Less than an hour later I introduced myself to another poet, John Kendricks, who had just been interviewed by *Viva*, a women's erotic magazine then popular in America. I remarked that the interview would probably help him get laid back in the States, but clearly, I was more excited about the interview than he was.

The next day, George had plans to reorganize one entire room—with me doing the heavy (and dirty) lifting of volumes off one shelf and onto another, without any noticeable improvement that I could see. Just...*different*.

On another evening I treated myself (since I was saving money on lodgings) to a chicken dinner with an egg sandwich, an orange, chocolate cake, and tea. I hadn't eaten that much food since I'd arrived in Frankfurt. Afterward, I returned to Shakespeare and Company and was in charge of the front desk the rest of that night. I'm as trustworthy as they come, but I wondered if George was being *too* trusting, considering he had no idea if I was a thief or even just bad at making change.

I had planned to leave for Dijon or somewhere else the next day, but in the morning Kendricks, the poet, asked me to cover for him at the front desk. He had an appointment at the gym, where he was training as a boxer. I explained that I was thinking of leaving for the next place, wherever that might be, because, after a week, I didn't want to overstay my welcome and take unfair advantage of George's hospitality.

"No, no," Kendricks said, laughing a little. "George likes you! Besides, he's had people stay here for a month or more. Trust me, you can stay as long as you want, as long as you help out around the place."

The bookstore was filling up with guests. Brad told me that George at times hosted as many as twenty visitors in the private-library guest rooms and various hidden Murphy beds. There had been just three of us on my first night; now seven warm bodies occupied the beds. I hadn't even had a chance to learn everyone's names. Some of the beds and their locations were preferable to others because of their size, comfort, or degree of privacy. George had assigned me the choicest sleeping spot of them all, for some reason: the "Famous Writers Bed." According to George (and I had no reason to doubt him), the bed had coddled the likes of Allen Ginsburg, Lawrence Durrell, and Henry Miller. Try sleeping in a bed like that!

On my last afternoon at Shakespeare and Company, I went for a final stroll around the neighborhood. *My* neighborhood, as I was beginning to think of it. Paris had turned cold and gloomy and blustery. The wind blowing across the Pont de Sully at the east end of the Île Saint-Louis was powerful enough to nearly bowl me over and chilly enough to make me sorrier than ever that I had no jacket. When I returned to the shop, George called me over to the desk.

"Mark, do you know Gregory?"

Gregory Corso, big as life, the ultimate beatnik, prison rat, poet-pirate, turned around to face me. Corso was the bad boy of the Beats, pals with Kerouac, Ginsberg, Burroughs, and the rest, a modern-day François Villon. He had stopped by the bookstore for a couple of hours while I was out walking that afternoon.

And now he was leaving.

"Hey, man," he said.

That was the extent of my conversation with the famous Gregory Corso. Well, I got a handshake from a legend out of the meeting. And he'd called me "man." You take what you can get—and that wasn't half-bad.

Ted Joans returned to the store that night, which lessened my disappointment about not getting to know Corso. Ted and I and a few other temporary tenants made idle conversation and drank wine well into the night. The ancient but deeply upholstered chairs and sofa were comfortable; the room was warm and lit by a couple of table lamps. I couldn't imagine a cozier place to be or a more congenial group. A French girl, an American girl, and a Swedish girl were hanging out, as were four guys besides me. The "writers' beds" were getting crowded. Sometimes romantically so.

I still planned to leave the next day for Italy, or at least in that general direction. George said he was sad to see me go, but that he understood the allure of Italy. He gave me the names of a couple of pensions in Venice (he pronounced the word *pawn-shone*, and I had no idea initially what he meant), but implied they were expensive by saying they were "worth it." When you're poor, you're alert to little clues like that.

In the morning, I said my goodbyes to a few of the literary lodgers I'd been friendly with, and then shook hands with George near the front of the shop, where he was engaged in the never-ending task of sorting books.

"You're a good man," he said, turning away as if I'd already left. "A good man. Come back and see us."

6

Pardon Me, Have You Any Gray Dijon?

Station deluxe - A feast in second-class - Acme spring-loaded train platforms - The rise and fall of the Italian campaign - Hygiene on hiatus - To points south

A time once existed, back in the mists of history, when unironic architects designed Temples to Transportation.

The Gare de Lyon was such a place. With its classical façade, enormous clock tower, and the vast plaza out front that allowed you to stand back and soak in the building's beauty and almost overwhelming amount of sculptural decoration, the terminal was as ornate as a Dauphin's chateau. The massive, warehouse-like main hall was bright, thanks to skylights and second-floor windows running the building's full length. People crossed the interior in every possible direction. I wouldn't have been surprised to discover some of them were walking in circles, if only to linger without loitering.

The clock in the tower chimed ten. I had already eaten breakfast, but I searched out the legendary Train Bleu restaurant anyway just to gaze inside. Gigantic, gilt-edged chandeliers hung so large and heavy they probably swung, imperceptibly, in sync with some celestial force, like glittering Foucault pendula. The high ceiling was ornamented with Parisian scenes painted on rococo-edged panels. Elegant travelers in their first-class finest, seemingly in no rush at all (unlike everyone else in the terminal), sipped on *café au lait* and daintily crammed buttered croissants into their perfectly toothed mouths. I glanced at the menu posted near the entrance and shuddered. Actually, I think I squealed. A coffee and a roll in that joint would have set me back several days' food budget. I backed out into the ticketing hall, hand firmly on my wallet, as if some high-class cutpurse were lurking about.

I'd taught myself the French word for ticket: *billet.* And I was pretty sure that "second class" translated as *de deuxième classe,* "one person" as *une personne,* and "to Dijon" as *à la capitale de la moutarde.*

I managed to book passage on a train leaving just an hour later. I could even understand the writing on the *billet* well enough to recognize the numbers of my train car, compartment, and assigned seat. Either that or I'd inadvertently bought a French Lotto ticket.

Before heading to the platform, I found a small Arab-run grocery store just off the plaza in front of the opulent depot. I'd noticed, when taking the train from Trier to Paris, that many of the travelers had brought with them the equivalent of a full picnic lunch, basket and all. I'd read that passengers sometimes even shared their bounty with one another. How charming! What a wonderful custom! I bought a loaf of crusty sourdough bread, some pre-packaged slices of salami, and a bottle of cheap red wine. Sophisticated, right? Who wouldn't want to share a picnic with me? *Voulez-vous manger avec moi, jolie mademoiselle?*

Large yellow signs hanging from the ceiling in the train hall indicated the location of the platforms, and I found mine easily. That didn't stop me from asking several waiting passengers, "*À Dijon, oui?*" Considering the responses I got, I'm sure I must have asked some of the same people twice.

As I looked around at the tracks and platforms, I began to understand the difference between a railroad *station* and a railroad *terminal.* At a station, the tracks ran alongside the ticketing office and waiting room; trains could conceivably whip right past a station without stopping, and in the case of express trains, frequently did. At a terminal, on the other hand, usually in a major, end-of-the-line city, the tracks came to an abrupt finale, often armed with a colossal spring-loaded buffer stop designed by Wile E. Coyote to prevent a runaway locomotive from jumping the track and winding up near the info booth in the main hall. Here, at the Gare de Lyon, as in so many European terminals, the trains pulled in under a protective cast-iron-and-glass "shed" a hundred feet high, full of light and often with traces of the weather creeping through the vast open end through which the trains chugged in and out. If the weather was cold and snowy, passengers on the platform had to wear their jackets. Train platforms, it seemed, even in a grand terminal such as this, were nearly as much outside as they were inside. Covered, yes, but not *indoors.*

If all these perhaps-less-than-startling insights evince an equally unnerving lack of basic knowledge for a twenty-two-year-old, it's because I knew nothing about trains from living in America. Where I grew up, in La Mirada, the old Mission-style train station had long since been taken out of use for passenger service and, by the late 1950s, had become the post office, where I would go on my father's shoulders to retrieve our mail every day.

To me, trains meant putting pennies on the track and then trying to find the flattened, elongated copper remains in the surrounding gravel of the track bed as a souvenir once the Atchison, Topeka & Santa Fe *San Diegan* had dieseled through.

MY TRAIN FOR Dijon arrived some ten minutes before our scheduled departure, and I settled into my compartment. Three thinly cushioned seats in the six-by-six-foot roomette faced three other thinly cushioned seats. The upholstery, however, was there for appearances only. Barely enough space existed between the facing benches for one passenger to avoid knocking knees with the opposite passenger, an acceptable closeness only if the opposing knees belonged to, say, Brigitte Bardot. Thankfully, only one other person sat with me in my compartment, and he didn't seem to care which was his seat number; he just shoved open the compartment's sliding door, looked at me with the same lack of interest he'd show to a kitchen appliance, and took the seat farthest away.

The train gave a jerk, and in seconds we were moving faster than I would have imagined possible, out of the train shed and into the late-morning light of France. Once in Dijon I would wash all my clothes (everything I owned was in the backpack I carried, so I didn't have much to launder), take a long hot shower (sponge baths were all I could do at Shakespeare and Company), and plan my trip to Italy with a bit more detail than "Venice, maybe Florence," which was about the extent of my Italian strategy thus far.

But I would miss Paris, especially Shakespeare and Company and the lively Left Bank. The experience had been memorable (as was, in a perverse way, my stay at Madame Daniela's Celebrated Establishment for Wayward Gentlemen), but everything was so expensive! Even having saved money by staying at the bookstore, I was fast going broke just on breakfast, beer, canned cassoulet, and the occasional splurge on a croque monsieur or kebab at a side-street café. Not a lot of economizing one can do from such a grim starting point.

The way my money was working out (more accurately, the way my money was *running* out), the less I thought I should go to Italy. After all, I had no appointment there. No one back home knew where I was or where I was heading. *Maybe I should go directly to Spain,* I thought. The distance wasn't much farther than to Italy. More importantly, from everything I'd been hearing, Spain was much cheaper than anywhere else in Europe. Hotels cost as little as ninety cents a night, a bottle of wine less than half that. If I were to take a train south to Avignon, it would cost fourteen dollars (or so I'd read); a ticket all the way to the coast, to Marseille, would run eighteen. Then I could hitchhike to Spain from there.

The rail trip from Paris to Dijon was scheduled to be only two hours long, so I began drinking the wine and eating the bread and salami shortly after the train left the terminal. My compartment mate sulked in the corner and seemed disinclined to chat; I refrained from asking brightly, "Hey, monsieur, how about rolling out *un peu du* that famous Gallic charm and sharing a European-style train picnic with me?" Instead, I uncorked the wine with my Swiss Army knife and drank right from the bottle. I chewed the bread directly off the loaf and ate the salami slices straight out of the plastic bag with my greasy fingers. That was me, all right: elegance on two legs, a regular Galloping Gourmet of the Rails.

I had no idea what the weather would be like in Dijon. I'd scanned the guidebook charts showing the average monthly temperatures and precipitation in some key European cities, but weather.com didn't exist in those days.

A person generally stuck his head out the window, looked at the sky, and *voila*, weather forecast. On this day, a light snow fell. The closer we got to Dijon, the heavier the snow came down.

Arriving in Dijon but before leaving the train, I put on a second shirt and my dashing reindeer sweater over what I already wore, then went into the station to find the tourist desk. The woman there gave me a map of the city and directions to the local hostel, the Foyer d'Étudiantes, an old gray three-story structure in a city full of old gray structures.

My private hostel room was fine, if unremarkable. It contained a large, sturdy metal desk with a reading lamp, a big closet with shelves, and a basin and mirror next to the bed. Your typical college dorm room—but it was the presidential suite at the Beverly Wilshire compared to my monk's cell at Daniela's Penitentiary.

I was conscious of my hygiene, or lack of it, because, as I sat on the bed, I got a whiff of my pits without even raising my arms. When you smell your own funk, you know things have gone too far. Humanity has every right to be appalled. I piled my dirty clothes onto the floor and decided to find a laundromat. Then I took a thirty-minute-long hot shower (unlike at some hostels, this one was free), letting the steaming stream massage my scalp and flow luxuriantly down my neck and back. When I stepped out to dry off, I felt like a Soviet commissar after a hot-house sweat and a birch-branch drubbing by a muscle-bound ogress named Zlata: fantastic.

That afternoon I met an American my age named Tony, who said Marseille was worth putting on my itinerary.

"Lots of bars down by the water," he said, fond memories almost visible. "Lots of girls walking around. Lots of places to stay. Pretty cheap."

Bars, girls, and cheap lodgings. And lots of 'em! Why else did anyone come to Europe?

The hostel served as the regular student dormitory for the University of Burgundy. No end of young people wandered throughout the public rooms. Tony said he had a steak in the refrigerator of the communal kitchen and offered to split it with me. In my pack, I had a can of ravioli, a half loaf of bread remaining from the train ride, and some slightly stale pastries from Paris, and brought them along to add to the repast. Tony produced two bottles of Burgundy wine, which we drank like water, and for dessert he brought out some strawberry-flavored yogurt. It may have been the best meal I'd eaten since I arrived in Europe. Hobo haute cuisine.

I AWOKE JUST after dawn to a day that was as gray as the surrounding streets, the sky drizzly with rain and sleet. A café took up a corner of the hostel's lounge, and I stopped there for a coffee and buttered bread. Croissants were available, but they were frozen and had to be heated. *In France?! Sacré bleu!*

Despite the miserable weather, Dijon turned out not to be as gray and dismal as I'd first thought. Tony and I crept around a tenth-century cathedral crypt, then saw the Manets and Guardis at the Palace of the Dukes. I marveled at Dijon's half-timbered houses, crumbling brick cottages, handsome merchant villas with their yellow-and-red-shingled roofs, and the ancient, warped, hand-laid stone streets that looked like they'd been mapped out by a bunch of amateur urban planners ripped on Beaujolais nouveau. With the gray misty sky, the Sunday afternoon silence, and few people on the streets, I easily imagined Tony and me as a pair of fifteenth-century gadabouts looking for mischief.

Tony returned to the hostel while I made a

reconnaissance mission to the train station to suss out my travel plans. A ticket to Avignon, it turned out, would cost sixteen dollars and to Marseille, twenty, more than I'd thought. I decided that I would go first to Avignon, pass by Marseille altogether, then continue by thumb to Arles, Nîmes, Carcassonne, and onward into Spain.

In other words, I didn't have a bloody clue.

7

Sur le
Pont d'Avignon

Bunking on an island in the Rhone - Why Aussies rule - Sofia and Isabetta - I protest - The fearsome pride of the Catalans - I learn to hate the Deux Chevaux - More kindness on the road - Rumble in La Rambla

The Auberge de Jeunesse was gone.

I'd arrived in Avignon, where I planned to stay at what I thought would be a comfortable and convenient hostel I'd read about. Someone on the street saw me looking disappointedly at the abandoned building and told me about a nearby campground that had a bunkhouse where a bed cost a dollar twenty-five for the night. The recommendation turned out to be a fortunate one, both for location and budget. The campground was situated on a bluff on an island in the middle of the Rhone River with a direct view of Avignon and its two-thousand-year-old fortress-like Roman walls.

The bunkhouse itself was more like an unofficial hostel than a place where a bunch of cowboys might bed down for the night. Some of the travelers were Swiss, some Germans, and a few Australians.

I quickly developed a fondness for the Aussies. They weren't necessarily the boozy, brawling brutes of popular reputation. They were, though, fiercely friendly, not at all shy, with a strong sense of humor.

I especially liked their habit of, as they said, taking the piss out of their mates, or what we would call good-natured teasing. That was how they judged a good bloke versus a wanker, by whether he could take some amiable ribbing and keep a smile—and maybe even dish it right back in an equally jovial manner. A bunch of us sitting around the hostel's social room got snockered on forty-cent wine while singing "God Save the Queen" and "Waltzing Matilda," which turned out to be rousing drinking songs.

The next day I ambled around the old town with two Englishmen, Ian and Alexander, and an American girl named Ess. For lunch, we bought some bread and cheese and ate it in a park. We somehow met two Italian girls who had moved to France for the adventure of it all. They were long-lashed, long-haired, and long-legged. Ian and I, using telepathy to coordinate our moves, soon left Alex and Ess behind, and steered the two Italian girls off on our own. Sofia was pretty in a classical way, with an intelligent-looking face; she was the sort of beautiful woman who could wear her hair up and, in an instant, pull off the librarian-turned-lioness routine. But the one I liked better was called Isabetta. She was what used to be referred to as voluptuous or what, in high school, my friends and I would have called *stacked*. That wasn't the sort of girl I usually went for, probably because they intimidated me. But Isabetta wasn't at all forbidding; she seemed to like me, too.

Both Sofia and Isabetta were sexy and cuddly, and I

soon found myself with an arm snuggled meaningfully around Isabetta's waist, which she seemed to welcome. At one street corner, she stopped and began to look in different directions, as if searching for something. She was so beautiful, and seemingly so unaware of just how attractive she was, that I leaned over and kissed her. She didn't pull away, and in fact moved her lips in concert with mine. Soon we were full-on making out right there on the street corner. I saw that Ian was doing pretty well with Sofia, too.

Sofia said something in Italian to Isabetta and pointed down the street. Isabetta pushed my hand off her waist and smoothed her hair.

"We must go," she said, her halting English charming enough to break my heart. "Our boyfriends, they wait for us."

Boyfriends?! They couldn't be much in the way of boyfriends, I thought, especially when the girls offered to meet Ian and me on Saturday night at a disco. But I would be leaving for Arles before that. I took a mental cold bath, kissed Isabetta goodbye, got an arrivederci peck on the cheek from Sofia, and stormed away, frustrated.

We hadn't gone far when we saw a student demonstration assembling. Pretty college-age girls were among the protestors, so Ian and I joined them. Someone called out to the group over an old-fashioned, Rudy Vallee-style megaphone; everyone picked up their signs and banners and began to march. About five hundred marchers made up the crowd, sizable for a relatively small city like Avignon. And we made a lot of noise! Shopkeepers and waiters came out to the sidewalks to watch. Passersby stopped and gazed at the chanting marchers.

"What are we protesting?" I shouted at Ian.

"No fucking clue," he called back.

He nodded toward the onlookers on the sidewalks. His

traveling buddy, Alex, stood at the edge of the street. We pulled ourselves out of the demonstration and joined him. He was gobsmacked, as he phrased it later, to see the two of us emerge from the loud and colorful protest group. As it turned out, he hadn't gotten any further with Ess than we had with the Italian girls. None of us was in a good mood.

By now the mid-afternoon sun made us uncomfortably warm, and I momentarily longed for the snows of Dijon. We bought some beer and walked to the river to drink it under the blue sky and hot sun and think longingly of Isabetta and Sofia and Ess.

AFTER AVIGNON, I thumbed to Arles for a few days and then to Carcassonne for a few days more, but it was time to make my way to Spain. I consulted my highway map, and trudged to a likely spot for a ride south—over the coastal Pyrénées, across the Spanish frontier, and onward to Barcelona on the Mediterranean, some two hundred miles away. I hoped to sleep that night in Barcelona, but I also knew of a youth hostel in Perpignan, sixty miles from Carcassonne, and a campground in Girona, Spain, sixty miles farther on from there. If I had no luck getting a long-distance ride to the Catalonian capital, I could divert to one of those two places. Maybe I was no General Patton, but I was learning the value of fallback strategies.

One French gentleman drove me to Perpignan, then a Catalan took me to Palamós on the coast, following a less-traveled road than my planned route, but the ride took me sixty miles, a good distance. I wasn't about to have turned it down. Besides, hitchhikers needed to make split-second decisions about accepting a ride. When the heavily accented Catalan man told me he was going to Palamós, on the coast, I replied, *"En España?"* He told me yes. My initial reaction was, *How far wrong could I go if I'm heading to Barcelona, Spain, on the coast, and this guy takes me to Palamós, which I've never heard of, on the coast?* In I hopped.

As we drove, the Spaniard told me about his home-land—and I don't mean Spain. He would have objected if I'd called him a Spaniard. He was Catalan! He was fiercely proud of Catalonia, a region that had flirted with independence for decades and reveled in its own identity. He couldn't tell me enough about how great Catalonia was. Its history was both tragic and heroic, its women were the most beautiful in all of Europe, its food was the most delicious on earth, and the landscape was so gor-geous it caused strong men to weep. He wasn't bragging, either; he was simply stating something he firmly be-lieved. He seemed eager to educate me, an American who probably knew nothing about Catalonia (he was correct on that point). He was merely providing facts for my ben-efit. The Catalans, he continued, were the wealthiest peo-ple in Iberia. Also, the most industrious, the best educated, and the most cosmopolitan.

As I feared, Palamós was not a promising launching point for a nonstop lift the rest of the way to Barcelona, still another sixty miles farther on. I got a couple of puny little rides along the water, then a third ride from a man who asked if I'd mind being dropped off at the main highway.

He too, unsurprisingly, was Catalan, but not nearly as hard-nosed about it as the earlier driver. He was proud but not boastful. We talked about King Juan Carlos and his attempts to offer Catalonia minor reforms to placate the restless people. Unlike the independence-minded Basque people and the active terrorist group, ETA, the Catalan people were largely peaceful, more apt to use political means than bombs to reach their ends. Still, between the

Basques and the Catalans, Juan Carlos had his hands full in that feisty northeast corner of the country.

From the highway, I got a ride the remaining distance to Barcelona. The driver was a personable Spaniard, though, at first, I assumed he was French because he was driving one of their comical Citroën 2CV cars. Its canvas top, which could be folded back for al fresco driving, led some people to refer to the vehicle as an umbrella on wheels. Often compared to the Volkswagen Beetle as an affordable car for the masses, the 2CV made the VW "bug" look like a fuel-injected Shelby GT500. Woefully underpowered, with a top speed of just 45 mph, the 2CV had a nine-horsepower engine, despite its full name, the *deux chevaux vapeurs* (literally "two horse steam," as in two horsepower). Many people called a 2CV "Le Duck," but whether because it tended to waddle when it braked or its ugly duckling appearance is unclear. Others simply called them Deux Chevaux.

Once in the city, the man insisted on driving all over town to find the best place to drop me off, finally settling on a neighborhood called the Barrio Gótico, or Gothic Quarter. With a name like that, I didn't argue. It was a Friday, after banking hours, but he knew the owner of a fancy small hotel in the area who would change money for me (I had no Spanish pesetas, just francs and Deutschmarks), then he bought me a coffee before shaking hands and saying goodbye, continuing on his long road to Valencia, two hundred miles farther south.

The warmth and generosity of strangers never failed to astonish me.

Getting settled concerned me, as the time was already seven p.m. and I was unsure where to find a hostel. I stopped at the first hotel that looked inexpensive (the clues I looked for: no lobby to speak of, maybe a sign out front with only one or two stars, a charmingly shabby appearance) and took a room for 160 pesetas. With a peseta worth one and a half cents, the nightly rate came to U.S. $2.40, not nearly as cheap as the hostel jungle drums had promised. The room wasn't worth more than that, either—a bare space with a weak overhead bulb, a saggy bed, shiny walls and bare tile floor with no rugs, a dresser with a mirror, and a writing table. That was it. I wondered for a moment if maybe Madame Daniela had franchised her unique lodging formula to Spain. But the location, on Carrer de la Boqueria right off the grand pedestrian promenade called La Rambla, couldn't have been more central. I went to the bare wooden desk and wrote in my journal.

You sat in your empty Barcelona hotel room with your thin sandals and no money, ignoring laughter in the street. A woman in the next room cried louder than before, and someone played a clarinet. The toilet next to the stairs didn't work; you felt part of a drama. The cheap Spanish rum from your rucksack nearly made you puke; you felt noble, misunderstood. Soon you left your room for a walk on the Rambla. After all, you thought, it's easier to be tragic where people can see you.

The action on the Rambla was like Dodge City on a Saturday night: drunks singing, tough guys scuffling with cops, hookers who weren't in the least shy about plying their trade. I sat on a bench in the center of the promenade and watched. The mood of the crowds was bizarre, as if a celebratory, alcohol-infused public event had just ended, leaving the intoxicated attendees too wound up to go home, still eager for diversion.

I sensed trouble afoot after just fifteen minutes of walking around.

Two men picked up a park bench that had not been bolted down, carried it across the street, heaved it through a shop window for no reason that I could fathom, then jogged away. Not five minutes later, forty or fifty people ran in my direction from farther down the Rambla. When they got to where I sat watching them, they seemed terrified of something. I stood and walked away from whatever might be behind them. Other people, seeing the scared runners, either fled with them or stood motionless against the buildings on either side of the avenue, as if imitating statues would camouflage them from the unseen danger. A Guardia Civil jeep stopped next to the smashed window. Two uniformed men stepped out and were soon joined by other policemen on foot. An officer spoke to the men, who pulled out their billy clubs and ran as a group down one of the side streets, ready to crack some skulls and kick some butt. Farther down the Rambla I could hear the sound of more glass breaking, shouts, and sirens.

Welcome to Barcelona!

I returned to my hotel and locked the door.

8

A Lot of Bull

*Spanish, as it's thpoken in Thpain - On the horns of a
bullfight dilemma - An unabashed Franco supporter -
Growing to love the Gothic Quarter - The pageantry of
the corrida - Frascuela! Frascuela! - So long, Barcelona
- Pesky hippies*

I 'll never be mistaken for a linguist. I didn't even remember that most Spaniards speak the Castilian
form of the language, in which they lisp the letter *s* and
spray virus-rich spittle thither and yon with each errant
fricative. Having learned Spanish in Southern California,
primarily from Mexican-born and Mexican-American
teachers, I found Castilian bizarre.

Soon enough I got over its dissimilarities to Mexican
Spanish, but I could never bring myself to speak that way.
Without the undervalued alveolar sibilant, a pick-up line
like "*Susanna, eres sexy*" becomes "*Thuthanna, ereth
thekthy.*" Out of the question.

Whenever I went down to the lobby of my crappy hotel,
I just used regular East L.A. pachuco Spanish honed to a
thick-as-a-brick sharpness in the cellar dives of T.J. Every
morning I would greet the desk clerk with a chipper,

"*Oye, vato, buenos días,*" and hand him my room key. In small European hotels, at least in those days, guests were obliged to drop off their room keys at the front desk when walking outside. I assume the rationale was to make it easier for the staff to enter your room after you'd gone out for the day and prowl through your luggage. Weighty, oversized key chains made it unlikely that a guest would accidentally put the key in his pocket.

In the morning, as I handed my key and its attached boat anchor to the clerk, I asked how much a bullfight ticket cost. I wanted to see a Spanish version, the original. I phrased my question flawlessly.

Somehow, and who knows how, the clerk misunderstood me.

He immediately picked up the telephone receiver and made a call. I thought maybe he was phoning a knowledgeable friend to inquire about ticket prices. As it turned out, he thought I wanted him to call Pullmantur and arrange for them to take me to a bullfight for 875 pesetas. Entirely too much! I said so to the clerk. He tried to convince me that the package he'd arranged was the best deal available, that I would be cheated if I bought my own ticket, and that I would get a terrible seat with no view of the goings-on. I was unmoved by his arguments.

He looked at me in a scientific way, deep in thought, brushing the knuckle of his right index finger under the seedy pencil mustache he wore. That cat was going to figure this out, one way or another.

"I am convinced," he intoned, lisping *s*'s all over the lobby, "it would be a tragedy."

He was putting on sales pressure. He'd dialed the telephone and spoken to a tour organizer, true, but now he acted as if he'd worked all morning and called in personal favors to find me a bullfight ticket and that I was being heartlessly cruel by declining his selfless assistance. I didn't want to create a scene but I wasn't about to be pushed into buying something I didn't want. I was alone in Europe, a knucklehead surfer dude from Southern California. If I didn't look out for myself, who would? And what did I care if the clerk lost a commission? (I felt certain that was the cause of his growing frustration.)

I told the clerk I was fully capable of finding my way to the *plaza de toros* and buying a ticket at the gate, which is what I did. I paid just 300 pesetas ($4.50) for a seat at the next afternoon's event, in the ninth row with, as it would turn out, a perfectly fine view of the arena floor.

Lunch that day was similar to most of my midday meals: a loaf of bread, some Gouda or brie (I had only ever eaten processed American cheese before coming to Europe), and a bottle of inexpensive red wine. I took the food to a bench overlooking the harbor at the end of the Rambla, and there met a fifty-six-year-old man wearing a beret who said he'd fought for Franco in the Civil War.

"Franco was for Spain," he said. "His love was for Spain. To organize us, to raise us up, to repel the Communists. That was his goal."

I was horrified (to me his admission was like confessing he'd fought for Hitler), but the man was sweet-natured. I'd noticed lots of military police on the street that afternoon; their helmets were eerily similar to those the Germans wore in World War II. Spain was a strange place in those days. The fascist dictator Francisco Franco, who had ruled Spain since 1939, had died only five months before I arrived. Although he had restored the monarchy just before his death, the country was still a pretty uptight place, with ugly mementos of its fascistic past.

"We don't like the Communists," the man said, making a weak smile and shaking his head sadly. "Franco kept the Communists out and brought back our king. There's no complaint."

I WAS GROWING fonder of the Gothic Quarter by the minute. The neighborhood was full of narrow lanes that twisted and turned at random. The sunlight seemed never to reach the streets, apart from the squares and the broad promenade, La Rambla. Some of the streets were too narrow to admit even the smallest of cars, the exclusive province of pedestrians and Vespa-mounted chain-snatchers. Every second-floor window had a balcony and every balcony had laundry drying in the shade next to an abundance of potted red and yellow flowers. The singsong of caged canaries carried from open windows.

I found myself on a street full of cheap saloons where beer cost only fifteen cents. Prostitutes, lining the sidewalk, did their business out of two hotels among the row of bars. On the other side of the street, a small group of men ogled the streetwalkers but were too shy or too poor to approach them.

What a place! I enjoyed the semitropical feel of Barcelona. The palm trees that decorated the main avenues and squares reminded me of home. Old ladies sold cigarettes from kiosks. Men and boys walked among the sidewalk crowds shouting, "*Lotería,*" selling lottery tickets to a hopeful public.

As the sun dipped, I grew hungry and bought a *bocadería Frankfurt* from a sidewalk seller. At a second-hand bookstore on La Rambla I purchased two English-language paperbacks. One was a Nick Carter espionage thriller titled *The Living Death,* "an exciting new killmaster spy chiller." The other was Ian Fleming's first James Bond novel, *Casino Royale.* I would save the likely better of the two, the Bond book, for later, and ditch the "killmaster spy chiller" if it didn't capture my interest after the first fifty pages. I always gave an author fifty pages; after that, he had to start giving back. Both books together cost only forty-five cents, so I didn't have much to lose.

CATALANS, AS A rule, don't enjoy bullfights, but enough of them do to support an arena in Barcelona. Generally, six bulls are presented to three different matadors over three hours. Because the arenas are open air, attendees have to consider whether to choose seats in the sun or shade (*sol o sombra*); the shady seats are more comfortable for such a long time, but the sunny seats are considerably cheaper. I sat in the sun.

I had been to a few bullfights before, in Tijuana, Ensenada, and Mexicali, and had read Hemingway's *Death in the Afternoon,* and even owned an early edition. But I didn't know the Barcelona matadors by name. Frankly, as long as the results were the same (the bull always dies), I could barely identify talented matadors from mediocre ones. Nonetheless, I loved the sound of the brass band introducing each new *corrida,* the enthusiastic crowds, the colorful costumes, the pomp and theatricality of it all.

On this particular afternoon, the first two matadors fought badly against fearlessly aggressive, beautiful bulls. The second of those two matadors was so sloppy at the kill that he stabbed and withdrew the sword three times before the animal, on its knees, finally succumbed to a knife blade across the spinal cord at the neck. The crowd booed and whistled and threw seat cushions into the arena to show their disapproval, even anger, at the matador's appalling performance. An elderly man sitting next to me held his head by his ears and moaned, his face, covered in gray bristles of whiskers, contorted as if in physical pain.

The star of the show that day was a matador called Frascuela, who was loved by the crowd. They cheered him frantically the moment he walked into the sunlight. He was showy, but no one could deny he was an expert at what he did. He was also unbelievably brave, or stupid, as he turned his back on the snorting bull several times and waved to the seats. Once, he lured the bull to charge, then dropped to his knees as the bull passed only inches away. When it came time for the kill, and the bull could barely keep his head up from being worn down by the picadors, Frascuela executed the animal with a swift and sure plunge of his sword, through the bull's neck into its heart, killing it instantly. *That* was the proper way for a bullfight to conclude (if you're having bullfights at all).

The audience went bonkers, the way Dodgers fans might go nuts to see their team come from behind with a grand-slam homer in the bottom of the ninth. Everyone who had a white handkerchief began to wave it—and from the looks of the arena stands, everyone but me had brought one. The judges awarded the matador two ears, which were cut from the dead bull and handed to Frascuela before a team of horses dragged the carcass away, leaving a trail of blood in the sand. The successful matador paraded and pranced around the outer edges of the arena floor, waving his arm like royalty, and tossed the bull's ears to people who seemed especially thrilled by the spectacle.

That night I was tired from all the walking of the day before and the excitement of the bullring that afternoon, so spent the evening in my uninspiring hotel room. When I collected my key from the front desk, the clerk, with a vague sneer, handed it to me without a word.

I pulled the cork on a bottle of cheap Spanish rum, then opened the window of my cheap Spanish room. A flute played poorly from the street, maybe from an untalented busker earning some spare change. Children played loudly in a nearby courtyard in the dark. Didn't they have parents to bring them inside at night and keep them quiet? I filled out some postcards to my parents and my aunt and uncle. I drank more rum, lay on the saggy bed, and slept.

TARRAGONA IS A historic city, a resort destination, with sunny beaches and fine weather. At least, so I've read. All I know is what it looks like while standing on the side of the road, waiting patiently for a sympathetic driver to stop for a disheveled hitchhiker. And such a driver did stop, but only after this hitchhiker had been waiting for two hours.

The driver and his girlfriend looked like all the hippies (eerily so) I had left behind in California. He was little more than a boy, with shoulder-length hair and a head-band; the beginnings of a baby mustache and goatee were barely visible but recognizable. The girl was stunning, with long straight blonde hair parted right up the middle. She wore a flowing white dress made of what looked to be muslin. Buttons held the front together, but she had fastened them only up to her sternum. Every time she turned in her seat to speak to me, she almost entirely exposed her breasts.

The girl immediately lit up a joint and passed it to me while the boy raised the volume of the Dead on the car's dashboard eight-track tape player. I half-expected them to start flashing me the peace sign. They were proud to tell me that the Rolling Stones were coming to play at a big stadium in Salou, near Tarragona. When they learned that I was from California and knew San Francisco well from having lived in nearby Marin County, I was afraid they would wet their pants with glee.

"You know Golden Gate Park?" asked the driver.

"Yes, I know Golden Gate Park," I said. "It's beautiful. I've been to concerts there."

"The Grateful Dead?" asked the girl expectantly.

"Oh yeah. And Jefferson Starship."

"What is Haight-Ashbury like?" asked the driver.

"It's very beautiful with many young people?"

I hated to disappoint him, but explained that it had deteriorated since the Summer of Love, well before my time, and had declined because of a heroin epidemic.

The questions went on and on, as if I were some sort of walking encyclopedia of hippie lore when in fact I barely caught the tail end of that period. Yes, I had attended concerts at Winterland and the Fillmore West, I said. No, I did not know Jerry or Grace.

They finally calmed down and gave me a chance to look out the windows. The passing countryside was a three-dimensional painting of scrub and desert mountains, cactus and ochre sands, women working in fields and burros pulling carts with children laughing inside.

When they dropped me off, the Spanish hippie chick smiled at me, a gorgeous, infectious smile. *What the hell is she doing with that dweeb?!* I almost asked her to continue on with me.

"You will have good luck with the auto-stop," she said, using the European phrase for hitchhiking. "The people in Spain feel sorry for soldiers and students, and always stop for them."

I must have been looking particularly sorrowful at that moment, because no sooner had the hippies driven off than two young men in a late-model Citroën station wagon pulled over for me.

The ride they gave me would dramatically change the course of my travels for the next two weeks.

The passenger rolled down his window and the driver leaned over and smiled.

"G'day, cobber. How ya goin'?"

9

Mal and Geoff, Me
Fair Dinkum Cobbers

*No friend of the police - Have any girls with you? - Bond-
ing with the Aussies - Lessons in architecture - The police
return - Invitation to Africa - Killing time in Algeciras -
The ferry to Ceuta - Border crossing headaches*

Then the cops arrived.
At this stage of my life, I was no admirer of the
constabulary. Doubtless, officers of the law in other cities
were sensitive, understanding, and friends to youth. Not
so the men and women of the Los Angeles County Sheriff's Department under the stern, no-nonsense leadership
of Sheriff Peter J. Pitchess. The deputy sheriffs, at least
through the 1960s and '70s, when I was a teenager, were
tough bastards who would take no guff from anyone.
They especially had it in for any young man with hair or
sideburns longer than his earlobe. Stop-and-frisk meetings were my primary interactions with the cops. If I was
simply walking on the sidewalk, I was always ready to be
halted by a passing prowl car, asked where I had been and

where I was going, shoved up against the hood, and patted down. No reason given.

A friend of mine, whose *nom du hippie* was Child, once flipped the bird at a sheriff's helicopter that was hovering over a field where he was smoking weed with some girl he'd met. The whirlybird set down in the field, while two sheriff's cruisers arrived out of nowhere to stop Child from running away. The chopper coppers took turns beating up Child while the other cops watched. They didn't even bother to roust Child for his weed. They just wanted to ball up their leather-gloved fists and smash his face in.

Support your local police!

Traffic citations were the bane of the hippies. Deputies could always come up with some far-fetched, half-legitimate reason to issue a ticket that they never would issue to a housewife or businessman, not in a million years. I once got a summons for failing to turn on my headlights at dusk. I got another for not coming to a complete stop (the famous "California rolling stop") at an empty intersection. I even got one for *driving too slow* on the freeway; I had been doing fifty-five in the middle lane when the limit was sixty-five.

When two uniformed officers with powerful flashlights approached Mal, Geoff, and me unexpectedly at our coastal campsite near Alicante, I figured doom was impending. They told us to stand up. Mal extinguished the camp-stove flame so as not to burn our supper. The cops spoke halting English, as if they secretly had been listening to us before making their approach and knew what language we spoke.

"You have any girls with you?" one of them asked, looking casually at our belongings laid out around the site. He seemed overly disappointed when I said no, we did not have any girls with us. He asked to see our passports. After he flipped through mine, he held it up like a preacher clutching a Bible at a riverside revival.

"You are delinquent," he accused, looking at me harshly. "You have no stamp to enter Spain."

I knew that I had no stamp. The Spanish immigration official had waved me and my driver through without even looking at our passports. I had no inkling that the lack of a stamp might have any lasting effect. When I explained what had happened, the cop seemed to lose interest.

Then they both walked over to the Citroën, which was parked ten feet away, and poked their heads into the open windows on either side.

"You have a nice car," said the one who hadn't spoken before.

"It's a very expensive car," said the first cop, the mean one. He had a dubious look. "How do boys like you have a very expensive car?"

I was surprised when Mal, the smaller but rougher-looking Aussie, snapped back.

"Look, mate, what do you want here?" he demanded. "Do you want to see my papers for the car? Did we do something wrong? Are there any complaints? Do you see anything suspicious? If not, we're prepping our tea and would like to eat now."

You go, dude! I was thrilled and terrified by his outburst. In L.A. such an eruption of indignation might have resulted in a billy club to the scalp, or one cop frisking you on the ground while his partner held you down with a knee in the small of your back. Things seemed to be different in Alicante, Spain, because the cops eased off their suspicion of us. Or so it seemed.

"Would you like some wine before you go?" I asked, trying to defuse the situation. "Or stay for some food? We were cooking chicken and rice."

Without answering, they walked away in the direction

from which they'd come, looking one last time around the campsite as they left. They were hoping to find something, but I couldn't imagine what.

"Good on ya, Mal," Geoff said to his pal. "But if you keep talking to coppers that way, we'll never make it out of Spain. Crikey!"

Our next encounter with the cops that night would be even more intense.

AFTER MAL AND Geoff had stopped for me that morning, we bonded almost immediately. I liked everything about them—their sense of humor, their far-ranging curiosity, their depth of arcane knowledge—and they seemed to like me as much.

Mal, the driver, and Geoff were recently graduated architects from Australia (or "Straya," as Mal called it). As adventurous as their countrymen's reputation, they had decided to postpone their entry into the working world and enjoy one last bash of youthful freedom. They planned to spend a year in Europe, financed in large measure by working as room attendants at a Zermatt ski resort over the previous winter. In exchange for meals, lodging, and a small salary they changed linens, scrubbed toilets, delivered room-service meals, and did any other laborious task they were handed by their superiors, who included everyone else who worked at the resort.

Denying themselves all luxuries during the work term, they saved enough money to buy a yellow 1976 Citroën GS 1220 Club station wagon and, once the ski season ended, set off on their journey.

I stayed with the Aussies that whole day, since they were going to Morocco and I was going most of that way, to Andalusia in the south of Spain. I even gave them two hundred pesetas for petrol, which wasn't much, but they seemed to appreciate the gesture.

Being architects, much of their sightseeing itinerary had to do with buildings, including the postmodern Muralla Roja, a red-and-pink Arabic-style apartment building that wouldn't have been out of place in the medina of Marrakech or Tangier. At least, that's what I imagined. The building, designed by Ricardo Bofill and now recognized as one of his most iconic works, had been completed just three years earlier in Calpe. Somehow Mal and Geoff had made arrangements to see inside one of the apartments, which was laid out like a cross, with the kitchen and bathroom at the center. The complex's multiple courtyards zigged and zagged like a maze and the Escher-like outdoor staircases were bizarre, disorienting, even psychedelic. I never even would have thought to visit the place on my own.

We decided to stop at a wide, deserted beach for a swim. The surf was still spring-chilly, but the unexpectedly clear water was refreshing and welcoming, especially considering my two-hour wait in the sun for my initial ride that morning. I hadn't showered for a couple of days, and I felt scrubbed and clean by the time I climbed back onto the sand and dried myself in the sun.

We drove mainly on side roads as we continued south. None of us was in a hurry to get anywhere in particular at any given time. If that little village off in the distance looked intriguing, we drove there and walked around. If somebody wanted a snack, we stopped at a market and looked at everything on the shelves, remarking on any unusual items that we couldn't get back home in Melbourne or L.A. Shortly before sunset we pulled off the road and found a remote stretch of beach just outside Alicante, with no outbuildings, lifeguard stations, picnic benches, fire rings, or any other signs of recreation. No private property signs, either. It looked like an agreeable spot to camp for free.

After setting up our respective tents, Mal and Geoff brought out their Coleman stove, which they lit in anticipation of cooking our dinner. I opened the first of two bottles of Rioja we had purchased at a *tienda*. The winds were calm and the sky was clear, I was clean, if a bit salty, and had two new personable companions. They had said I could travel with them the next day, if I wanted. What had started as a lousy morning was concluding on a splendid upbeat note. That is, until the police ambushed us.

After the cops left, clearly frustrated at not having found whatever they'd been looking for, we returned to preparing our supper. We all felt so greatly relieved after the clash with the cops that we were almost giddy as we ate and drank.

We had barely finished our meal of chicken, rice, and vegetables in a spicy tomato sauce, and were starting to clean up, when two more cops surprised us, rushing at our campsite quickly from behind a thicket of trees. It hadn't been more than forty-five minutes since the other pair of cops had left us.

The one who spoke first was old and gray-haired, and was plainly the man in charge. He waved his hand in a motion indicating that we should stand, and, of course, we complied. He let his eyes roam around our campsite, inspecting every detail without moving, then spoke.

"Who else is here with you?" he asked, in English, but his question was more like a statement, as if to say that he was *certain* someone else was with us but out of sight.

"*Solamente nosotros,*" I said. "*No hay nadie más aquí.*"

My Spanish was basic but effective. I sensed the stiffness leak out of the man's posture when he heard me speak. But he wasn't done with us just yet.

"*Quiero buscar en su auto,*" he said, looking directly at me.

"He wants to search your car," I told Mal and Geoff. "The way he asked, I get the feeling we don't have to let him, if *for any reason* you don't want to."

I hoped they understood my emphasis. I sure didn't want to get popped because they were holding any sort of dope. But they both shrugged, as if to say they had no objection.

"*Pásale, señor, por favor,*" I said, telling him to go ahead, and that the car's owner gave his permission. "*El dueño alla dice es no problema.*"

Our ready willingness to be searched eliminated the last of the officer's resolve. Like the two cops who had preceded him, he gave a lackluster peek into the car's interior through the windows, shining his flashlight inside for perhaps thirty seconds before turning back to me.

"*Cuidado, joven,*" he said, quietly and just to me, holding up a finger in warning—although of what, I had no idea. "*Cuidado.*" Be careful, young man. Be careful.

And with that, the two policemen walked purposely back into the trees. We could hear their car engine rev in the distance, then everything was silent until Geoff looked at Mal and me and said, in shocked relief, "Fu-u-u-u-uck me dead!"

"And bury me pregnant," added Mal, at which point he pulled a joint out of his shirt pocket, lit it, and took the deepest toke I'd ever seen a man take in my life.

WE ROSE EARLY—Mal and Geoff in their two-man tent, me in my smaller pup tent—and had a simple breakfast of buttered bread and instant coffee, taken black.

I was enjoying the company of my two new companions more with each passing day. Mal was a little brassy and a little bossy to his friend, but I also saw in him a core of insecurity, as if his forthright nature was emotional camouflage. Geoff, I was surprised to learn, had been raised in China by his wealthy parents. He had a stiffness to his body that troubled me; when he looked to one side, he would turn his entire torso, as if he had injured his neck and couldn't twist it. Geoff was an ardent photographer, and extremely proud of his Leica M3 Rangefinder, which he carried in a sturdy leather case constantly strapped to his shoulder, even when we were eating.

My new Australian friends had a long list of buildings they wanted to see, as would be expected of eager young architects on holiday. They may not have known it, but they were opening a new world to me. I'd been interested in architecture only in the sense of seeing something different than the tract houses and shopping malls of the suburb in which I was raised. That set a low bar. A twenty-foot-tall Paul Bunyan statue planted in the parking lot of a tire store had always thrilled me. As a youth, I'd enjoyed the faux windmills over the Van de Kamp Bakery restaurants in the area. The colossal raised glazed above the donut shop near Los Angeles International Airport never failed to amuse me. These, to me, represented the heights of building design. Keep your Frank Lloyd Wright; we've got giant donuts!

You can readily imagine my reactions, then, to castles overlooking the Rhine, a two-thousand-year-old Roman gate in the center of a medieval city, and the looming presence of Notre-Dame Cathedral. Way, way better than an oversized fiberglass tribute to Paul Bunyan.

At Alicante's ninth-century Castell Santa Bárbara, built by the Moors to protect against the Castilians, Mal and Geoff talked in terms I was unused to. *Crenellation. Parapet. Cantilever.* The words sounded vaguely like English, and I was fascinated. Listening to them at the castle and on the previous day at the Muralla Rioja, I began to understand that they appraised a building as a collection of *components*, not merely and superficially as a single unit, the way I looked at buildings. I began to pay attention when they talked.

Throughout the day we stopped at more intriguing places that the boys had mapped out during their bleak winter of cleaning Swiss toilets and being bossed around. We walked the hilly streets of Mojácar, a stunning example of southern Spain's white villages. *Cubism. Minimalism. Grouped houses.* I gained a deeper appreciation of the Cathedral of Murcia by walking a foot or two behind Mal and Geoff and letting their excited observations wash over me. *Spanish Baroque. Rococo. Arcosolia.*

As much as the buildings, I loved the landscape through which we passed. In the province of Murcia, unlike the countryside I had come through farther north, the cacti, sage, chaparral, and high rocky mesas reminded me more of Arizona and New Mexico than California. Entering Andalusia, the landscape and the people took another turn. The climate and topography were even more desert-like. The setting wasn't the only thing that had changed; the centuries seemed to have transformed as well. Elderly women in black dresses with matching shawls and clunky shoes pulled donkeys tied with ropes around their necks. Oxen towed wooden gypsy wagons that lumbered precariously down dusty roads.

In Granada (a mecca of Moorish architecture, as I was to learn), we agreed to stay in a hotel, both so we could bathe after our swim in the ocean the day before and to get an early start visiting the city's attractions before heading to the next place, wherever that might be. The first few hotels we looked into didn't have hot water, but the one-star Hotel Niza in the center of Granada had all the basics we wanted. Mal and Geoff got a double room with a full bath; I got a single next door without facilities, but would use the shower in their room. Breakfast was included in the price of three dollars for the two rooms.

We found a restaurant around the corner, on the narrow lane called Calle Navas, where we ordered bread, paella, eggs and potatoes, fruit, and ample wine for which we paid a dollar twenty-five apiece, service included. My budget was holding steady. I was beginning to like Spain.

We ambled after our meal to nowhere in particular and everywhere in general. The sun had not yet set. I was charmed by the flowers in all the windows, the cast-iron balconies, the fruit-bearing orange trees alongside the stone-paved streets, and the lively locals who laughed as they crowded the walkways and squares. Mal and Geoff slowed a bit and chatted in low tones as I walked ahead. When they rejoined me they apparently had come to a decision of some sort.

"Look, mate," said Geoff, the sweeter, meeker of the two, "we've just been talking. We're planning to go to Morocco, if we didn't already tell you. Well, you seem like a good bloke, we all get along, and if you're willing to contribute a bit for petty at the servos now and then, we were thinking maybe you'd like to come along with us. You know, if you want to."

Morocco! Paul Bowles. William S. Burroughs. Bogart in *Casablanca*. Hashish. As mesmerizing a picture as that country was in my imagination, I hadn't even considered putting the North African kingdom on my itinerary for fear of it being just a trifle *too* remote and backward for hitchhiking. What was I going to do, stand on the side of a sand dune with my thumb out, waiting for a camel caravan to come by? Conceivably I could take buses, true, but they were few and unreliable and had to cross long distances between major cities.

Geoff and Mal saw the thrill on my face, and Mal picked up with the invitation.

"We'll spend a week or ten days in Morocco," he said, "then we'll take the ferry back to Spain, maybe go into

Portugal for a while, and be in Paris by June. What say, cobber?"

"Absolutely," I said, not at all sure what *petty* and *servos* were. "That's just great. The only condition is that we split all our expenses evenly. Gas, tolls, hotels, campgrounds, meals, the ferry, the works."

Later, I wondered what my decision would mean about traveling to Italy, Bavaria, and the Netherlands, all of which I was eager to see. But right there, that night, in the middle of Granada, Spain, I was living in the moment. I would go to Morocco.

The first thing the next morning we loaded our bags into the Citroën and ate our breakfast in the small lobby restaurant of the Niza. The waiter charged us for an extra cup of coffee we didn't have, so I felt justified in taking the bath towel I'd already liberated.

We went first to the Alhambra, which should be listed as one of the wonders of the world. The interior was like the inside of a psychedelic marshmallow—every wall full of intricate stone carvings, the vaulted ceilings dripping with alabaster stalactites, the floor built from great slabs of marble. And all the time, I was learning: *horseshoe arch, muqarna, interlacing motifs.*

THE ROAD LEADING from Granada to Algeciras, where we would take the car ferry the next day, passed through mountains with vast olive orchards. We drove past Torremolinos and Málaga, but both were so modern and uninspiring that we didn't even bother to stop. The beaches we passed could have been lifted straight from California and seemed to have some decent surfable waves. Too bad we had no boards.

In Algeciras, we drove straight to the ferry ticket office to see about a reservation, but the man behind the counter was not optimistic about our chances.

"No ferries," he said. "Not today. Not yesterday. Maybe not tomorrow. The rough seas. You come back tomorrow."

Just in case the ferry would be back in service, we made a reservation for the first boat out, and paid the equivalent of five dollars each for the ticket, including the car. The price was much more than we had expected. We agreed that we'd sleep in the car that night to save money. Mal and Geoff would fold back their seats as much as they could, and I would sleep on the bench seat behind them. The prospect sounded uncomfortable, but would allow us to drive straight onto the ferry as soon as we could the next morning and avoid paying for a hotel.

We rose around seven and went immediately to the ticket agency to see if the ferries would run that day. The agent said that all indications were good, but the first departure had been pushed back, so we still had time to kill. The man gave us some papers we would need to submit to passport control on departure. At a kiosk, we ordered coffee and donuts, and as we ate them admired the views across the harbor to Gibraltar and its famous rock on the other side of the bay. Mal dug out a boxed game of Parcheesi from the back of the Citroën, and we played several rounds at a picnic table while sipping our coffees.

The signal came, a blasting horn, alerting passengers to board the ferry, but first we were obliged to enter a drive-through passport check. Once again, I was hassled by someone in authority about not having the proper stamps in my visa pages, but I was learning that in such confrontations meekness and an air of cluelessness were more likely to get the desired results than anything like argumentativeness or assertiveness. Fortunately, I didn't have to try hard to play the role of a befuddled American tourist. We drove onto the boat.

We had chosen to arrive in Ceuta, an autonomous

Spanish city on the North African coast, rather than in Tangier, because the ferry was cheaper, not because the port offered much to see. A pinch-faced immigration officer, who curiously avoided eye contact, directed us to complete and sign various forms before stamping our passports. For some reason, cars seemed to require more paperwork than people did. We waited in line, filled out forms, waited in line to submit them, then received more forms to complete. The entire process took an hour, despite that only fifty arriving passengers occupied the cavernous customs hall. I couldn't see the sense of going through immigration formalities simply to travel from one Spanish city to another, even if it was on another continent. Imagine if Americans had to pass through passport control when flying from San Francisco to Honolulu.

The immediate area around Ceuta's port was unattractive, even outright ugly, full of warehouses, rusting steel gates pulled across access roads, and dumpy little houses on potholed streets. Not even the pleasant weather could add any luster to the place. The settlement seemed to exist for no other reason than to serve as a transit depot for goods and people. I understood how such a port would be profitable to the Spanish government by levying tariffs at both ends of the movement of goods between two continents. I could also see why any tourist landing there would want to leave in a hurry, which is what we did.

Mysterious Morocco awaited.

10

Morocco Bound

Camel poop is squishier than you'd think - Gas coupons - Mad for the Rif Mountains - Bad vibes in Moulay Idriss - Wabi-sabi, baby! - The result of raising a child on Wonder Bread and TV dinners - Didress of Fez - Souks, dye vats, carpets - The Great Djellaba Fiasco

Almost immediately after leaving the border checkpoint, we came across a wizened, near-toothless grandpa in an ankle-length robe towing a camel by a rope.

We pulled over and persuaded the old man, in exchange for some wadded-up Spanish pesetas, to let us take turns sitting on the camel for photos. He had us remove our shoes—I assumed to avoid hurting the hideous, slobbering brute—commanded the drooling devil to kneel, then demonstrated how to wrap our legs tight against the camel's rear haunches, lean forward, and hold onto the hump. The position reminded me of a jockey on a Thoroughbred, hunched over with knees high from the short stirrups, but this smelly primeval chaos-monster had neither saddle nor stirrups, just a flea-flecked hide and a fat-filled hump. I volunteered to go first. After all, I was quite the horseman, if you counted my half-dozen hour-long trail rides on worn-out glue fodder at a suburban stable in Long Beach when I was ten.

How hard could it be to ride a camel?

The butt-ugly ungulate sensed my mastery of the situation. I climbed into position, expertly clamped my legs as instructed, and grabbed a couple of handfuls of camel fur, which was about as pleasant as clutching your father's weekend whiskers. The spittle-stained Satan of the Sahara turned its head 180 degrees to stare at me with its malevolent, cow-like eyes. With a shout from the camel driver, the varmint rose from its crouch, quicker than I'd expected, and immediately, petulantly, squatted back on its belly. As if in a bizarre gymnastics event, I rolled backward and did a neat little flip off the camel's ass. With an *ooph!* they could have heard at Rick's Café Americain 250 miles away, and with such precision you'd have thought I was aiming for it, I landed in a pile of camel crap.

Instead of riding the Ship of the Desert, I'd tumbled into the shit of the desert.

Funny thing about dromedary dung. It resembles a bunch of overly large Concorde grapes, but brown and dry-looking. I'm here to tell you that looks can be deceiving in this particular aspect of animal husbandry. Physical contact, whenever possible, should be avoided. The poop had squished all over my Levi's 501s. But hey, I could now say I had *ridden a camel*! Well, I nearly *sat* on one while an elderly man held tightly to the rope around the fiendish quadruped's neck, but why split camel hairs?

Mal and Geoff declined to give it a go for themselves after my Olympic performance, and we returned to the car. I'm afraid I stunk up the place when we continued onward. We had nothing with which I could wipe my clothes clean. We had no paper towels, and the toilet paper we carried was dangerously low, so we didn't want to waste it on camel waste. But Mal and Geoff acted as if they were about to die from the odor. Geoff began to gag, nearly ready to vomit. I sat in the backseat and tried to look angelic. *Smell? What smell?* Eventually, Mal pulled over and shut down the engine.

"Find something," he pleaded. "Anything."

I tried to scrape off the residue with a rough-edged stone from the side of the road.

"When it dries, I can brush it all off," I said optimistically. "Let's just roll the windows down and not worry about it."

"I've a better idea, mate," Mal called from the driver's seat. "Why don't you sit on the roof of the car? Your trousers'll dry faster and we won't have to smell that bloody goona."

Down the road we went, soon growing used to the smell of my manure-slathered jeans.

MAL, GEOFF, AND I, on the crossing from Spain, had agreed on a rough route for this leg of our journey and an even rougher timetable. We all hoped to see the most well-known cities, especially Fez and Marrakech; the boys also had in mind a few places of architectural interest that I'd never heard of. We figured to make Agadir, on the coast, the southernmost point of our trip, and from there loop back north along the coast to Tangier. But if we had to pass up one of the midway destinations because we'd lingered too long at another, so be it. If we wanted to extend our Moroccan sojourn by a day or two, so be that too. We would rise when we awoke, eat when hungry, and sleep wherever was convenient at the end of a long day. The idea was to have some fun and see unusual things without any time pressure. But I was a natural clock-watcher, list-maker, and calendar-keeper. Random fun without a schedule? I wasn't sure I could handle it.

Tetouan, a forty-minute drive farther south, was the first city of any size we came to. We stopped there to cash some traveler's cheques and to buy gas coupons that were good for a thirty percent discount. There I got my first good look at daily life in Morocco. The costumes worn by the men of Morocco were like nothing to be found in America or Europe. Many of them sported a red fez with a tassel on top, like Sydney Greenstreet in *Casablanca*. They wore ankle-length, long-sleeved, hooded robes called djellabas. Their shoes were most odd of all: lemon-yellow leather slip-ons with long pointy toes called *babouches*. The women wore brightly colored wraps, many had heavy bundles on their backs, and quite a few had fabric pulled across the lower half of their faces in the Islamic style.

The road out of Tetouan led through the lush, rough Rif Mountains, which were unexpectedly green and moist. Roadside streams rushed into large rivers. Eucalyptus trees and open fields of tall green hay swayed in the wind. We'd climbed out of the harsh desert into Shangri-La. The higher we ascended on the mountain road, the cloudier the sky became until soon rain began to fall. Everywhere, herds of sheep and cows grazed. Plentiful too were lone donkeys tied to fence posts. Gray-whiskers in djellabas, holding tall shepherd's crooks, watched their flocks nibble on grass in the deep green valleys. The Rif Mountains. I had never heard of them the day before. Now they were my favorite place on earth.

We descended to a broad plateau that looked uninhabited. The rain continued here, but the greenness of the mountains was gone. We saw no signs of agriculture or any other cars, just a desolate landscape. This was the home of Volubilis, a remarkably preserved Roman city founded in the third century B.C.

We were the sole visitors that day—whether because of

the rain showers or the site's remoteness, I didn't know—but we felt privileged to have the place to ourselves, to walk along its wide stone streets without bumping into other people. Floors of the ruined houses still retained intricate mosaics of fish, dolphins, angels, and gods. Our path took us under elaborate arches and between columns leading to altars. We came to a high point in the ruins and simply stared at the history at our feet, none of us wanting to break the magic by speaking. Overhead, the drifting rain-laden clouds lent a suitably somber backdrop to the panorama of this outpost of a once great but long-dead civilization.

Today Volubilis is a popular tourist destination, thanks to its 1997 designation as a UNESCO World Heritage site. And because of the security and preservation precautions required to earn such a distinction, Volubilis can no longer be climbed and poked about the way three young men once did in the spring of 1976.

We drove to the small hilltop town of Moulay Idriss, two miles outside Volubilis. A more inhospitable place I had never seen. A young boy, perhaps twelve years old, offered to guide us around, saying he could speak English, German, French, and Arabic, but the place didn't seem large enough to require a guide. Looking around at the people and the buildings, the calendar might have read 1676 as easily as 1976. Dirty, grungy men huddled here and there, smoking pipes in doorways of crumbling mortar, listlessly weaving baskets, whispering with one another, or just staring. Mainly at us. An elderly man crossing the street seemed to be aiming straight at me, then purposely bumped me with his shoulder. What could I do? He was seventy, at least. Grampy-bashing couldn't have been popular in Morocco. I bought a piece of nougat candy in a little shop, and the woman behind the counter treated me as if I had just walked out of a spaceship. I got the sense that Moulay Idriss was not a popular spot among Western tourists, at least not in those days, because these people seemed unused to outsiders. I never liked being conspicuous in a crowd, but in our shorts, flip-flops, and gaudy T-shirts, the three of us certainly stood out in Moulay Idriss.

"Let's go back to the car," Geoff said, which we did without debate.

Meknes, a partly walled city some thirty miles farther south, was a different matter. Maybe because Meknes was larger than Moulay Idriss, and other Westerners were milling about, we no longer felt like below-the-line actors in the first reel of a horror movie. We found a campground just inside the old city walls and set up our tents, but left our gear in the locked car, then walked to the market street for some sightseeing and to have dinner.

We assumed that because we were parked in a campground and the car doors were locked, our belongings would be safe. And this time, they would be. But our fatalistic approach to security would ultimately be our undoing.

The boys were eager to see something called the Bab al-Mansour, the main gate to the city's medina. The gate was a massive entrance through the city walls, with fifty-foot-high wooden doors and a palace-like appearance boasting mosaics and scrollwork on every surface. No question, the drive to Meknes was worthwhile for that alone.

We approached the structure close up, then stood well back. We walked its breadth to see it from every angle. Geoff and Mal used some new words on me, but also told me what they meant, like zellige tiling, the glossy, rough-edged tiles on the gate's façade. I pointed out that the tiles seemed less than perfect, considering this structure was built at the behest of a sultan.

"That's just it," said Geoff, gently, explaining without being teacherly. "There's a *wabi-sabi* charm that's just delightful. And it will be even more so in another hundred years."

Wabi-sabi, a Japanese aesthetic that perceives beauty in the imperfect and impermanent, has been my favorite phrase ever since. Not least of all when describing my wardrobe.

"See those columns on either side?" Mal asked. He pointed to two white marble posts whose material and design were completely different from the rest of the gate. "Notice that they're crowned with Corinthian capitals?"

I didn't know what either *Corinthian* or *capital* meant. Mal explained briefly and to the point. Then he went on.

"The builders brought them here from Volubilis," he said, happy to see my interest. "They were part of the ruins we just visited." He turned his gaze back to the gate. "Amazing to think that the architects who built this beautiful gate three hundred and fifty years ago felt they had to embellish their work with something they thought was equally or even more beautiful and from a completely different civilization."

A month earlier, I would have looked at the Bab al-Mansour and said, "Gnarly." Now I could remark on the *wabi-sabi* charm of the zellige mosaics and the brilliant ode to architectural artistry through the unexpected juxtaposition of Roman Corinthian columns and indigenous Islamic design elements. Not a clash of communities, but a commemoratory commingling of cultures.

"See the calligraphy?" Geoff pointed to some Arabic lettering among the scrollwork. "It says, 'I am the most beautiful gate in Morocco. I'm like the moon in the sky. Property and wealth are written on my front.'"

I was stunned.

"You...you read *Arabic*?!" I asked.

But no. Geoff had written a paper on the Bab al-Mansour, and had never forgotten that phrase. His memory of the research he'd done was the driving force behind our stopping in Meknes. I gathered that Geoff and Mal didn't ditch class in architecture school often.

Later we walked without purpose through the winding brick lanes of the old medina, stopping in the souks and remarking on the odd use of colors painted on the shopfronts and houses. They were pink and green and red and an odd shade of blue, every color of the prism.

"But all pastels," Geoff emphasized. "That's what I find unique. Not a garish color among them."

Back in La Mirada, only mothers and girlfriends and kids taking art classes used the word *pastel*. And Geoff wasn't self-conscious about it either.

"How about getting a bite in this place? It's nearly time for our tea," Mal said, pointing to a shabby eatery filled with men in djellabas. "Strikes me as an interestingly filthy place to sample the local victuals."

At that stage in my life, food was not a major concern other than getting enough of it to fill my belly. Growing up, we ate a lot of frozen TV dinners and Chef Boyardee canned spaghetti. Our idea of a healthy snack was toasted Wonder Bread palette-knifed with an inch-thick coating of Market Basket margarine and sprinkled generously with off-brand cinnamon powder and two heaping spoonfuls of C&H Pure Granulated White Cane Sugar straight out of its sixty-four-ounce bag. My divorced mother was a full-time technical editor for Hughes Aircraft, working long days between her morning and evening commutes. Expecting her to prepare fancy dinners was unrealistic. The most sophisticated meal she cooked in those days was something she called "hamburger noodle bake," a simple casserole that tasted better than it sounds.

In the years since I left home at eighteen, I ate like most

college students eat—peanut butter sandwiches, McDonald's french fries, entire sleeves of Ritz crackers, spaghetti with tomato sauce, chips and dip, and lots of boxed macaroni and cheese.

The only foreign food I ever ate (and not nearly as often as you might think a Californian would) was Mexican, mainly tacos. And those weren't tacos from some suitably decorated place called El Sarape or Rosa's Jardin de Guadalajara, with a fountain out front and "Cielito Lindo" playing over the loudspeakers. No, we went to Jack-in-the-Box, the omnipresent fast-food joint, for our greasy tacos.

Even during my first few weeks in Europe, I had survived largely on uninspired foods like bread, simple cheese, pre-sliced meats, and any American staples that came my way at breakfast. An adventurous diner I was not. A croque-madame, with a fried egg on top of what was basically a ham-and-cheese sandwich, was about as reckless as I got.

As I peeked into the literal hole-in-the-wall in which Mal suggested we eat, my stomach began doing flip-flops even before entering. But in for a penny....

Mal, who was happy to take charge, indicated to the waiter that we wanted three of whatever that man sitting next to us was having, along with bread and three pastries. The main dish was a kind of bean stew, hot and spicy and filling. The bread was fresh, crusty outside, and like a cloud within; dipped into the stew, it metamorphosed into something approaching the sublime. The pastries didn't disappoint either; I still don't know what they were made from except that they were sweet and chewy with an aftertaste of almonds, a brilliant end to a simple meal. When the waiter came to take our money, he confused us by holding up a thumb, as if giving us a signal that everything was OK.

"I don't understand," Geoff said. "Why is he holding up his thumb? Are we supposed to hold up our thumbs back to him?"

"No," I said, though I wasn't positive. "That's how some people count one on their hand. I think he means we owe him one dirham."

"Each?" Mal asked, as if I were some sort of Moroccan dining expert.

"We'll see...."

I dug out a one-dirham coin from my pocket and tentatively handed it to the man, who took it and walked away, seemingly satisfied.

"Guys," I said, "I'm pretty sure we just paid one dirham for all three meals."

Twenty-two cents for all that food! But none of us was completely certain that we had paid in full—or whether the waiter had gone to the back room to find the scimitar reserved for deadbeat customers. We stood up slowly, edging our way through the low tables, ready to return with cash in hand at the first angry shout from a cleaver-carrying cook or the whoosh of a rolling pin sailing past our skulls.

THE CLOUDS DIDN'T dissipate overnight. We awoke to a gray and chilly morning without sun. Mal seemed to enjoy cooking for us; Geoff and I were glad to oblige him, especially first thing in the morning. Soon we were enjoying platefuls of fried potatoes and fluffy scrambled eggs, along with tin cups of instant coffee, all of which fortified us well for our day's goal: to explore the mysterious, timeworn imperial city of Fez.

We parked in the newer part of the metropolis and entered the old town on foot. We had no map of the cacophonous, crowded medina, so we set out in search of the tourist office. We were like blind men in an unfamiliar house, feeling our way cautiously, without knowing exactly where we were going. A young man on a small, 125cc dirt bike (nothing with more than two wheels could motor through much of the medina) saw our confusion and stopped next to us.

"Where do you go?" he asked matter-of-factly. "I am Didress."

He looked to be no more than twenty years old, small, sturdy, and good-looking. I liked his confidence. I told him we were in search of the tourist office.

"Come with me," he said, and walked his motorcycle slightly ahead of us.

No way could we have found the place on our own, I realized. Into one alley, out into a square, down a side street, and into another alley. Then with a flourish, Didress waved his arm toward a glass-fronted shop front. Unfortunately, the tourist office was closed, but whether for the day or momentarily was unclear.

"I guess we should just wing it," I said to Mal and Geoff.

Geoff looked comically at our surroundings in mock horror. Men led donkeys down the narrow lanes. Weird women in full hijabs or scarf-covered heads and long black dresses floated by, wraithlike. Three young men, as if in an acrobatic act, sputtered past on a rusty scooter. Some sort of reed instrument played from a second-floor window. I fully expected a muezzin to call from a nearby minaret, as we had heard early that morning in Meknes.

"I will guide you," Didress said quietly. "Three hours, ten dirhams."

We had little need to consult one another, and quickly agreed to his offer. We liked Didress immediately. His manner of dress and speech was Westernized. He wore blue jeans, a black T-shirt, and a black vest. He could speak English, French, and Arabic. He was at ease with us, and eager to show us his city. And if he made a back-door commission on anything we purchased, you had to expect that.

I couldn't help but feel sorry for all the donkeys we saw. They were omnipresent. The people used them as they might use a wheelbarrow, but without as much concern for the animals' well-being. They were loaded to the breaking point with stacks of firewood, sheets of leather, mountainous bundles of wool, crates of spices, and, for all I knew, plastic pouches of opium hidden in gunny sacks of soybean meal. A garage for donkeys, where vendors could leave their animals during market hours, recalled a typical parking lot in an American city.

As we walked to what Didress said was the largest mosque in Fez, the unpaved lanes were wet and slick with mud and donkey shit. The threat of slipping was constant. We watched from outside the mosque as locals washed their feet, hands, and faces in a long basin near the entrance. Because we were non-Muslims, we weren't allowed inside.

I had never in my life been denied access to something because of who I was, except for the time they wouldn't let me into Les Girls topless bar in Norwalk because I was only seventeen. My feelings were mixed. True, I was in a foreign country, having to abide by the customs of strangers. But having grown up a white Christian male in a largely white Christian society, I couldn't have fathomed what discrimination might feel like.

Didress sensed my discomfort, and led us through the puzzle of streets to a decommissioned mosque. He knew the location of a staircase that allowed us to reach the mosque's rooftop, where we looked out over the entire medina. The panorama brought to mind a 1940s fantasy film starring Sabu, full of flying carpets and wicked viziers with pointy black beards. We could see the tattered roofs of the shops, the green slate domes of mosques, the fourteen minarets spread across the old town, and the massive city walls.

Back on the street, all the males looked similar: mostly old, stubbly bearded, missing teeth, wearing turbans (or fezzes, if they were well-to-do), and djellabas. Those robe-like cloaks ranged from shabby, moth-eaten wool to elegant milky-white silk. The shops in the twisting tiny streets were, quite literally, holes in the wall, much like the restaurant in which we'd eaten dinner the previous night. In many cases, the entries were cave-like mouths in the fronts of the mud-walled buildings, openings about ten by ten feet and two feet off the ground. I couldn't imagine how all these elderly Moroccans were able to climb inside. Then I realized that many locals didn't enter the shops, but merely stood at an entrance, placed an order with a shopkeeper inside, and completed the transaction without ever leaving the street. Not all of the building fronts held shops. In some of them, I saw old men at work—spinning pottery, working a loom, or just sitting, talking, and smoking.

As Didress led us among the curious sights of the casbah, we had picked up a silent companion: a severely cross-eyed boy about ten or eleven years old. He wore simple cotton gym shorts, a dirty T-shirt, and no shoes. He stayed with us for half an hour, never speaking, and never approaching us when we tried to lure him closer. He was like a stray dog, eager for food and companionship but afraid of being kicked. I pulled a one-dirham coin from my pocket and held it out to him, but he was too shy to reach for it. I flipped it in the air and caught it in my fist, ala George Raft, and the boy laughed. Then I flipped it again, but this time toward him. He caught it on the fly, jammed it into his pocket, then turned and ran away, the last we saw of him.

Coming from a sheltered life as I did, a life in which my family knew where I was at any given hour of every day until I was in my middle teens, I was stupefied by the freedom allowed to young Moroccan children, some barely more than toddlers. In the California suburbs, the cross-eyed boy would never have been allowed to wander the way he did. We saw a few kids sitting in front of a mosque. One of them, not even old enough to attend school, removed a cigarette from his pocket, lit it, and began puffing away, as casually as a full-grown man.

Didress escorted us to a carpet store, since Mal and Geoff had made some vague suggestions about wanting to buy one. Sure, why not? They had a car and could tie a carpet to the roof. The salesman greeted us with handshakes and a hug for Didress, and led us to a showroom in the back. He had us sit on a bench against a wall, then called to someone in Arabic. A woman dressed conservatively in a long-sleeved, ankle-length caftan came out carrying a pewter tray with a tea service. The salesman poured each of us a small cup of mint tea and began to boast about the wonders of his carpets—the superlative quality of the wool, the expertise of the weavers, the artistry of the designs. Geoff and Mal appraised some of the rugs on display, but their enthusiasm had waned. They seemed bored. The salesman noticed their growing inattention and ordered his servant to unroll another rug, then another, then another. In no time, ten large carpets had been presented to us, their history explicated as each was unveiled. Mal asked the prices of several, and told Geoff they were too high. The salesman began to look desperate. His eyes landed on Didress, who set down his tea and walked over to where we stood.

"You will not find better prices," he said. "They will carry a carpet to your car. It is *not* a problem. *This* is your place to buy a carpet."

I liked Didress, but his hard-sell tone of voice was un-appealing. Mal and Geoff seemed turned off as well.

"Please," said the salesman. "This place, originally a mansion for a very rich man. Come, see upstairs."

Curious, we followed him up a flight of stairs to a large room where four teenage girls were operating a loom with what looked to be silk threads of various colors. That was the extent of the tour, then we walked back to the show-room.

"Now, we find you a carpet," said the salesman, as if he had just overcome a major sales hurdle. "You tell me what you want. Colors, patterns. We have it."

But Mal and Geoff were done. I was just along for the amusement of it all, so I joined them as soon as they headed for the street. The salesman looked extremely per-turbed, and split his gaze back and forth between us and Didress.

Once outside, we rambled through byways and back al-leys and crowded shopping streets until Didress led us to a dealer in blankets and leather goods. Again, we were invited to sit in a parlor and were served mint tea as hire-lings presented us with an array of leather belts for our inspection and approval. As we examined them and nod-ded our heads noncommittally, the shopkeeper and Didress passed me a long-stemmed pipe of smoldering hash. I took a lengthy hit and passed it to Geoff, who in-haled deeply. Mal shook his head, and Geoff handed the pipe back to me. I ended up smoking the rest of the bowl myself while Mal tried on several styles of belts and se-lected one to buy.

We returned to the street, where the intensity of the col-ors and odd sounds and smells were magnified by the hash.

Didress was eager to show us the eleventh-century Chouara Tannery, still operational after nearly a thousand years. Young boys of nine or ten, with multi-hued dyes on their faces, hands, and feet, carried wet leather to the far corners of the complex. Men hauled recently tanned hides over their shoulders to the edges of the building's second-story parapets, where they draped the skins over the sides to dry. Dozens of men and boys wearing only shorts and turbans boiled cow hides in huge stone cauldrons of red, blue, and green dye. Smoke and steam hung close and thick to the ground, and the stink was terrific, enough to hurt your sinuses. We climbed to the roof, from where we had another wide view of Fez. We could also observe the courtyard where the dyeing was taking place, the men laboring like animals in the sun, as if we were looking at a painting from a book on antiquity.

"You want djellaba?" Didress asked as Geoff flipped through some of those garments hanging from an awning in front of a clothes shop. "Not here. This place is not good. Quality is bad. Prices are too high. Come."

Then he led us around the corner to a different clothes store with the same merchandise. He gave a warm greeting to the shopkeeper, a pimply teen, then turned to us.

"Best prices," he said. "Please, have a look."

Although we went inside, the Aussies were tiring of the purchasing excursion, and almost immediately turned to leave. In a panic, seeing their lack of interest, the salesman started laying out djellabas faster and faster on the counter, assuming that surely *one* of his garments would appeal to these visitors. But he had priced his goods too high, with nothing costing less than twenty dollars. Mal and Geoff made their way outside. In desperation, the shopkeeper told me he would drop his prices to seventy-five dirhams each. I saw one that I liked, a thigh-length, roughly woven, striped cotton djellaba with a pouch in front, like the Baja hoodies popular with California surfers and hippies. I was still conscious of the fact that I didn't have a jacket, and this would do fine. As a veteran haggler in the curio markets of Tijuana, I offered forty dirhams. He countered with sixty-five. I stuck to my price and made as if to leave. The young man grabbed me by the arm.

"You guys bargain more than Moroccans!" he said curtly, pocketing my forty dirhams and placing my purchase in a paper sack.

I caught up with my friends, but we had hardly taken more than a few steps when an angry man ran up to us from behind, grabbed the bundle out of my arms, and began cursing furiously in Arabic. He looked back toward the shop doorway, where my hapless salesman now stood, clearly the target of his boss's wrath. I grabbed my package out of the man's hands and narrowed my eyes to look tough. Then we went on our way while the boss continued to vent his anger at the sheepish shop clerk.

"The man was not angry with you," Didress explained. "The boy who sold you the djellaba gave it to you very cheap because he planned to keep the money and not record the sale. He was stealing from the owner."

"What'll happen to him?" I asked, wondering if they still chopped off the hands of thieves in this part of the world.

"Nothing," Didress said. "The boy is the nephew of the owner. The owner will watch him more closely from now on. Nothing more."

11

The Pink City
and Beyond

*The angry watermen of Marrakech - I'm instructed to go
fuck myself - Toothsome tagine - Shirtless in Ouarzazate
- That's public-school math for you - How are things in
Essaouira? - Rick's Place - A travel education*

Ack!" Mal shouted in mock alarm. "Bloody ankle bit-
ers! Get 'em off! Geoff, save me!"

A dozen or more children, ages somewhere between
five and ten, swarmed us as we entered the narrow dark
alleys of the Marrakech medina.

"Monsieur! Monsieur!" they shouted as they grabbed
our hands.

The kids appeared harmless, and were probably hoping
for nothing more than a coin or two tossed to them. We
were fully aware, though, that even a nine-year-old street
urchin could race away with your wallet in hand, never to
be found. The potential for having your pocket picked in
the crowded casbahs of North Africa (as well as on the
thronged thoroughfares of Europe) was real; we were

vigilant about wearing our money belts, and proactively carried nothing of value in our outer pockets.

A shopkeeper came out of his minuscule electronics store and chased the kids away with shouts and waves of his hands. He was perhaps thirty years old, dressed in Western-style slacks and a button-down shirt. When the children ran away, he turned to us, smiled, and bowed slightly before returning to his shop. He hadn't even tried to sell us anything.

Mal and Geoff were eager to see the Saadian Tombs, a sixteenth-century royal necropolis considered by many to be the apex of Moroccan architecture during the 150-year reign of the Saadian dynasty—as you no doubt already knew. Not that *I* had a clue. But my architect friends hadn't led me astray up to now. Spooky tombs in the back alleys of Marrakech? Lead on, Macduff (as we serial misquoters are wont to say). The trouble was that we couldn't find the building; we continually turned into dead-end lanes or unintentionally retraced our steps. *Hey, didn't we just pass that ironmonger five minutes ago?!*

To understand why it might be difficult to locate a massive mausoleum in Marrakech, consult an aerial map of the city's historic core, the medina. The settlement was built on an oasis nearly a thousand years ago, and continued doubling in size century after century without apparent need for zoning regulations. Almost since its founding in 1062, Marrakech had been a capital to one degree or another—of its region, of a dynasty, of an empire. There were palaces aplenty, grand civic buildings, lavish homes of the long-gone sharifs, handsome mosques, secret gardens, and public squares. Crammed among them were rude houses and stinky tanneries, metal-roofed *souks* whose stalls of fruit, clothing, and spices seemed to go on endlessly. Thousands of centuries-old lanes, passageways, and footpaths meandered as if laid out by a cock-

eyed opium smoker. Modern, straight-as-an-arrow boulevards cut along the edges of the historic quarter but were
of little directional value to visitors feeling their way
through the depths of the city's chaotic core. No, the cat's
cradle that was Marrakech wasn't easily negotiated by
first-timers from the West.

The city of Marrakech, then as now, was rigorous about
its requirement that all tour guides be licensed, so, of
course, we hired an illegal guide, figuring he would be
less expensive and more apt to show us the "real" Marrakech. Like Didress in Fez, Nassim was in his early twenties and wore Western-style clothes, but was, unlike
Didress, tall and lanky. His English wasn't as good as our
previous guide, but good enough.

Nassim said he always began his excursions by visiting
the markets, called *souks*, which were jammed with small
kiosks. The plain-dirt pathways between the stalls had
rope netting overhead to provide a measure of shade from
the desert sun. We saw the yarn market, the djellaba market, the spice and leather and brass markets. The basket
market had a clean, fresh aroma of dried reeds and straw.
I bought some cut-rate souvenirs—rings for my brothers,
colorful scarves for my mother and sister—but wanted to
see everything more than to buy anything.

Among the oddities that morning were men walking
about in the strangest of costumes. They wore blazing red
djellabas with patterned vests. On their heads were wide-
brimmed, conical pink sombreros adorned by brass ban-
gles that jingled as they walked and scores of multi-hued
tassels that swayed dramatically as the men moved their
heads. Draped from their shoulders on string were small
brass drinking bowls. Some of the men rang brass hand-
bells, others shouted out in a sing-song fashion, and a few
did little dances, but they all managed to call attention to
themselves.

"They are *guerrab*," Nassim explained. "The water-men. Their costumes, very traditional."

The watermen could be found in market squares throughout the country, selling drinks of water to pass-ersby from goatskin bladders (many still covered in thick goat hair) strapped to their backs. Mal and Geoff imme-diately brought out their cameras and began to snap away, but the men seemed agitated at being the subject of photos without having given their permission, and outright angry when the boys declined their request for payment, which they made by rubbing a thumb across their fingers. The *guerrab* were more interested in earning tips from posing than in actually selling water. Their aggressive behavior began to alarm me, and Nassim seemed to agree. He hus-tled us away and said something curt over his shoulder to the men in the complicated pink hats.

Nassim pointed out minarets ("None can be taller than the tallest palm tree," he said), mosques, and more mar-kets. Marrakech was much more commercial than Fez, and we saw far more European and American tourists. Storefront signs spelled out their proffered goods in Eng-lish and French as well as Arabic. The wide avenues that separated parts of the medina were modern. But tourists, the souvenir shops that appealed to tourists, and the broad boulevards carrying busloads of tourists were not why we had come to Marrakech.

"Let's go to the tombs now, mate," Mal said to Nassim. "I've been wanting to see them since we got here."

Finally, we arrived at the Saadian Tombs, where many long-forgotten monarchs are buried. I could appreciate the craftsmanship of the patterned tile floors, the complex carvings around the arched doorways, and the ghostly chill in the shadowy tomb room, but overall I wasn't im-pressed. Mal and Geoff failed to take me to architecture school, so I imagined they were mildly disappointed too.

We paid off Nassim and ate lunch at a small eatery in the core of the old city. The restaurant wasn't too clean, but we took seats and ordered anyway: salad, french fries, bread, and lamb shish kebab. (The next morning, I had mild diarrhea, but figured I was just paying the price of culinary acclimation.)

Afterward, we walked aimlessly around the Djemaa el-Fna, a massive square edged by *souks,* mosques, European-style shops selling perfume and leather goods, and scores of cafés. Hundreds of people milled about, lounged at the café tables, or browsed the merchandise at the market stalls. On Thursdays, a camel market was held in the square, but we had missed it. Too bad. We could have shown the locals the correct way to pose for a picture while sitting on a camel (as long as the animals were tied with a rope held by a funny old man).

Elsewhere in the expansive plaza were booksellers in booths that stocked used paperbacks published in every language conceivable. You could walk into shops offering the same skullcaps that many of the local men favored, as well as belts, jewelry, and bright yellow pointy-toed *babouches,* all overpriced. It would be better to search deeper in the medina for such things.

As we passed a leather-goods store in the busy square, a man of about fifty standing in the doorway stepped toward me and took a firm hold of my wrist.

"Mister, come inside," he urged in an unctuous tone. "Please, best prices. What do you want? Wallet? Belt? Purse for your wife?"

As he pitched his oily patter, he pulled insistently on my arm, trying to get me to enter his shop. I don't mind being touched, but I dislike being grabbed. I yanked my wrist out of his grip with a sharp tug.

"Get outta here!" I said, with what I hoped was a threat in my voice.

Mal and Geoff had unwittingly walked on ahead of me and didn't see what had happened. I walked purposely toward my friends and away from the shopkeeper and two men who had joined him.

"Fuck you!" the man called after me in good English, following me and raising his hand in a gesture that was more Italian than Moroccan. "You go and fuck yourself!"

Now Geoff and Mal saw the commotion and waited for me to catch up to them. I said not to worry, that everything was fine, but Mal wanted to go back and have it out with the shopkeeper and his mates.

"I think they'll calm down if all three of us go back," Mal said, steaming mad and looking in the shopkeeper's direction. "Unless they want a barney."

I had never heard that word before, but I knew what Mal was implying. The men saw the three of us staring at them, and walked purposely back into the shop. Instead of challenging the rowdy retailers to a fistfight, we chose to move along (reluctantly, in Mal's case) without starting a major international incident and ending up in a Moroccan hoosegow on assault charges.

A dozen Black Africans dressed in white robes and black fezzes with long black tassels pounded on a variety of hand drums in the center of the Djemaa el-Fna. They stood in a row while one after another of them jumped in front of his fellow drummers and did a wild, contorted dance in time to the pounding. The leader of the group eyed the growing crowd that surrounded them and quickly moved to anyone who snapped a picture and made them pay one dirham for the privilege.

Another crowd had gathered around three young acrobats, teenagers, who balanced one another on their knees and shoulders, flipped their partners into airborne somersaults, and tumbled across the stone-floored square while their mates leaped over them, Superman fashion, and did shoulder rolls as they landed. The audience was enthusiastic in its cheers and applause, and readily filled the boys' tip hat with coins and paper.

Not so well received were the snake charmers. I had always thought that sort of serpent bedazzler was the province of India, but at least one two-man team had come to Morocco that afternoon. The shirtless, shoeless performers, visibly poor and dirty, sat on the ground on either side of a rude basket. One of them played a simple reed horn that could produce only three or four different notes, while the other lifted the top off the basket. A cobra rose slowly from its enclosure until its head was two feet above the container's rim. The man with the horn began to play livelier, and his partner picked up a hand drum, patted it twice with his palm, then spun it slowly in front of the cobra, as if to hypnotize it. The cobra, though, had seemed tired from the moment it poked its head into the sunlight. I wondered if it had been drugged. The snake charmers failed to attract any onlookers, and we turned away.

"What are we going to see next?" asked Geoff. "Aladdin and the genie?"

"Ali Baba and the Forty Thieves, more like it," Mal replied.

WE ARRIVED LATE that night at our pre-selected campground in Ourzazate, set up our tents, and walked to a clean modern-looking restaurant with a lighted sign and large windows in front. The server recommended a traditional Moroccan dish he called chicken *tagine*, which proved to be the most savory stew I had ever eaten. Of course, as a college student, my idea of stew came in a can with a Dinty Moore label.

The man who served us the food was also the owner of the restaurant, fluent in English. He had overseen the preparation of the *tagine* himself, and seemed glad of our interest. He left our table for a moment and immediately returned from the kitchen holding a wide shallow clay bowl with a conical ceramic top.

"This is a *tagine*," he said. "When you cook food in a *tagine*, the food is also called *tagine*. You are eating chicken *tagine*."

"It's delicious," I said. "What's in it besides chicken?"

I had noticed olives, but I knew nothing about the other vegetables or the spices.

The man set the *tagine* next to my bowl and pulled up a chair from another table to join us.

"The *tagine* comes to us from the Romans," he said, "so we have had a few years to get it right. You can cook lamb *tagine*, fish *tagine*, vegetarian *tagine*, or, like you have here, chicken *tagine*. The chicken, first I remove the skin, then I rub with pepper, turmeric, garlic, paprika, saffron, and *ras el hanout*." He looked at us quizzically. "I don't know this word in English. But only the best spices, or why should you bother? In my kitchen, we leave the chicken like this overnight, in the refrigerator, of course. The next day, we place the chicken in a *tagine*, add lemon, onion, olives, potatoes, peas, carrots if we have them, maybe cauliflower. Some days have different vegetables than other days, depending on the market. We cook for one hour and one-half and then…"

He stood up dramatically from his seat and flourished his arm at our table.

"We bring to you!"

With all the new foods I'd been eating and learning about, I figured I'd be giving James Beard a run for his money by the time I returned from this trip.

We paid the bill, thanked our kind host effusively, and waddled back to our campsite, where we crawled into our sleeping bags and allowed a food coma to slowly put us to sleep.

Ouarzazate proved to be an open, airy, desert town. The temperature was already ninety degrees F. by mid-morning the next day, so we removed our shirts as we walked around. We found a place that sold discount gas coupons, and were surprised when the clerk said we could buy coupons only once every ten days. That meant we would have to pay the regular price of 1.83 dirhams per liter, or about U.S. $1.60 a gallon, instead of the discounted price of a dollar a gallon. I'm good with maps and mental arithmetic. I calculated that we had driven some six hundred miles so far, and had roughly another eight hundred miles before we ended our Moroccan sojourn, in Tangier at the country's northern tip, on the Strait of Gibraltar. Mal had said the Citroën got a respectable twenty miles per gallon, fully loaded.

Let's see, petrol in Morocco is sold by the liter. There are about four liters per gallon. Based on our mileage, we're getting about five miles to one liter. We still have 800 miles to drive, which divided by five is 160. Interesting coincidence, considering the price of gas. Multiply 160 by U.S. $1.60 per gallon.... No, wait, multiply 160 by the price per liter, which is about forty cents. Okay, then figure out the difference between what we'll be paying versus what we would have saved with the coupons....

"Well?" Mal asked, clearly worried about the fuel budget. "What do you reckon?"

"I *reckon* petrol for the rest of the trip back to Tangier will cost about one thousand four hundred dollars."

The boys looked horrified. I was joking, of course, but too often I wear a serious expression when I'm kidding around.

"No, no," I said, "I didn't mean it. I figure we'll need about a hundred and sixty liters to finish out the trip.

We're paying the full price of one point eight three dirhams per liter, which comes to about three hundred dirhams, which is about six hundred and forty U.S."

The boys looked hugely relieved.

"So how much more are we paying than we would with the coupons?" asked Geoff.

I put up my hands in mock surrender. My head hurt too much already, and I wasn't even positive I had calculated correctly. Besides, I was too busy worrying about how I would pay my share. In fact, I couldn't. The remainder of my stay would be unsustainable. I would be flat-out broke before my scheduled flight home, which couldn't be changed, nor did I particularly *want* to change it. I had no credit cards, nor any practical way to ask for money from home, especially since I was moving from place to place almost every day.

My father was a school teacher and my mother was a technical editor; they had no extra money to send, though they would if they'd had it. No, I couldn't see a way around it: I would have to have a pointed talk—and soon—with Mal and Geoff about the realities of my money situation.

We had no plans to stick around Ouarzazate, a pleasant-enough sandstone city on a hillside, but made for Agadir on the coast, about two hundred miles away or, as I was starting to think of it, about twenty dollars away.

Wait a minute, I thought. *Twenty dollars?! That can't be right.*

"Geoff," I called from the back seat. "Do you have some paper and a pencil?"

He fumbled around in the glove compartment and handed me a notepad and ballpoint pen. I began scribbling furiously. I did the figures twice to be sure. If Agadir was two hundred miles away and would cost us twenty dollars in gas, and if our overall journey from Ouarzazate to Tangier was eight hundred miles and the Citroën got twenty miles to the gallon and we were paying the U.S. equivalent of $1.60 per gallon…

"Guys, I just figured the numbers again," I told them, still not entirely certain of my math. "Gas isn't going to cost us six hundred and forty U.S. the rest of the way. I put the decimal in the wrong place when I was doing it in my head. I think we'll spend more like sixty-four dollars on gas."

Mal pulled to the side of the empty road, put the car in park, and slowly turned to look at me. His gaze was leaden.

"You bloody bastard!" he shouted unexpectedly. "You motherfucker! You scared the shit out of me. I figured that was it. We'll have to sell the car and buy a bloody camel."

Geoff reached across to put a hand on Mal's shoulder, then turned to me. "He's just taking the piss out of you, mate," he said. "No worries."

When I looked back at Mal he was smiling.

"I'm joking with you," he said as he turned back to the road and put the car in gear. "But I wasn't joking about scaring the shit out of me."

The drive through the brown brush-covered desert between the rugged, black, snow-capped High Atlas Mountains to our north and the indigo Anti-Atlas to the south was solemn, serene, and we were quiet for much of the ride.

About three hours after pulling out of Ouarzazate, Mal turned to look at me without pulling over or even reducing his speed.

"Six hundred and forty dollars!" Then he turned back to his driving. "Bloody American public education."

AGADIR, ON THE ocean, was a modern European-style city

with little to distinguish it from an industrious town on the edges of Paris. The most productive fishing port in Morocco, Agadir also claimed to be the Biblical location where the whale vomited Jonah onto dry land. The medina was so well hidden that we never found it. On the beach, we met a young Canadian who told us he'd been hassled by cops in Casablanca while camping freestyle, and had been pitching his tent in official campgrounds ever since, which sounded rational to us.

We wasted no time in Agadir and continued north along the Atlantic shore, arriving in the town of Essaouira at ten that night, nearly twelve hours after leaving Ouarzazate. We quickly set up camp (at an official campground).

We paid a boy one dirham to take us to the closest restaurant with the best food. He led us to a simple concrete structure with no signage. We surely would have passed it by if we'd been on our own. We removed our shoes on entering and placed them on a rack by the door alongside the shoes of the other (all male) diners. We sat on the floor, on straw mats, at a table that was no more than eighteen inches high, where we ordered couscous, lamb *tagine,* bread, and mint tea. The total bill for the three of us was seventeen dirhams, or about U.S. $3.75, but we'd been too worn out from driving to find an affordable eatery.

While we were inside, the weather had deteriorated. We weren't more than half a mile from our campsite, but wind-driven rain nearly soaked us by the time we returned. That was bad enough, but when we got to our spot, we saw that a rivulet had formed near Mal and Geoff's two-man tent and had started to leak inside. I'd unwittingly left my tent flaps open, exposing the lower half of my sleeping bag to the rain. The night was miserable. When I awoke the next morning, I saw that Mal and

Geoff had left their watery lodgings to sleep in the front seats of the car.

Essaouira, in the morning, proved to be an attractive place, whose quaint walled old city had few tourists that we noticed. Most of the markets catered to the locals, offering little in the way of curios but instead were rife with bright plastic items of all sorts, colorful and cheaply stamped out—buckets, shoes, dustpans, stackable chairs, side tables, and other housewares.

Continuing on our journey north, we pointed the Citroën toward Casablanca and got on the highway by ten. A handful of towns along the way seemed potentially amusing, but ultimately offered nothing to sidetrack three road-weary rascals. More noteworthy than the dusty settlements we passed were the camels. They seemed to be everywhere. I counted at least thirty of the ugly exotic stinkpots as we drove, some working in fields, some on the roadside hauling cords of wood or sacks full of produce, others tied to a tree or fence post.

As we neared Casablanca, I couldn't help but think of the eponymous film that made Humphrey Bogart a household name. I'd seen *Casablanca* several times and enjoyed its exoticism. I looked forward to visiting the dreamy, spy-filled city for myself, complete with fez-topped fat men in white linen suits and sneaky characters selling stolen letters of transit.

When we drove into the city at three that afternoon, the sun was shining but rain was nonetheless falling from scattered cumulonimbus clouds. We followed directions to the Syndicat d'Initiative in a 1920s-era column-fronted building on the wide Boulevard Mohammed V. The efficient girl at the counter, at our request, promptly handed us a tourist map and gave us directions to the youth hostel in the ancient medina.

A group of local musicians was playing traditional

Moroccan tunes in the hostel's interior courtyard, which was furnished with comfortable-looking sofas and chairs. A cast-iron rail lined the interior balcony of the second floor; items of clothing and bath towels of many different colors and patterns were hung there to dry by the travelers occupying the upper-floor rooms. The courtyard walls were lined with hand-painted tiles. Potted plants lent a well-tended hominess to the place. We paid three dirhams each in advance for a triple room, unrolled our sleeping bags on our respective mattresses (having declined the proffered sheets because of the extra fee), and went outside to inspect the town.

Boulevard Hosali was lined on both sides with tourist-trinket stalls. A boy standing on a corner sold me seven etched-brass bracelets for five dirhams; at less than twenty cents apiece, they would make for simple gifts when I got back to California. A grotesque man who continually snuffled when he talked sold Mal a more elaborate bracelet with what seemed to be semi-precious stones for ten dirhams. The man saw me observing the transaction, and when Mal left with his purchase offered to sell me the same bracelet for five dirhams. The man was disgusting, but a bargain's a bargain, so I bought it.

"How much did you pay for that," Mal asked when I caught up with him.

"How much did you pay for yours? Ten?"

"Yeah, ten."

I hesitated, then said, "Me too."

We enjoyed the medina, which had a far more old-world atmosphere than one might have thought, considering the modern metropolis that surrounded it. Like me, the boys were generally familiar with Bogart and *Casablanca*, and we had fun picking out places and people that could have fit into the film.

"That restaurant could have been Rick's Café

Americain," Geoff said, pointing to a façade that didn't in the least resemble the nightclub that in reality existed only on a Warner Bros. sound stage.

"Are you kidding me?" I countered. "Have you even *seen* the movie? On the other hand, that guy over there, the little man on the corner who looks so worried? He's nervous because he's carrying the stolen exit letters."

"Peter Lorre!" Mal replied. "Absolutely."

The short stocky man waiting hesitantly to cross the street did indeed bear some resemblance to the movie's slippery crook Ugarte.

That night, we dined on *steak frites* in a Parisian-style bistro in the city's new quarter, then returned to the hostel for a good night's sleep. Tomorrow we would be in Tangier. The day after that we would again be "safe" in Europe. But very soon, we'd be wishing we'd stayed in Morocco.

12

We Wuz Robbed

My stuff isn't for sale - To Spain again - Bad news from Italy - An Andalusian idyll, until it wasn't - Calamity strikes - Victims caravan - Recovery in Seville - Ramos looks like a goner - Cheerio to a couple of bonzer blokes

H ow much do you want for this?" the Moroccan customs inspector asked after extracting a Kodak disposable mini-camera from my backpack.

I couldn't believe it. The customs agent was bargaining with me for my stuff. I had a hunch that he wanted me to give it to him as a gift in exchange for not searching my backpack too thoroughly. But I'd been stopped and squeezed by enough Mexican cops on excursions to Hussong's Cantina in Ensenada to recognize a shakedown.

"Not for sale," I replied, since I had no contraband.

He frowned and dropped the disposable camera rudely on the inspection table, then prowled through the depths of my pack with renewed gusto.

A stubble-faced officer in a dirty uniform had told us to walk through the pedestrian checkpoint while the Citroën was being searched. We didn't trust the safety of our belongings to inspectors rifling through the car without us present, so I brought along my backpack into the Immigration Hall, Mal carried a day pack with his valuables, and Geoff as always slung his cherished Leica across his shoulder.

On the Spanish side, as we entered Ceuta, the process was less stressful. An inspector absently looked through the window at our gear and kicked each of the four tires, presumably to be sure they were hollow and not crammed full of smuggled Moroccan blonde .

The strait crossing was as smooth as the previous one, and I had time to consider my plans for the next few weeks. I'd already decided that I would part ways with Geoff and Mal in a day or two. Although they were excellent road companions, I found being one of a trio stifling. We ate only with one another, traveled only with one another, went sightseeing only with one another. Traveling with the Aussies had its benefits, and they were nothing if not agreeable sidekicks, but I felt subject to their plans, not my own. I had come on this trip in the first place to meet a variety of people as much as to see new things.

I figured I would remain with the boys for our visit to Seville. From there I would go on, alone, to Córdoba, Toledo, Madrid, Pamplona, San Sebastián, and I knew not where else. Unfortunately, Venice was now out of the question. A newspaper someone had left behind on the ferry carried an article about a major earthquake in northern Italy a few days earlier. My Spanish wasn't good enough to translate the entire text, but what I could understand made clear that many people had died and the destruction was widespread. I didn't fully realize it at the time, but what became known as the Friuli Earthquake, centered just north of Venice, registered a devastating 6.5 on the Richter scale. More than five hundred people were dead, a thousand were seriously injured, and at least

eighty thousand people were left homeless in the surrounding villages.

Come for the holiday, stay for the Apocalypse!

From Algeciras, we got onto the backroads and wandered through the towns and villages without any specific
plan. The boys were fascinated by Andalusia—its architecture, its Moorish-Spanish culture, and its unique cuisine. Along our way, we ate *carrillada de cerdo* at a tapas
bar in Arcos de la Frontera, drank sherry in Jerez, admired
castles on hilltops, and finally arrived at our campsite in
the town of Dos Hermanas, ten miles south of Seville.

It had been a splendid day, "a beauty arvo," as Mal
called it in his catchy if baffling Strine slang. The weather
had been sunny and warm, the sights had been visual de-
lights, and the food we'd eaten had been superb. An almost perfect day.

And a perfect set-up for a brewing disaster.

I DIDN'T KNOW what time the man began shouting. I was
in my pup tent, sleeping soundly, when his frantic calls
rattled me awake. I sat up to climb out of my sleeping
bag, and immediately saw a tear, about two feet long, in
the roof of my tent. Moments later I saw another tear,
along the entire bottom of one side. Disappointed, and
wondering if and how I could sew up the gapes, I tried to
imagine what I had done to cause them.

But first I had to see what the shouting man wanted. He
was now directly outside my tent. For some reason, I
thought he must be Señor Ladrón, the campground
owner. Had we pitched our tents out of bounds or screwed
up some other way?

I duck-walked out into the open just as Mal, in his bi-
kini underwear, and Geoff, in full pajamas, crawled into
the early sunlight from their tent. The man turned out to
be another camper. He was talking so quickly in Spanish

that I couldn't understand what he was saying. We realized soon enough, though, that something was wrong by the tone of his voice and the fact that he was pointing, with some alarm, at the Citroën. We hurried to the car, which appeared to be just as we had left it. But no. Something was out of place.

"Guys," I said. "Look at the windshield."

There *was* no windshield. The rubber molding around its edges had been cut off and removed. The windshield itself had been lifted out, fully intact, and placed gently on the grass beside the driver's door.

Mal moved around to the rear of the car. I heard him say, "Oh no, oh shit," then he raced back to the front and reached through the windshield opening to unlock the passenger door from the inside. He climbed into the car and scrambled to the back seat.

"They got it all," he shouted desperately from inside. "They took fucking everything!"

We had been the victims of a theft overnight. Big-time victims. The thieves had waltzed away with my backpack, which held all my possessions except for the few items in my tent. I still had my money belt and passport, but not my clothes, my mess kit, my maps, my notebook, my cheapo disposable cameras, or the souvenirs I'd purchased over the past couple of months. All gone. Geoff began going through the papers that the thieves had left untouched in the glove compartment and elsewhere in the car. Thankfully, he found both his and Mal's passports, the car ownership papers, and, to our complete surprise, Mal's wallet, full of money, which was hidden under the driver's seat.

"There are some things over there," said the man, who indeed spoke some English. "Perhaps they are your things."

The three of us ran in the direction he pointed. On a

wide patch of grass about thirty yards away some of our possessions were tossed around like trash. The scene looked as if the thieves had grabbed whatever they could carry, brought the loot to this spot, and then went quickly through it all to determine what was worth running off with and what could be left behind. Heister triage.

My yellow backpack was among the detritus. The bastards had sliced it open with a knife or razor blade across the front rather than simply unclasping the flap on top. They had also, inexplicably, cut one of the straps in two, which I had to tie in a knot to make the pack usable again. The knot, unfortunately, rested squarely against my left shoulder. But I was euphoric to discover the only things they had taken from my bag were a pair of pants, my rain poncho, the Moroccan scarves and bracelets, and my eyeglasses. (The rest of my stay in Europe would prove to be a little blurry, but not catastrophically so.) Geoff lost his two hundred dollar watch, forty-five dollars in cash, all his clothes, the suitcase that held everything, and, worst of all, his beloved Leica. Mal too lost a camera, along with his clothes and a beautiful leather suitcase that I'd admired since I first saw it. For me, the theft was a bummer; for Mal and Geoff, it was just short of ruinous.

When the cops arrived, they bawled out Señor Ladrón, a sweaty Zero Mostel lookalike, who seemed abashed, his eyes shifting from the cops to us victims and back.

"The policeman is angry with the owner," said the man who had first alerted us to the theft, "because the campground was robbed just this way seven weeks ago."

Two teenage girls from Portugal were among the victims. They said their tent had been razor-sliced along its base and their tape deck had been stolen through the opening while the girls were asleep inside. Now I understood where the rip in the roof and base of my own tent had come from. Someone had silently cut the holes with a razor, peeked inside, saw a six-foot man asleep there, and decided to let it be.

The cops took our statements and drove away, leaving the bereft victims numb, trying to decide what to do next. Mal and Geoff still had their clothes from the night before in their tent, so at least they could dress properly. The Portuguese girls and Mal and Geoff figured they would need a copy of the police report for insurance purposes (I had no insurance coverage of any kind, not even medical), so the owner offered to lead us to the police station where the report would be filed.

Señor Ladrón walked back to his office and returned with a little Vespa scooter that sounded like a mad hornet and spat out smoky exhaust. We followed next in our airy, windshieldless car, and the petite Portuguese teens came up behind in a dented Seat 124. Two other victims, Dutch college students riding ten-speed bicycles and wearing racing regalia, completed our motley caravan. Anyone watching us pass by would have thought us a pretty poor parade. The Vespa was two sizes too small for its fat owner, and could go no faster than fifteen miles an hour; Mal had to continually pump the Citroën's brakes to avoid rear-ending the scooter. The Dutchmen would race ahead of our sad spectacle, not even steering, their hands blithely on their hips, then wait for us by the side of the road to catch up. The smoke from the Vespa chugged directly into our car through the open windshield. We were such a comical-looking crew that there should have been calliope music in the background.

The police station in the town of Dos Hermanas was housed in an uninspired modern two-story municipal building on a street lined with uninspired modern two-story buildings. We waited inside for two hours until the boys finally got copies of the report.

Back at the campground, I discarded my tent, now

useless to keep out the weather. We figured out a way to place the windshield in its original position so that, barring any significant bumps in the road, it would stay in place if we drove slowly and carefully. The solution was temporary but effective. Mal planned to steer with his right hand and reach through his open side window with his left to hold down the windshield as we drove. Geoff rolled down his window and placed the palm of his right hand on the windshield's opposite side. We abandoned the scene of the crime and drove ten miles north to Seville, where we sniffed out a cheap hotel. We took a ground-floor room that had only two beds; the room was behind the noisy hotel kitchen, but the price was too good to pass up. The three of us flipped a coin to see who would get a mattress and who would sleep on the floor. Mal got the floor.

By that time, the day was too late for any meaningful sightseeing. Mal and Geoff took the car to an auto-glass shop the hotel clerk recommended, where they managed to have a new window seal applied in just over an hour. They also bought some inexpensive clothing to replace what was taken, including, for Mal, a too-small T-shirt with the slogan, *"Todo va mejor con Coca-Cola!"* But those were costs that hadn't been anticipated in their budget. The Australians, like me, had to watch their spending more than their couture.

We ate a bare-bones supper at a bare-bones bodega near our bare-bones hotel. You had to hand it to the Australians. Despite their losses and the damage to the car, they managed to keep up their spirits. Over dinner, not even twelve hours since discovering the robbery, they were ready to horse around.

"You know what hurts most?" Mal said as we ate, looking at Geoff. "The pictures you took."

"Which pictures?" Geoff replied.

"The ones with *me* in them. The film in your camera bag. I would've liked to have seen those. Many other people would have appreciated them as well. People enjoy looking at pictures of me. Tragic loss. Tragic."

Geoff frowned, then shot back, "Well, I think the bigger loss is the photos *you* took of *me*! The angels must be weeping right now. That's how we get rain, you know."

Mal dramatically stopped eating, with his mouth still open, then slowly lowered his fork back onto his plate.

"Are you daft?" he asked in exasperation. "There were no bloody photos of you, mate! Flamin' hell, you've got a face like a dropped pie! One photo of you would have shattered the lens!"

And they went on that way, and we laughed about other things, and we all ordered more beer, and life seemed almost normal again.

God, I love Australians.

IMAGINE! I SLEPT until ten-thirty *in a hotel bed*! Having camped throughout Morocco and Spain for most of the previous two weeks, a lumpy mattress in a half-star hotel was a comparative luxury. Plus, not having to rise with the sun to "make good time on the road" was delightful. And this from a man who does not lightly use the word *delightful*.

After our late breakfast, the three of us marched off to see the premier local sight: the Alcázar of Seville. Since it was a fortress-palace like the Alhambra in nearby Granada, I assumed the Alcázar would be as stupefyingly beautiful. I was disappointed. The rooms were repetitious, the ornamentation clunky. I didn't have the architectural language to articulate why it didn't compare.

"Probably because it's Mudejar style," Geoff suggested. "The Alhambra is Islamic, designed by Moorish architects, built by Moorish craftsmen. This palace was built by King Pedro after the Spanish reconquest of Andalusia."

He noted the similarities—horseshoe arches, intricate Islamic ornamentation, highly stylized Arabic calligraphy, the placement of water features—and the key differences.

"Mudejar is a blend of European and Islamic design," he continued. "There are elements of Gothic, Renaissance, and Romanesque styles. Plus, this place has been extended, renovated, and redecorated countless times over the past five hundred years."

Once again, I was able to look at an old building in a new way.

Next on the list was the Seville Cathedral. Geoff called it the third largest cathedral in the world.

"Correction!" Mal interjected. "Third largest in the *known* world."

"Do you think maybe there's a larger one in some undiscovered part of darkest Africa? Or under the sea and we just haven't noticed it yet?" Geoff asked with a smile on his face and a jovial sneer in his voice.

"Then why don't you just say it's the third largest in the entire universe?" Mal shot back.

"You mean *the known* universe, I think," Geoff answered, slicing his countryman with a verbal *touché*. "And I don't say it's the third largest in the universe because I have no information that leads me to believe that Martians are Catholic, so why on earth, or on Mars, would they build a cathedral?"

They could go on like that for an hour at a stretch and never tire of one another. I really liked these guys.

The cathedral, seen from the outside, looked to me like a great warty bug, though I admired the bell tower, an iconic symbol of the city. Inside, the columns were massive, oppressive, anything but graceful. After the stylish delicacy of the Islamic architecture I had seen, the Seville Cathedral struck me as neither grand nor inspiring. Just...*big.*

THE PLAZA DE Toros Real Maestranza, the largest and most important bullring in Spain, was in the city center, a short walk from both the Seville Cathedral and the Alcázar. The fights were not so good that day. An onlooker didn't have to have *afición* to identify a lousy matador. Our seats were in the first row, so we saw everything clearly.

The only one of the three matadors that afternoon who had any demonstrable skill was the bullfighter Ramos, but he was a poor killer. In the second of his two *corridas*, he made an especially good pass, then in a show of bravura turned his back on the animal, raised a right hand to the crowd, and strolled in the opposite direction. The bull, however, had stopped and turned much more quickly than Ramos realized, and the matador was unprepared when at last he saw the bull charging at him from behind.

The bull, impervious to the frantic movement of the matador's cape, caught Ramos between its horns and tossed him four feet into the air. When Ramos hit the ground, the bull dug into him with its right horn. The other matadors and members of Ramos's *cuadrilla* rushed into the ring to distract the bull. I thought Ramos was a goner for sure, lying where he fell, not moving, as the bull was lured away by the other men.

Unexpectedly, despite bleeding from the waist, Ramos rose to his feet. He must have lain on the ground to collect his wits before standing up again to face the thousand-pound beast that had nearly finished him. He wasted no time in preparing for the kill as the other toreros returned to the edges of the ring. The tension in the crowd was tight, as the fight now had become personal, so to speak, between man and bull. Ramos took his position, the bull charged, and the sword pierced the back of the animal's neck, driving straight into its heart. The bull fell to the ground, dead. Just to be certain, as always, a *puntillero* approached from the outer edges of the ring and severed the bull's spinal cord with a sharp-edged knife. A team of horses entered the ring and dragged the bull out to be slaughtered, leaving a trail of blood.

Mal, Geoff, and I were thrilled as well as horrified by what we had seen that afternoon. We went to a beer café just outside the arena that attracted a boisterous crowd of *corrida* aficionados.

"Don't think I like bullfights," Geoff said. He had looked squeamish at several points during the day's event. "I just don't see the point."

"He only likes the matadors' tight trousers," Mal said to me. "If it was just matadors prancing about, he'd be fine with it."

"Bugger off, dipstick," Geoff said with a smile.

A group of ten or twelve men and women, clearly several drinks ahead of us, began to clap as one of the women launched into a flamenco dance. She danced furiously, her arms swinging, accompanied by no music, just the clapping of hands in a steady three-quarter beat.

THE NEXT MORNING was bittersweet as I watched my companions collect their now-meager belongings to leave the hotel. I liked them each, despite their completely different personalities. Mal was the brassier of the two, and always tried to outdo his traveling partner in everything, whether exhibiting knowledge of architectural history or simply getting in the last fart joke when they were taking the piss out of one another. What made it all okay was that Geoff, in his quiet way, would often end up getting the better of his friend. Geoff was the gentler of the two, soft of voice, and sympathetic in his expression when he listened to you talk about something personal. How they got along so well was anyone's guess. Two halves of the same Australian personality, I suppose.

On the street, the boys put their remaining gear into the back of the Citroën. We hugged and gave each other smirks that seemed to express our feelings of sadness, but also gratitude for the memorable times we'd shared—exploring mysterious Volubilis, attempting camel rides, negotiating the spider web of dark alleyways in Fez and Marrakech with Didress and Nassim, joking nonstop as we drove endless backroads the long way from Alicante to Agadir, and even helping one another get through the emotional trauma of the campsite robbery.

As Mal started the engine, Geoff rolled down the passenger window.

"Cheerio, mate," he said quietly. "Mind how you go."

Mal leaned across the front seat and with a big smile on his face shouted, "Hooroo!"

And they drove off. My friends were gone.

13

The Welsh Girls Chapter

Hay wagon transportation - Reasons to have a wife -
Flowery streets of Córdoba - The drunken dwarf dislikes
me - Distance is relative - Gwyn and Jane - Late arrival
in Madrid - "I too was young once"

A skinny teenage boy stopped his farm wagon at the
roadside when he saw me. His cart, pulled by a
mule, carried a half-dozen bales of hay. The wagon
wheels were painted bright red, and I saw smears of red
paint on the boy's trousers. A friendly dog was with the
boy, walking beside the wagon. The dog hopped confi-
dently over to me and sniffed my ankles curiously.

"*No hay mucho tráfico aquí,*" the boy said. "*¿Adónde
va?*" There isn't much traffic here. Where are you going?

When I told him I was on my way to Córdoba, he indicated I should climb aboard, that he would take me to a
better place for hitchhiking. "*Cinco kilometros, más or
menos.*" Five kilometers, more or less. The problem, for
me, was that the wagon had no seat. The boy had been
standing on one of two poles that extended in front of the

wagon and attached to the mule's harness. I removed my pack and tossed it into the back with the hay, then hopped onto the opposing pole, grasping the edge of the wagon box with both hands. I worried whether the additional weight might be too much for the lone mule, but the road ahead of us was flat and smooth, and the boy himself showed no concern.

The only time I almost fell off my narrow balance beam was when the mule first began to walk, starting with a jerk, but I quickly got my sea legs, and even began holding onto the wagon bed with one hand only, as the boy was doing. The boy, of course, had no choice, because in his free hand he held the reins.

A drainage ditch paralleled the side of the road. The dog walked between the cart and the ditch, and barked in warning whenever the mule seemed to veer too close to the trench. Some dog.

"*Mula, mula, mula!*" the boy shouted in encouragement, shaking the reins.

We went on that way for several miles. The boy was bringing the hay to his father's ranch, he said, which was not far. As we bounced pleasantly along, he began to sing quietly, an unexpectedly somber melody whose words I couldn't make out. Again, the dog barked a warning, and again the boy shook the reins and called out, "*Mula, mula, mula!*"

Two cars passed us within minutes of one another, frightening the mule, but the boy wasn't alarmed. The mule seemed to want off the tarmac and onto the safety of the roadside, but because of the wide ditch, he couldn't leave the pavement.

At last, we came to an intersection with a larger road that had two lanes of traffic in each direction. Surrounding us were farm fields and almost no trees. The boy pointed to the left and said Córdoba was that way. I jumped down from my perch, grabbed my backpack from the cart, and thanked the boy.

"Vaya con Díos," I said with a wave as he, the mule, and the dog crossed the intersection and carried on in the direction they'd been heading.

A truck came toward me, seemingly heading on the road to Córdoba, but at the last moment turned right onto the smaller road, going the same way as the boy. Almost immediately I heard a commotion from that direction. I hurried over to where the boy was now standing on the road, the dog barking furiously beside him, and the wagon on its side in the ditch, the mule still attached. The boy hopped into the ditch and began to kick the mule in the stomach.

"Hey, hey, hey!" I said in protest.

The mule's eyes were wide with panic, and it flailed its legs to no purpose. Two men working in a nearby field ran over to help. I had no idea how I could assist, but the men seemed to know what to do. They unhitched the mule's harness, which allowed the animal to scramble up on its own. The mule didn't appear to be hurt seriously, or even at all. Together the men managed to right the small wagon, with little help from me. They and the boy loaded the hay back into the wagon. The boy re-harnessed the mule. Before I knew it, the wagon was rolling down the road again and the men had returned to their field.

LUCK WAS WITH me. A traveling wholesale shoe salesman who looked to be in his middle or late forties stopped his sedan just beyond where I stood and honked. He was going all the way to Córdoba. He was focused on making lots of money, blathering on as if he were twenty years younger and experiencing the first flush of success in the business world, not a middle-aged man who already had been earning a salary for a couple of decades. At first, he could talk about nothing else—how good a salesman he was, how he was earning so much money ("You see my car," he said, as if introducing supporting evidence), and planned to earn much more.

"You have a wife?" he asked. He spoke in a mixture of Spanish and the little English he knew, once he realized the limitations of my rudimentary language skills. "It's important to have a wife, for many reasons. You should be married. You can't have everything, but you can have a wife."

His comments put him in a thoughtful mood, and he said nothing for a time.

I had expected the climate of Andalusia to be desert-like, but between Seville and Córdoba the land was fertile. The terrain outside Córdoba comprised miles and miles of gently rolling farmland nurturing crops of wheat, cotton, and sunflowers.

"My wife makes problems for me," the driver continued, as if he hadn't paused for the past five minutes. "Also, she is very ugly. But she sings well."

We arrived in Córdoba, where the salesman let me out in the heart of the charming Moorish city.

"And remember," he admonished again, but with a friendly smile, "when you get back to your country, you must find a wife!"

El Arcangel, near the city's cathedral, looked to be an affordable hotel, so I went inside to ask about a room. The front-desk clerk called to a maid and told her to show me one for my approval. (I learned early on in my travels that you should always look at a proposed room before accepting it.) The maid was a little person, a dwarf. Her head reached only to my waist. She was cross-eyed and appeared to be drunk. I don't think she liked me. When she opened the door to the room, she slammed it against the wall with a bang.

The room was tiny. I could touch three of the four walls without leaving the bed. The bath, as usual for my class of hotel, was down the hall. I was more than happy with the choice of room, though, because the hotel had an attractive flower-filled courtyard. The location, smack in the middle of the historic core, couldn't have been more convenient for sightseeing, dining, and bar-hopping. The price was good at two dollars a night.

The maid leaned against the door jamb, her arms folded against her chest. When it appeared that I wasn't going to object to the room, she sniffed loudly, turned on her heels, and marched quickly down the hall.

Córdoba was smaller than its better-known sister, Seville, but humanistic in size, easy to get around. The old section, whose colors were white and brown, and many of whose crumbling sandstone structures sprouted weeds from their walls and rooftops, blended well with the new city as opposed to being ringed by a modern metropolis that hemmed it in. The same Guadalquivir River that coursed alongside the Seville bullring flowed here too.

Córdoba had a raucous daily market in the Plaza de la Corredera, bordered on three sides by handsome arcaded nineteenth-century buildings. The slaughterhouse reality of Europe's open-air markets was, like the bullfights, both thrilling and horrifying. Blood oozed off the edges of display tables. The cold dead eyes of fish stared indifferently at the shoppers. Delicious smells clashed with vile odors. The pavement was wet and strewn with the detritus of vegetable bins and fish guts.

But Córdoba was also a flowery city as much as Seville was. Every other window and balcony burst with pink and purple blooms. I found myself in a part of town in which horses were trained and traded. The men wore flat-topped, stiff-brimmed felt hats and waist-length jackets, the sort that I had always associated with the wealthy

Spanish rancheros who settled California in the eighteenth century. Afterward, I got lost in the labyrinth of streets at the east end of town.

The day had been enjoyable, but somehow not as fun as when I was traveling with Mal and Geoff. They would have been happy to keep me on board. Had I made a mistake to separate from them?

MY SITUATION WAS about to improve considerably the next day after I left for Madrid, 240 miles away. In America, people drove that distance on a whim, to visit an elderly aunt, to enjoy a new amusement park, to get a better deal on cartons of cigarettes at an out-of-state Indian reservation. They might even drive back home *on that same day,* "depending on traffic." And that's fine when the freeways have four or five lanes in each direction and are as unbending as a Southern Baptist's moral compass.

Traveling in Europe by car was different in those days. Superhighways were rarer than now. Major roads, once outside the exurbs, were often one lane in each direction, and curved as necessary to avoid mountains, rivers, and other natural impediments. They sometimes passed through small towns, slowing traffic, instead of diverting around them. A 240-mile drive from Bakersfield to Stockton could be done in three and a half hours (or less, with a radar detector), but might take double that time in Europe. Add to that the uncertainties of hitchhiking, and you could expect the travel time to be closer to ten hours or more. And that's *if* the hitchhiker arrived at the final destination at all, or ended up sleeping in a glade by the side of the road for failure to get one last ride.

That's why you should always like hitchhikers: At heart, they're authentic optimists.

From the Arcangel, I walked out of town for three or four miles until, at about nine, I found what I thought was a decent spot to hitch a ride. Many cars and many hours later, I had barely traveled thirty kilometers.

Then fortune sprinkled some pixie dust on my thumb.

Gwyn and Jane, as I learned later, had driven their Vauxhall Viva from their homes in Swansea to Dover, where they took the car ferry to Calais. They had been traveling in France and Spain for two weeks. From their chat, I gathered that they had been pawed and propositioned by strange men at every gas station, supermarket, and public square from Calais to Cadíz. Yet they hadn't lost their smiles or enthusiasm for the road.

They were both twenty-one and had been working at non-career jobs when they decided to make their big trip to the Continent, the first for either of them. The unwanted attention they caused was no mystery. They both had reddish blonde hair down to their shoulders, milky white complexions, and slim, shapely bodies. They could have been sisters, and they were gorgeous. But their beauty was inside too. They knew they were attractive—how could they *not* be aware?—but were sweet and unassuming. A major drawback, though, loomed, as far as I was concerned.

I couldn't, at first, understand a word they said.

When I climbed into the Vauxhall at the side of the road, I did as I always do: I smiled politely, tried to look as unthreatening as possible, and said my destination in the local language, whether mumbling *Ich möchte nach Koblenz* in Germany or *Je veux aller aux Carcassonne* in France. You didn't have to master a foreign tongue to memorize stock phrases like those, and the locals seemed to appreciate such linguistic efforts—tortured though they might have been.

I had seen enough red-haired and blonde Spaniards to mistake Gwyn and Jane for locals, so greeted them as I would anyone else that day.

"*Me voy a Madrid,*" I said. "*Pero creo que es muy lejos para llegar hoy.*"

I wasn't surprised when they didn't understand me. Many Spaniards didn't understand my attempts to speak their beautiful language, limited as I was to the present tense, a narrow vocabulary, and an absurdly macho refusal to lisp. But when the young women themselves began to speak, I thought they must be French. Their sentences were lovely and lilting, interspersed with cute giggles. Somewhere in what they said I thought I discerned a word or two of English.

"*Français?*" I asked.

"Welsh!" said Gwyn, behind the wheel, looking at me briefly in the rear seat then turning her eyes quickly back to the road.

"From Wales!" said Jane, proudly. "Great Britain!"

They enunciated each vowel slowly and carefully, as if I didn't understand English.

"I'm from the U.S.," I replied. "California."

This delighted the girls no end, and they began to jabber again in what at first I took to be the Welsh language. Soon, though, I understood they were speaking English but with strong Welsh accents. They were talking in the same language, or at least some species of it, that I did.

Over the next hour of driving, my ear tuned to their speech, and soon I could understand nearly seventy or eighty percent of what they said. We talked about everything and nothing, where they had been and where I was going, what life was like in California and what distinguished the Welsh from the English. We stopped for coffee twice en route to Madrid, and arrived in that city at eleven p.m. We parked the car on a well-lighted side street off the Puerto del Sol, then went in search of a restaurant or even a snack bar.

For all the talk I'd heard about the late hours of supper in Spain, we spent twenty minutes searching before finding a reasonably priced *fonda* that was still open. As the food was being served, I asked Gwyn and Jane if I could go on with them the next day as they traveled to Burgos, and they were pleased that I asked, smiling and agreeing immediately. I was starting to think that they liked me in a boy-girl way, not just as an amiable travel companion.

HUNTING FOR A hotel in a strange city near midnight is a lousy predicament. You can't avoid a gnawing sense of desperation. I had visions of my fruitless late-night hotel search when I'd first arrived in Paris and ended up sleeping in the bushes of the Square René-Viviani. I asked at the front desks of five hotels, but all were full. On the sixth try, we were lucky. The man at the desk wanted to charge us six hundred pesetas for two rooms—four hundred for a double room for the girls and two hundred for a small single for me. Gwyn said something to Jane, and Jane said to me, "Let's share a room, save the extra money."

"*Necesitamos solamente una habitación,*" I said to the clerk quickly, before the girls could change their minds, "*con dos camas grandes o tres camas individuales.*" We need only one room, with two large beds or three single beds.

"The price is five hundred pesetas," he replied, in Spanish. The man was dressed in a suit and tie, despite the late hour, and was immaculately groomed. He looked to be my father's age or so, perhaps fifty, and I wondered if he were the hotel owner.

"That's not possible," I said, balking at the price. "You said one room for the women was four hundred. We will pay you four hundred." I tried to sound reasonable yet firm, but the man just shook his head and made as if to turn away from the desk. I explained we were poor young people. Didn't he perhaps have something on a higher floor that cost less money?

He relented, and we handed him our passports, as was customary in European hotels so that the identities of every hotel guest could be submitted to the police, in case a wanted criminal were hiding out. I always wondered how many wanted criminals were caught that way. Not many.

As he took our proffered I.D.'s and passed me a key with a heavyweight key ring, he said to me, "There are four beds in this room. Please use only *your* beds."

As it turned out, we would use only two. We picked up our luggage and turned for the stairway when the clerk stopped me.

"Sir, you want one room only," he said. "Clearly, you are young. So I give you one room for you and the two young women. But no noise. I understand you want one room, but no noise. I too was young once."

14

Leaving Madrid

Should I stay or should I go? - Radio taxis to the rescue - Second thoughts about splitting up - Goodbye, Gwyn, and you too, Jane - A town without a center - What the hell am I eating? - Big boys don't cry

T hings didn't transpire exactly as I'd planned the next day. The girls had a friend, an exchange student they knew from high school, whose family lived near Burgos, where Gwyn and Jane had been invited to stay.

"I'm sure they'd be glad to have you too," Gwyn said. "I hear they're very nice."

No doubt. But I never liked to impose, and didn't want to invite myself to be an unwanted houseguest.

Surprise! We've brought a tame hippie along with us. He's a bit dirty, but you don't mind putting him up for a few days, do you?

After Burgos, the girls and their friend planned to travel to Bilbao, where the friend had an apartment; Gwyn was certain I would be more than welcome there as well. But I hadn't planned to see either Burgos or Bilbao. Also, Gwyn and Jane would want to spend much of their time with their friend. What I *really* wanted before leaving

Spain was to see Pamplona, the setting for Hemingway's *The Sun Also Rises.* And that's what I decided to do.

When I told Gwyn about my plans to split up from them once they reached their destination, she looked especially disappointed. Her reaction almost made me change my mind again.

THE ROUTES FROM Madrid to both Burgos and Pamplona overlapped for a hundred and fifty miles, so we agreed that I would travel with them for that distance, then continue hitching from there.

With our passports and luggage in hand, we returned to the trusty Vauxhall Viva after a light breakfast at the hotel. But getting to the car was one thing; getting the car out of Madrid was something else. My unwieldy map of Europe was useful for choosing routes between cities, but useless in providing details of city streets. We were completely turned around, uncertain even of the direction from which we had arrived in Madrid.

At a traffic signal, we stopped for a red light. A taxi came up alongside us. The driver's window was down, so I called out to him and asked directions for the road to Burgos. The man understood, and seemed eager to help. Too eager, I guessed, because he removed the *Libre* sign from the window and flipped down the flag on his dashboard meter. *Was he going to charge us for directions?!*

Before I could say something, he had driven ahead of us so we could follow him. I told Gwyn to stop alongside him at the next light.

"Mister, I'm sorry, but we can't pay you," I said. "We are lost and need to find the road to Burgos, but we have no money for you."

He frowned at first, then shrugged, raised his bushy eyebrows, and said, "*No es importa.*"

We followed him to a large plaza that apparently connected with the road we wanted, because he pointed ahead of us, as if we should keep going in that direction, and waved goodbye. We tentatively continued onward, though we were still in the depths of metropolitan traffic at rush hour. Barely had we passed the plaza when another taxi pulled next to us. The driver gave a honk and a wave. In the back of the cab was a passenger.

"Are you the ones going to Burgos?" he called through the window, in perfect English.

We all nodded, then he zipped ahead and waved for us to follow.

We figured that the first cabbie must have radioed this one and asked his help in escorting us out of town. He made a quick turn into a narrow side street, disgorged his passenger, and continued ahead, with us following closely behind. He led us to the outskirts of the business district, then pointed emphatically at a traffic sign that said "A Burgos." Amazing. We drove slowly around the taxi. When we were even with it, the driver turned to us with a big smile, then clasped his palms together and shook his hands in a victory symbol.

The longer we drove that morning, the prettier Gwyn got as I watched her from my spot, sitting cater-corner in the back seat. I was having third and fourth thoughts. Around one o'clock we stopped at a picnic area off the side of the road, and gathered the bread and cheese we'd purchased shortly after leaving Madrid. Gwyn took my hand as we walked to a picnic table.

At last, just past three, our paths diverged, and the girls got out of the car with me. I hugged each of them, kissed them, shook their hands, and hugged and kissed Gwyn a second time, and then they were gone.

Those sorts of intense, brief friendships on the road were going to give me high blood pressure, I thought. The excitement of meeting someone new, whether male or female, of getting to know each other, of sharing adventures big and small, often in less than twenty-four hours, was the heady high that led to a disappointing emptiness as, ultimately, they drove away. The emotional ups and downs of hitchhiking were taking a toll on me.

A SALESMAN (I never did find out what he sold) picked me up two hours later, although for the life of me I couldn't figure out why. He expressed no interest in a conversation other than to say, "Alsasua," which I took to mean a town farther up the road. In the event, Alsasua was a strange little place. It looked to be full of nothing but four- and five-story modern apartment houses. A handful of them held a business of one sort or another on their ground floors, but, unless you needed a shoe store or realtor, they were few and uninteresting. I couldn't find the center of town; I began to doubt there even *was* a downtown. I found only one hotel in the village, where the price for a single room was three hundred pesetas, which I wouldn't pay.

At a nearby grocery, I bought some pre-cooked canned meat, oranges, and beer, then walked a mile outside town on the Pamplona road. I set up camp in an overgrown apple orchard that was far enough back from the street that I wouldn't bother anyone or be seen. As the sun went down, it turned cloudy and cold. I put on my Moroccan djellaba. When the light dimmed too much to read by, I brought out my dinner, and opened the can of meat. The choice of entrée had come recommended by the grocer.

"*Buen precio,*" he had said. "*Muy sabrosa.*" Good price. Very tasty.

But when I saw the contents of the container, I almost broke camp and stormed back to the shop. The "meat" comprised fatty pieces of animal stomach, complete with tube-like openings, in a rich, savory tomato sauce. I tried to eat a bite-size portion, but I could barely keep it in my mouth long enough to chew, let alone swallow the horrid flesh. It was organ meat! You don't recommend organ meat without a frank and open discussion. I couldn't imagine the offal would have been improved by heating it. I threw the repulsive viscera under a bush, ate one of the oranges, and drank some beer.

On the previous night, I had shared a room with two sexy young red-haired Welsh women at a hotel in one of the great capitals of Europe. Tonight, I was eating cold, gelatinous ferret innards out of a can in a windy weed-strewn orchard just beyond the hopeless depths of some Spanish Podunk. A boy of the 1950s and '60s, I had been raised not to cry.

The training came in handy that night.

15

Tío Tom

Smoke gets in your eyes - A pub crawl of epic proportions - The discovery of Spanish tinto - Tío Tom, my culinary instructor - How to treat a waiter - Snails and mucus on the half shell - Legless beggars make lousy runners

U rdiain was as attractive as Alsasua was not. I was in the province of Navarre now, and the architecture was unrecognizable compared to that of Andalusia. The buildings here looked like Swiss ski chalets. I had three *cafés con leche* and two donuts at a cantina, then strapped on my tattered yellow backpack and returned to the road, hoping for a fast ride to Pamplona.

My first lift that day came from a young construction worker who insisted he was not a Spaniard; he was a Basque. He admired the ultra-violent Basque Liberation Front, the ETA, and was certain that one day País Vasco, as he called the Basque country, would separate from Spain. I think if he had taken me farther he would have tried to recruit me as a bomb-thrower. He dropped me off a short time later, offered me a cigarette, and wished me luck.

I had tried cigarettes when I was in high school and college, but had never started a habit. In fact, I disliked them. Europe, however, taught me, encouraged me even, to be a cigarette smoker.

In Europe, in those days, smoking was permitted in bars and grocery stores, while driving in a car with children or waiting in line at the bank, everywhere but in church. And I'm not even sure about church. Smoking was as popular with young imbibers as older ones; the youth hostels I stayed at reeked of cigarette smoke. Europeans loved their cigarettes so much that pot smokers would sometimes empty the tobacco from a cigarette, blend it with weed, refill the hollow tube with the mixture, and toke up that way to get the taste of both marijuana and tobacco. When I tried that once I was nauseous and dizzy for the next four hours.

Part of the European smokers' etiquette was the formal exchange of cigarettes on meeting someone, just like in old movies. A gentleman removes an elegant silver case from the inner breast pocket of his dinner jacket and offers a cigarette to another man. The second man graciously accepts the proffered tobacco, removes his *own* engraved case, and hands one of his cigarettes to the first man.

"Please," he says, "you must try one of *mine*. I have a man in Ankara who gets them for me."

At campgrounds and in hostels, people constantly offered me cigarettes. I never saw a single person during my entire time traveling in Europe who opened a pack without offering to share. It just wasn't done. Fortunas from Spain, Gauloises from France, Kings from Denmark, Mayfairs from England, Sweet Aftons from Ireland—cigarettes of all kinds, all lengths, with and without filter tips, in cellophane wrappers and in sturdy boxes. You never saw so many cigarettes. People even smoked in restaurants *while they were eating,* taking puffs between bites and swallows.

The problem for me was that, as I said, I didn't smoke. After only a few days in Germany, however, and especially in France, I realized what an uncouth lout I must have seemed when I declined a cigarette offered by a new acquaintance, whether in a hostel dining room, across a cookfire at a campsite, or over a glass of Mosel Riesling at a country *weinstube.* Conscious of the poor reputation of "Ugly Americans" on the Continent, I tried receiving a cigarette with a polite "Thanks, I'll save this for later," but that was no better than my flat-out rejecting it. I began accepting cigarettes, taking a few puffs, and surreptitiously snuffing them out when the other person wasn't looking.

That still wasn't enough, of course. I was expected to offer a cigarette of my own in return. So I began to buy cigarettes. I received one, I gave one, we both lit up. The social compact was complete. The future of Europe was secure.

Some of the cigarettes I was offered were worse than others, either too harsh or flavored with menthol. Soon I developed my favorites—Players from the U.K. and Gitanes from France. And then I found myself lighting up a cigarette not to share a smoke with a newfound friend but to kill time, to do something with my hands, or just because they were there. I began to *like* the taste and smell. By the time I returned to America I was a full-fledged smoker.

Thanks, Europe!

With the Basque radical's cigarette dangling from my mouth, I continued on the little-traveled side road to Pamplona. For two hours I walked alongside that two-lane blacktop, doing my little twist-turn-thumb dance whenever I heard a car approach from behind.

Finally, a young guy with longish dark hair and an eager smile stopped for me. He was handsome, like an actor, with a strong jaw and long bovine eyelashes.

"Pamplona?" I asked before climbing inside.

He instantly caught on that I spoke English.

"I'm going all the way to Pamplona," he said. "Come in."

I retrieved a pack of Fortunas from my shirt pocket.

"Care for a cigarette?" I asked.

"Thanks," he replied, then handed me a pack of British Woodbines from his own pocket. "Try a Woodie. They're strong but good."

His name was Higinio, or Gini, for short. The same age as I, he lived in Pamplona. He had no job, but I gathered that he didn't need to work to support himself. I didn't pry. He was driving a sporty two-door job that I learned later was a 1976 Seat 1200 Sport Coupé, or *Bocanegra,* as Gini called it because of the black front grill.

Arriving in Pamplona, I asked Gini if he knew where I could find the local youth hostel, and he frowned.

"You have no reservation someplace?" he asked, and I shook my head. "My friend has a small hotel. Good location. He will give you a good price."

Into the old town he drove, barreling down the narrow cobbled streets, and stopped in front of an unpretentious inn. Gini told me to wait in the car while he spoke with the front-desk clerk.

"You can have a room for one hundred and fifty pesetas a night," he said when he returned. "Can you pay that?"

That was about $2.25, not much more than I would have paid at a hostel, so I agreed.

"You can check in and put your things in your room," Gini said. "I'll wait here, then we can have a beer. I know some good places."

I ran up to my room, which was spare but clean, then

hurried back down, eager to discover whatever charms Pamplona held.

At the first pub, Gini ordered Cinco Estrellas. At the next he called for Alhambra 1925s. Then he ordered Estrella Galicia and Cerveza Reinas at the next pub and the next. He wanted to school me in the variety of Spanish beers.

As we left the fourth pub in search of another, Gini turned to me with a serious expression.

"I think," he said slowly, almost wistfully, "we should switch now to wine. Do you agree? Red wine!"

So red wine it would be (Gini called it *tinto*), a glass at each of three successive cafés. We tried Jumilla, Tempranillo, and my favorite, Rioja. Gini knew where each wine came from, what distinguished them, and why he preferred one over another with certain foods. My wine knowledge was limited to half-gallon jugs of Bali Hai. Anything Gini told me about wine would be an education.

By now the time was three, when all good Spaniards should be savoring their midday meals. Gini went home to eat, while I had *steak frites* and salad on my own. We met up again at five, which had given me time to return to my hotel (I barely remembered its location), change clothes, and freshen up.

Back in the center of old Pamplona, at another bar, Gini introduced me to Tío Tom, a local man of about sixty who was not related to Gini, despite his name (*tío* is Spanish for "uncle"). I liked Tío Tom instantly. He had a dark-gray walrus mustache, a well-lived-in face with smile lines at the eyes, eyebrows thick enough to comb, and a Falstaffian zest in everything he did.

"*Joven!*" he called to a young waiter. "*Tres más cervezas aquí.*" He slammed his meat-like fist on the table. "*Pronto!*" Then he roared with laughter to indicate that he wasn't serious about demanding quickness.

Tío Tom leaned over to me and said under his breath, "It's always good to have a waiter be a little afraid of you, but you must always leave him a tip."

In all the years since then, I have never been rude to or terrorized a waiter, but I have found that a somewhat stern, businesslike start to a waiter-customer relationship while holding a menu leads to more professional service. Then smile and leave a nice gratuity on your way out. Well, it has worked for me, and it certainly worked for Tío Tom, because the teenage waiter was back at our table with three Cinco Estrellas on a pewter serving tray less than sixty seconds later.

Gini told Tom about my travels, from Frankfurt to Paris, Avignon, Barcelona, Marrakech, Tangier, Granada, and more. Tom (his full name was Tomás, but he preferred the Americanized form) seemed to have a new-found fascination with me.

"I think we should have cognac, to celebrate your arrival in the finest city in all Europe," he said in English almost as good as Gini's. When the cognac arrived, poured into tulip glasses, Tío Tom raised a toast and said with great drama, "To Pamplona!"

Tom and Gini decided that I needed to eat snails and mussels, after I confessed I'd never tried either. All I knew about snails was that snooty people at expensive, white-cloth French restaurants in Manhattan ate them in *New Yorker* cartoons. (Impatient diner to waiter: "Why are the escargots so slow in coming tonight?!") And mussels, to me, were just mucus on the half-shell. But before I knew it the three of us had left the *cervecieria* for an elegant café near the main square, Plaza del Castillo, with linen napkins and flowers on the tables.

Tom ordered the mussels, a huge porringer of them, served family-style. I watched the older and younger men so I could follow their example, as I had no idea how to eat a mussel. Tom held a mussel in his left hand and broke off the upper half of the shell to use as a spoon, sliding it under the meat attached to the bottom shell. Then he raised the loosened mussel and slurped it into his mouth. He placed the empty shells into one of the smaller, individual bowls that had been set before each of us. Gini ate his first mussel in a similar manner, so I followed suit.

The mussels didn't taste as I had feared, but were delicious. I tried to isolate the multiple flavors that spread through my mouth as I chewed. While I ate, Tom looked at me curiously, then seemed satisfied as I ate my second and third ones.

"Tío Tom," I said, "these are great. What are the flavors I taste?"

Tom looked at Gini with a what-can-you-do shrug.

"I've spoiled him," he said, then turned back to me. "This is the best *marisquería* in all of Navarre. You will find mussels cooked like this only here, in this place. The olive oil is the best, golden, extra-virgin, *aceite de Navarra*. The onions and tomatoes, only the freshest. The best dry white wine, from Rueda. A pinch of saffron, but not too much! This is Pamplona, not Bombay. The juice of fat Valencia lemons."

Tom poured each of us another glass of white wine from the bottle of Verdejo he had ordered. I was woozy from all the drinking, but not so intoxicated that I was unconcerned about the cost of everything we were eating and drinking. Tío Tom had paid for our beers at the bar earlier, and Gini had paid for most of the drinks we'd shared before that, but this restaurant looked like a different level of pricing than the humble drinking establishments we'd visited. I needn't have worried. When the bill came, Tom stood up and casually threw a wad of pesetas on top of it.

"And now" he cried, "snails!"

Instead of another upscale restaurant, we went to a tavern-like place where Tom ordered three beers and a platter of snails. Where I grew up, our backyard garden was often infested with snails. They were so plentiful that we sometimes had to buy snail poison. I hated the look of them, the trail of gunge they left behind, the antenna-like eyes that retracted when you poked them, the *crunch* and squirminess when you accidentally stepped on one with your bare feet as you crossed the dewy front lawn in the evening. To eat one of those slimy boogers? The mere thought churned my stomach.

I was agreeably surprised to find the snails were not served whole. After cooking, they had been removed from their shells, chopped up with garlic butter, tomato sauce, bread crumbs, and spices, and cooked some more in a pan. Then the mixture was spooned into the empty shells and served on a platter. Tom and Gini ate them in much the same way they had eaten their mussels, by picking one up, sucking the contents out of the shell (with some help from their tongues), then tossing the empty husks into a separate bowl. The garlic-and-tomato sauce was so piquant that I don't think I even would have known the dish contained something as foul as a snail. I was pleased with myself. I could say now that I had eaten snails. Without vomiting.

We walked to a tiny lane, no more than twelve feet wide, called Calle San Nicolas, lined for several blocks with *cervecerías, vinotecas,* Basque-cuisine restaurants, pizzerias, and cocktail bars. It took me a minute to realize my hotel was on this same street. The *calle* was filled with hundreds of pedestrians out for a good time on a Friday evening. Tío Tom led us to a bar, but before we entered, a beggar with no legs, seated in a wheelchair by the entrance, grabbed me by the arm and began talking quickly. I couldn't understand him, and looked to Gini for help.

"He's telling you that he's running with the bulls to-day," Gini translated. "He says he will run in your honor but he wants you to give him some money."

"Should I give him something?"

"Give him ten pesetas," Gini suggested. "No more."

From my pocket I brought out two five-peseta coins and handed them to the man. As soon as he grasped the money, he ignored me and started calling to the passersby that he was running with the bulls and wanted money.

As we took seats at a table inside, Tío Tom told me that years ago the man would don a beret and red neckerchief during the annual Feria de San Fermín, which featured the colorful running of the bulls through the city streets to the bullring. He would get ferociously drunk and beg for money, telling tourists that he would run on their behalf for a small contribution. Nobody believed it, of course; no such tradition existed as running on behalf of someone else.

"Then the man lost his legs," Tom explained. "About five years ago, more or less, from diabetes. First one, then the other. And so, of course, after that he would beg every day, saying the same thing to the tourists, even when the *feria* was over. But people here give him a little money. He gets food from some of the restaurants. He has enough to drink."

What a sad, sad story, I thought.

"How do you know him, Tío Tom?" I asked. "Just from living here?"

"He used to be my cousin," Tom said, then slapped the table loudly and "demanded" three more beers, *pronto!*

As we continued walking from bar to bar, Gini and Tío Tom would point out the streets through which the bulls ran during the fiesta on their way to the bullring. On this street, you needed to be at least a hundred meters ahead of the first bulls. Whatever you do, don't fall on the other street because you are likely to be gored or trampled. On the street over there, by the old telephone exchange, was where a local man was killed by a *cornada* during the previous year's *encierro,* as Tom and Gini called the running of the bulls.

We ended up at Café Iruña, one of Hemingway's favored drinking establishments. Gini waved to a couple of *chicas* he knew, one of whom was an old girlfriend, who joined us at our table.

Her name was Adelina. Gini called her Ady. She was stunning, like a model, with brown eyes that glowed, a massive mane of dark-brown hair that tumbled across her shoulders, and a figure that would have made any man in the Plaza del Castillo stop and turn. *Gini,* I thought, *you idiot! How in the world did you let this one get away?*

Then Ady looked at me, and I felt a moment's sexual frisson. Until, that is, the next thing that came out of her mouth.

"I see you have a new friend," she said to Gini in flawless English, then looked at me with a sly smile.

I didn't like the sound of that.

"No, no," Gini said, defensively. "No, I just met Mark today. He's hitchhiking around Europe."

Adelina appraised me again, but seemed unconvinced of whatever suspicion she was harboring.

Gini called for more beers, but Tom raised his hands as if in surrender.

"Thank you, Gini, but not for me," he said. "You young people can drink beer all night, no problem. It's not the same for an old man. I no longer have the kidneys or liver of a thirty-year-old. I have to go home."

We all stood as Tom climbed out of his chair to leave.

"Tío Tom," I said, reaching for his hand, "it has been an honor to meet you. Thank you for the wine, the mussels, the snails, the…"

He shushed me with a fingertip placed on my lips.

"*Escúchame, joven,*" he said. "This is important. Everyone likes you. You have many, many years ahead of you. Promise me you will never lose it."

"Lose what?" I had no idea what he meant.

He took my shoulders in his thick carpenter's hands and pulled me to him in a warm embrace.

Then he walked out the door.

Adelina looked at me as we all took our seats again.

"A little bit of Tomás can be a lot," she said, almost dismissively.

Despite her beauty, I immediately stopped lusting after her.

I have vague memories of a non-serious arm-wrestling match, still more beer, and an overly long, completely unrequested explanation from Gini about why I would not see him tomorrow, as he had to be in Zaragoza early in the morning on some errand for Tío Tom. We left the bar and had a pleasant stroll to my hotel while Gini and Adelina held me up by the elbows. Adelina instructed me to kiss her on both cheeks, Gini and I embraced and exchanged addresses, and I went off to my room.

16

La France Redux

*Pushing a Deux Chevaux - The French frontier by foot -
Trilingual conversation - Dreaming of England - Mont-
Saint-Michel - Ferry instruction - Another cold supper -
Why are the French so generous?*

I was thankful for every ride I ever got as a hitchhiker. Except for the one on the morning that I left
Pamplona.

A student at the Universidad de Navarra driving a Deux
Chevaux kindly stopped for me and promptly ran out of
gas, just minutes later. I suspected he knew he was dangerously low on fuel. The two of us, somehow, had to
move the car up a slight incline for a quarter of a mile to
a service station.

There's only one way to describe the difficulty in pushing a car uphill: goddam freaking arduous. The driver po-
sitioned himself on the left side, so he could steer through
the window with one hand and push (a little too lightly,
in my opinion) with the other. That meant I got the heavy
load, shoving with all my might from the car's ass end,
threatened at every step with a runaway 2CV knocking
me down and leaving Michelin 125R15 tire tracks down

my back. I told the driver to open his door and push from between the door and the driver's seat, so that he could quickly hop inside and put on the brakes, in case the weight of the French clown car became too much for us. By the time we got to the top of the rise, I was sweating worse than an obsessive sunbather slathered in Hawaiian Tropic Tanning Butter.

Finally, with a full tank, we drove north through the Pyrenees and its picturesque pueblos. The student gave me a ride to the Spanish-French frontier at Irun, fifty miles from Pamplona. Apart from the uphill pushing, the travel day had gotten off to a good start.

I crossed the Bidasoa River marking the border, went through an efficient customs check on the Gallic side, and walked for a couple of kilometers to get away from the usual traffic jumble that accompanied almost every border crossing. A short time later a new Mercedes W123 driven by a stunning blonde German woman pulled to the side of the road to give me a lift. Unfortunately, she was accompanied in the passenger seat by her boyfriend. They were driving to Poitiers, three hundred miles north. In fact, they were only stopping in Poitiers for lunch, and planned to continue on to Dusseldorf, a total distance of eight hundred miles in a single day. Those were two determined Germans! Even the Wehrmacht panzer divisions could average only fifty miles a day.

She spoke German and English. Her boyfriend spoke Spanish and German. I spoke English and a little Spanish. You can see where this is going.

"You have a very nice car," I said, in English.

"It's not as nice as I thought it would be," she replied, then said something to her boyfriend in German.

In Spanish, the boyfriend said to me, "It's a terrible car. I don't know why she ever bought it. But if you're German, you want a Mercedes, I suppose."

"But they have a very good reputation," I replied in Spanish. "What's wrong with it?"

The boyfriend said something to the German, who said to me in English, "I should have gotten the bigger engine." If you want to know how to kill time on a four-and-a-half-hour car ride, I have an idea. But I wouldn't recommend it. My head began to hurt after an hour.

I camped that night outside Poitiers on a bed of leaves in a grove of trees. My plan was to camp at least three or four times in the coming week to save money for the ferry to England. The chief drawback to camping that way, though, was the sheer boredom. Of course, I didn't want to pay for a site at a campground, which would have undermined the whole reason for camping in the first place. So I had to seek shelter in some out-of-the-way spots where I wouldn't be seen, in case I was unwittingly on private property. That meant being far from the bars and restaurants and crowds that I found so much fun. Camping rough also meant doing without plumbing. Being a scrupulously clean young man (growing up, I would sometimes take two showers on a particularly hot day), and a faithful fan of Thomas Crapper's singular invention, I didn't particularly look forward to these nights in the woods.

In the morning I walked to the opposite side of Poitiers to continue hitching north toward the English Channel. My hope was to spend the next month or so in England, which to me was as iconic a destination as anything on the Continent. I wanted to see Big Ben and the Changing of the Guard at Buckingham Palace. I longed to drink a pint of cask ale on a warm evening in a country pub, preferably one thatched in traditional straw. I wanted to stroll the quads of Oxford and meander along hilly footpaths from hamlet to village, passing through the pastures of kindly farmers who would wave to me.

God, I was an idiot. But a romantic one, at least.

The rides dried up, so I began to walk in earnest. The knot I'd been forced to tie in my pack's left strap, a result of the Seville robbery, dug into my shoulder. Most of the time when I wore the backpack, I was either standing in place or walking only a short distance. But from Poitiers I ended up walking fifteen kilometers over four hours on the road to Rennes (or the road to ruin, as I began to think of it, considering my painful shoulder). Finally, I could take it no more. I found a grassy spot far from the road and any houses and made my camp there.

The weather had warmed, so I spent a comfortable night outside. I awoke early and got my first ride of the day from a young businessman who drove me through Rennes and put me on the road to Mont Saint-Michel, a place he recommended with enthusiasm.

"You will thank me in your prayers," he said with a smile.

I reached that storybook destination in two successive rides, and marveled at the sight. Mont Saint-Michel was a village, topped with a spire-filled cathedral, that clung to the slopes of a steep mountain that rose inexplicably from the edge of the Atlantic in northern France. But what made it even more wondrous were the tides. At low tide, you could walk to the village across hundreds of yards of beach sand and mud flats, while at high tide the village was surrounded by water. In the early days, anyone wanting to travel to or from Mont Saint-Michel had to time his travels with the tides. Later, a causeway was built to allow communication between village and shore twenty-four hours a day, and that's the road I followed toward that fairy tale come to life.

The dreamlike Gothic abbey-cathedral that crowned the mountain could be seen from everywhere. The village itself was small——hardly large enough even to be called a village—and fantastically old, with narrow cobblestone lanes that spiraled around the mountainsides. The houses, hotels, and restaurants were like an illustration of some long-ago fable, made of stone and wooden beams, with flowers in the windows and iron lanterns at the doorways. One could walk through the entire village in an hour, so I didn't linger.

I thumbed it back to Pontorson, from where I had diverted to Mont Saint-Michel, and quickly caught a ride to Falaise, then another from a young engineer to the beachside casino town of Deauville. The engineer spoke English well, and was happy to show me points of interest along the way. When he found out I planned to visit the U.K., he said I might be able to take the ferry across the Channel for free.

"The auto ferry is expensive," he explained, "so to attract customers they allow the driver up to five passengers at no extra charge."

At least, that's how it worked the last time he'd taken his car to England. My heart was leaping in my chest. The ferry, for free.

"Of course," he continued, "I suppose it depends on which ferry company you choose, which port you leave from, which port you arrive at."

My heart thudded to a halt as fast as it had fluttered to racing speed. I had figured on one ferry company, and one route, Calais to Dover. I hadn't done my homework.

"You can take Brittany Ferries from Cherbourg, Saint-Malo, or Caen. All go to Portsmouth. P&O Ferries has a popular one from Calais to Dover. That route has the most ferries. You can also choose to leave from Dieppe or Dunkerque, but I can't remember if both go to Folkestone or one goes to Newhaven. But it hardly matters what they were doing last year or even last month; they change their schedules so frequently."

The young engineer was giving me plenty of options, but that's not what I wanted. *Give me clarity!* I wanted someone to tell me what to do, and I would do it.

"Well, which one did you choose?" I asked, figuring I would simply take whichever ferry he had taken.

"No, no, no, that will do you no good," he said. "I took the ferry to Plymouth, from Roscoff. But Roscoff is in Brittany, four hundred kilometers in the direction you are coming from."

Even so, he'd given me hope. Of course, a car ferry would let passengers travel free. Why not? A universal policy. I was certain of it. Probably. I tried talking myself into a positive state of mind. In any event, I would continue onward to Calais, since more ferries left from there than the other ports.

I CAMPED THAT night on a wooded hillside in sight of the ocean and the resort town of Trouville. I was well hidden there, so decided to risk building a small cookfire. Dry wood wasn't easy to find, though. The twigs and branches I collected were either green or wet. For about thirty minutes all I could get from the wood was thick smoke. Finally, but barely, a flame caught hold. I quickly opened a can of pork with sauerkraut and a smaller can of peas, all of which I poured into my lone cook pan. I hadn't eaten all day and was ravenously anticipating this meal. Often, when I would buy a can of meat, what poured out was unidentifiable and sometimes inedible. But as I considered the sight of the pork and sauerkraut in the pan, the saliva began to flow across the roof of my mouth. I was like a famished Elmer Fudd, looking at Bugs but seeing wabbit fwicassee. I would simmer it slowly, I decided, rather than just heat it at full flame as I often did when I cooked at home. I would let the juices from the pork simmer teasingly, giving them time to meld with and deeply flavor the sauerkraut. I wanted the peas to soften slowly to the point where they would nearly fall apart even before reaching my mouth. My stomach growled.

I had just begun to smell the aroma of the slowly heating meat when the small pyramid of wood I was urging along collapsed on itself, smothering the fire and shooting up a cloud of white smoke. It would be cold comfort for me that night.

HONFLEUR, HOME OF the Impressionists, charming harbor town, artistic muse, had barely changed in a century. Monet and Sisley learned the techniques of plein air painting there from Boudin, how to capture the dance of direct sunlight on water. Baudelaire dreamed of living there. Erik Satie composed there.

Of course, I knew none of this when I took a table at a waterfront café overlooking the docks and boats. I simply knew a picturesque town when I saw one. The shingled, exposed-beam Church of St. Catherine had been designed and built by the city's carpenters following the Hundred Years War, and, unlike so many of the Mudejar and Gothic cathedrals I'd already seen, was woody and homey. The belfry of the separate, adjacent bell tower reminded me of a windmill. The winding streets were narrow and filled with brightly painted shopfronts holding galleries, antiques stores, *bar-tabacs,* and attractive small hotels that I could only dream of affording.

I had slept well the previous night in my hillside bed of ivy, but was still disappointed about my failed pork-sauerkraut dinner. I hitched out of Trouville on the two-lane coast road that connected to Honfleur, and stopped at that artistic Mecca only because that's where my first ride let me out, just twenty minutes later.

From Honfleur, two young geology students, a man and woman, stopped for me en route to Le Havre. There followed a ride to Dieppe with three young men who spoke no English, and of course, I spoke no French, but they stopped and bought me several beers anyway. Two sexy French girls gave me cigarettes and drove me to Eu an hour and a half farther along the coast. The day was getting on toward dusk, but I continued thumbing, getting two more rides to Abbeville, an administrative center of little interest to tourists.

I walked out of town on a road leading to Boulogne so I could get a good jump on hitching a ride in the morning, but could find no attractive place to camp. The ground was flat for miles, farmland, with no groves of trees to provide shelter and to hide me from the view of curious passersby or the police. For lack of anything better, I set up housekeeping in a gully on the edge of a furrowed field, next to what seemed to be the one tree for a hundred miles.

Who was I kidding? It wasn't a gully. It was a ditch to channel rainwater. I was sleeping in the rural equivalent of a gutter. A farmhouse rooftop shone in the moonlight just a half-mile away, so I dared not build a campfire for fear of alerting the farmer to a trespasser among his cabbages and beets.

I'd had too many cold camps lately. But I wasn't upset about it. I was too excited.

Tomorrow I would be in England.

17

Footpath to Goudhurst

Choppy Channel - Dover solo - Riding in a firebomb - Bloody Syrians - The Hitchhiker's Tale - That's not a trail! - Drinking in the shadows of the Hawkhurst Gang - London in sight

The "passengers ride free" policy didn't apply in Calais. A ticket for the two p.m. departure cost sixteen dollars, but I paid it gladly. I'd earned the right to spend such an exorbitant amount by sleeping outdoors much of the past three weeks, too often forgoing the comforts of hot showers and soft beds. I freshened myself up in the public bathroom on the boat, knowing I'd be passing through immigration on arrival at Dover. Looking like the wrong half of The Odd Couple on acid and smelling like a pigsty were unlikely to provide me with an expedited passport check.

The crossing was rough, and I wasn't a good sailor. I clutched the railing most of the voyage, ready to hurl. But when I spied the famed white cliffs of Dover, I instantly cheered up. England! More than any country on my itinerary, this is where I wanted to be.

Customs was fast, and nobody seemed put off by my unshaven and rumpled appearance. I don't know why. I certainly wouldn't have let me in.

Before I could even get my bearings, I found myself walking through the town, eager to see England. Signs were in English! People were speaking English! How refreshing.

Apart from the fabled cliffs and the imposing castle on a bluff above the city, Dover was an unremarkable transit hub. But at that moment, to me, that port city represented the home of King Arthur, Sherlock Holmes, Robin Hood, and Queen Victoria. Everything was invisibly stamped with the words "Made in England." An English chemist shop! Not a pharmacy, a chemist! And that drinking establishment? Not a bar, but an honest-to-goodness British pub! I may have even begun to sing "Rule, Britannia."

The youth hostel was closed until six p.m., and I decided not to wait. I would sleep rough again, the better to conserve money for when I arrived in London. I had pretty much seen all one could see in Dover, so I walked out of town into a lush tree-filled countryscape, where I hoped to make camp. I went to sleep early, laying out my bedroll in a soft patch of grass on a forested hillside—in England's green and pleasant land.

Canterbury was my goal the next morning, for no other reason than that I had once attempted to read *The Canterbury Tales*. But I was leery about accepting that first ride, from a tanker truck hauling gasoline. I envisioned the next day's newspaper article: "Unfortunately, the driver had just picked up an American hitchhiker near Dover moments before the fiery crash. Because of the fury of the inferno, the passenger could be identified only from dental records." But in I climbed nonetheless.

The driver looked to be in his early forties, with a bit of a gut and a frightening nonchalance behind the wheel. I was about to ask him whether a driver pulling petrol shouldn't be a little more, I don't know, *alert and possibly terrified?* But before I could figure out a way to phrase the question without seeming thankless, he had something he wanted to get off his chest, apropos of nothing that I could tell.

"Bloody Syrians," he said in an accent that was thick enough to make me sit forward and concentrate on each word individually, thus putting me in the mental position of always being a split second behind his meaning. "You know why they cut off only one hand when they punish their criminals, don't ya?"

"Because it's such a horrible punishment, I guess," I said. "As a reminder to others of the price you pay for breaking the law."

"No, mate," he countered, disappointed in me. "That's not it at all."

We were approaching a roundabout, but he showed no signs of slowing the mobile firebomb he was driving. I was ready to say something when he downshifted, braked smoothly, and handled the circle without blinking. Clearly a pro. But I guess they don't give combustible loads to truckers with learner's permits.

"No, ya see, they do it to make the bloke eat and wipe his arse with the same hand. It's nefarious-like, see? Diabolical is what I call it. Diabolical, that's what that is. What kind of people even *think* of something like that?"

I had to admit I'd never considered it with such a morbid spin. But then, I hadn't given the issue of Syrian crime and punishment much thought period.

The driver, whose name I never got, proved not to be well-educated, but he went out of his way to be friendly and chatty. I hoped he was being genuine, and not just talking his head off because he had driven all night and was on the verge of falling asleep with the massive motorized Molotov cocktail in our backseat ready to consume us with its sulfurous flames.

THE CANTERBURY HOSTEL, about a half-mile from the city center, was unlike any of the hostels I had stayed at on the Continent, housed in an old, three-story, weirdly shaped brick mansion that had seen better days. The wood trim was splintered and in need of paint, and the bushes and grass at the entrance had not been maintained. Inside, the hostel was rife with the usual morning activity of such places—young people arriving and leaving, cooking their breakfast in the communal kitchen, packing up their gear.

After registering at the front desk, paying my overnight fee (one pound fifty, or about two dollars U.S.), and stowing my pack, I walked into Canterbury, eager to discover what the ancient place had to offer. As usual, my first stop was the train station, where one could usually expect to find a tourist office in a city of any consequence, and pick up a map and any helpful brochures.

The cathedral, Canterbury's chief claim to prominence, dated to 597 A.D., though reconstructions in the 1100s provided its present-day appearance. The interior was enormous, unimaginably vast for a church, full of chapels and medieval doors leading who knew where.

The tomb of the Black Prince—son of Edward III, hero of the Hundred Years War, the epitome of knightly chivalry—was arresting, topped with a full-length effigy of the mustachioed prince in fighting armor. The elaborate tomb of Henry IV was equally startling in the detailed carving of the marble graven image on its top. Unlike most kings, he had asked to be buried at Canterbury rather than Westminster Abbey because of his devotion to St.

Thomas Becket, the martyr who was murdered in the cathedral.

The rest of Canterbury didn't merit the same attention as the church, and appeared to be struggling to retain its historic character. New apartment buildings, bright super-markets, and tourist hotels tended to hide or overshadow the Grey Friars House, the Weavers House, what little re-mained of the old city walls, and even a section of Roman pavement.

HITCHHIKERS ROUTINELY DID a lot of walking. It might sound counterintuitive, but long waits by the roadside and a strong urge *to go* sometimes resulted in a hitcher walk-ing a mile or more along the road, if only to "find a better spot" or from sheer restlessness. So when I saw a sign saying "Footpath to Goudhurst" that pointed into a woods, I decided to follow it instead of standing idly at the edge of a little-traveled country road.

Goudhurst might have been the prettiest village in all England, my guidebook said, ridiculously picturesque. More than two hundred of its buildings were listed among the country's historic sites. Half-timbered houses lined the serpentine lanes, I'd read. Ancient oast houses with high conical roofs, where brewers once dried their hops in kilns, loomed over a charming duck pond. A tilting wood-frame inn stood adjacent to the twelfth-century St. Mary's Church and its hundred-and-fifty-foot-tall tower.

The day was warm, and I was in no rush, so I decided to walk the rest of the way, especially because I was eager to try an English footpath for myself. I'd read about them before leaving for Europe, and was intrigued. The foot-path network extended to all four corners of England and Wales, usually connecting one village to another through easements on private properties. Many of the paths had been in use for centuries, and in that time the law had granted pedestrians the right of way through those lands—farms, open fields, forests, fenced pastures, and whatever else man or the English countryside could throw in their way. Better yet, horses, bicycles, and anything other than human feet weren't allowed. Walkers only.

Holding up my map for a minute to better judge the direction of north, and to keep myself oriented on the path, I began to hike. The hilly dirt trail was no more than five feet wide at first, barely enough for two oncoming hikers to pass one another, and led through rolling farm fields of what I took to be wheat, then brought me through a cherry orchard. A sudden bend in the path took me into some deep woods. The pleasant sounds of streams and breezes amid the shadows were so soothing that I didn't even mind the knot in my backpack strap digging into my shoulder.

Coming out of the trees, I entered a cattle pasture that required me to open and shut a metal gate so the animals didn't escape. I followed what I thought to be the path, passing by cows casually chewing their cud, and came out the other side, where I opened and closed a gate like the other. But then the trail petered out. I thought I saw it continue at the bottom of the hill, but when I got there a barbed-wire fence blocked the way, with the path on the other side. I decided to gently, carefully, climb over the barbed wire—there seemed to be enough give to let me move it as necessary—rather than search for another way to reach the continuation of the footpath.

As I pushed down on the uppermost wire, I carefully swung my right leg over the top and planted my foot firmly on the opposite side, then just as carefully lifted my left leg over, cognizant of my responsibility to propagate future generations of Orwolls. When I came to another barbed-wire fence no more than one hundred yards on, I began to doubt whether I had chosen the right trail.

Nonetheless, the path continued on the other side, so again I climbed over the fence without emasculation.

The trail, by now, was more a wish than a reality. I came to a three-foot-wide, fast-rushing, ankle-deep stream with no simple way to cross it other than to wade or attempt a jump onto the muddy far bank. In my effort to leap across, I accidentally kicked a rock and stumbled onto my knees in the middle of the creek, leaving my shoes and lower pants legs soaking wet. As if it couldn't get worse, I was forced to crouch as the "trail" led me into a patch of thorny bushes that cut my hands and face. My backpack continually got caught on the thorns, so, with some difficulty, I slipped out of it and carried it in my arms, leaving me with no way to protect my face against the branches that scraped at me. In so doing, I unwittingly dropped my map of Great Britain out of the pack's side pocket. I was now wet, dirty, directionless, and bleeding.

"This," I decided, "is *not* the footpath to Goudhurst."

An hour later I limped into that village, which was so utterly unlike what I'd read of it that I felt betrayed. The quaint Elizabethan brewing settlement I'd envisioned was just so-so. It didn't appear to have two hundred buildings in total, let alone two hundred listed ones. It looked flat-out boring, with one shop (a newsstand) and an admittedly alluring pub, the Star & Eagle. The pub had been built as a monastery in the reign of Henry IV and had once been the headquarters of a notorious eighteenth-century band of smugglers, the Hawkhurst Gang. On this afternoon it proved to be a charming-enough drinkery for one Mark Orwoll. I took advantage of the beer break to clean myself up in the pub's bathroom, and decided to carry on hitchhiking, this time to the larger, ideally more interesting town of nearby Royal Tunbridge Wells.

But even that small city wasn't enough to entice me, especially since it had no hostel and I couldn't find an affordable hotel. Not surprising. Royal Tunbridge Wells was what the Brits called posh, full of private polo grounds, private clubs, and private schools. As a spa resort town, it had been the preferred holiday home to the haute monde since the 1700s. Originally called simply Tunbridge Wells, the town gained its "royal" appellation in 1909 from Edward VII in recognition of its popularity among the extended royal family. No wonder I couldn't find any two-dollar one-star hotel rooms with a bath down the hall.

What to do? I bought some regional maps and retired to a café to consider my options while under the influence of a much-needed hamburger and some baked beans. Then it occurred to me.

London Town.

Well, of course. Dreams of that world capital were what had spurred me toward England. What was I doing farting around in these crummy little towns when what I wanted was to witness the majesty of the Thames, check out the groovy stores on Carnaby Street, go to the free museums, see bobbies on bicycles two-by-two, and sit in a stained-glass-shadowed pew in Westminster Abbey?

Also, I had written everyone back home to let them know I would be in London around this date, more or less, and to contact me at Poste Restante, Trafalgar Square. Who knew, maybe there would even be a letter waiting for me.

The time was just past three. London was only forty-five miles northwest. With a good ride, I could be there in under an hour. In fact, two gents picked me up the moment I stretched out my thumb. They were going to London themselves. When they found out I'd never been there, they took no little pride in showing it off.

"Give 'im the Cook's Tour, Benny," said the passenger, waving his hand forward like a cavalry officer.

They drove me past the Houses of Parliament and Hyde Park, to Buckingham Palace and around Trafalgar Square, to Piccadilly Circus and over to Marble Arch. They seemed to be having as much fun trumpeting the grandeur of the city as I was in seeing it.

Why are people so nice to me, I wondered for the thousandth time? I could give or do precisely nothing in this world for these guys, or the dozens of other people, in Germany, France, and Spain, who had given me rides, offered travel suggestions, bought me meals and drinks, and made friendly chit-chat that always boosted my spirits. Horrible things happen in this world. Evil people roam the Earth, looking to cause ill. I know that. But I will never be persuaded that the human race, at its core, is anything other than kind and generous. And yes, I still believe in Santa Claus and the Tooth Fairy.

So there.

18

Like a Pendulum Do

London highs - Blood in my pee - The old overshadowed by the new - Green grassy quads of Oxford - Cities, towns, villages, and hamlets, explained - Salisbury Cathedral - The problem with America - Stonehenge

The next day I wanted to see everything, and I wanted to see it all at once.

I witnessed the Changing of the Guard at Buckingham Palace, regal, full of pomp and tradition (and crowds). I hustled from there down Birdcage Walk to Big Ben and the Houses of Parliament, where I was able to enter through Victoria Tower to see both the House of Lords and the House of Commons, picture galleries, the Queen's Robing Room, and St. Stephen's Hall. (Imagine showing up unannounced at the U.S. Capitol and having someone escort you around the joint.) Several dozen hippies had taken over the square below the statue of Eros at Piccadilly Circus. I marveled at the Nelson Statue atop its column in Trafalgar Square, picturesquely backdropped by the elegantly spired Church of St. Martin-in-the-Fields and the domed and columned National Gallery.

At the large post office just off the square, I stopped at the general enquiry desk, but the clerk told me he had no mail for me. ("Maybe tomorrow," he said, cheerfully, responding to my look of disappointment.)

A light rain began to fall, and cars turned on their headlamps, giving the afternoon a moody edge. A more conducive setting and atmosphere could hardly be imagined to go in search of 221B Baker Street, home to the fictional private detective Sherlock Holmes. I'd assumed Baker Street would be a charming Victorian lane full of handsome lodging houses like that owned by Mrs. Hudson, Holmes's landlady. Instead, I found a wide commercial avenue with truck traffic. The detective's street number had been concocted by Conan Doyle, but where it *would* have been, had it existed, was an unassuming three-story house at the street's northern end, hard by Regent's Park. I stood across the street, looking at the upper windows, imagining Holmes and Dr. Watson in their second-floor study interviewing some hapless crime victim (and Watson glancing surreptitiously at the shapely female client's well-turned ankle).

Back at the hostel in Earl's Court, I had a long talk with a young Englishman named Rupert and his wife Matilda (married couples at hostels were rare) about Ken Kesey and *One Flew Over the Cuckoo's Nest*, the Acid Tests, the Merry Pranksters, and Neal Cassady, which led to Jack Kerouac and Allen Ginsburg, my chats with Beat poet Ted Joans at Shakespeare and Company, and my blink-and-you'd-miss-it introduction to Gregory Corso.

I hadn't begun to exhaust my London to-do list, so the next day I carried on by visiting the British Museum of Natural History and the Victoria and Albert. At Trafalgar Square, I found once again no mail at the post office. I went to a movie theater and saw the longest, most boring film ever made, *Barry Lyndon,* visually stunning though it may have been.

In truth, I had gone to the movie theater not out of any

great desire to watch Ryan O'Neal in tricorn hat and frilly lace, but because I needed to sit down for a while. I'd been noticing a numbness in the front of my right thigh, in a spot about as wide as my fist, ever since I'd walked the nine or ten miles out of Poitiers. Then yesterday, after walking what I estimated to be seven or eight miles on the streets of London, I noticed a pink tinge in my urine. Blood. I was sure—well, pretty sure—that the constant pounding of my feet on the rough pavement might have temporarily broken a capillary in my ankle, and that a good rest was all I needed to recover. Take it from Dr. O.

Later I bought a used paperback copy of *All The President's Men*. Back at the hostel, I read several chapters in a comfortable chair in the lounge. I marveled at the life of a journalist. I had always regretted not joining the staff of the *Trojan Shield* at William N. Neff High School. A couple of my buddies were on the paper, writing album reviews and having a blast. I had once published a letter, while in high school, in the La Mirada *Lamplighter,* of which I was proud. (I was defending youthful musicians who, a previous letter-writer had implied, were responsible for the theft of a local church's public-address system.) I should have pursued that, I thought.

I would have been good at it.

AFTER A WEEK, on my final day in the capital, I walked clear across town to see the Tower of London and Tower Bridge—from the outside, as I couldn't afford a tour ticket. While I was in the East End I went to the Church of St. Mary-le-Bow to hear the hour chime. (By tradition, one must be born within the sound of "Bow bells" to be considered a Cockney, so now I could at least consider myself an honorary one.)

My map was full of undeniably atmospheric street names straight out of Dickens—Cheapside, Little Trinity

Lane, Poultry, Cornhill, Threadneedle—in a section of
London referred to simply as "the City." How disappointing to discover nothing like the Six Jolly Fellowship Por-
ters tavern or Mrs. Chivery's tobacco shop and instead
have to walk among rows of glass-and-steel towers housing banking headquarters, bond traders, insurance bro-
kers, and international shipping agencies.

I have since come to cherish my visits to London. I've
been there perhaps twenty times in my life, and love it
passionately. But it isn't an easy city to unpeel. At least,
it wasn't easy for me in 1976. So I decided to hitchhike
to Oxford the next day, and got one ride the entire distance, a little more than an hour from central London.

Now, this is more like it, I thought, as I walked down
random streets in the heart of the famed university city.
Its size was easily negotiable on foot, and the architecture
ranged from medieval to high Victorian, with almost
nothing built since the First World War.

To show you how untutored I was in my travel
knowledge, I hadn't realized that Oxford University comprised forty-five separate colleges and "private halls,"
each with its own buildings, masters, curricula, and tradi-
tions. At Christ Church College, I roamed through the
picture gallery, where I saw several paintings by Rubens
and Van Dyck. At the Sheldonian Theater, designed by
Sir Christopher Wren, I climbed to the cupola with its
360-degree views of the city's spires, enjoyed the mag-
nificent ceiling mural of heaven opening up its glories,
and listened to an organ recital.

Out back of the colleges were vast meadows, especially
near Christ Church, Merton, and Magdalen colleges. I
was particularly smitten with Magdalen, which they pronounced "maudlin." Students actually wore caps and
gowns for routine events like exams, and I saw more than
one running down a brick lane, clearly late for a lecture,

robe flailing behind, his hand frantically holding down the mortarboard on his head.

I WANTED TO see Stonehenge, the mysterious Paleolithic worship site made from massive standing stones. The nearest hostel to that monument, which sits by itself on a broad plain, was in Salisbury. And so we set off, my thumb and I.

My last ride that day was with a man who seemed concerned that I didn't know the different classifications of English settlements. Here was a man who had plenty of knowledge but, from his colorful grammar and syntax, not much education. Still, he appeared to be successful in whatever line of work he was in. He dressed conservatively in a button-down long-sleeved shirt, khakis, and what looked to be expensive driving shoes, and drove a late-model Land Rover. You didn't get one of those by being a bum.

"Ya see, first and foremost, you have your cathedral cities," he said, "cities that have a cathedral. That's what makes 'em cities, ya see, not how many people they got.

"Then there's your towns, like," he continued. "They can be bigger than cities, but if they ain't got a cathedral, they can't be cities. It's disturbin' to many of 'em. So, your towns can be either just regular towns or market towns, where the people used to come to buy everything from a tin of biscuits to a team of horses. They must have a church and shops and like.

"Then come the villages," he explained. "The villages, they must have at least a church and a pub and maybe twenty or thirty houses, like. Some of 'em is what they call green villages, ya see. They have a village green, like, at the center of the village, which is common land for the entire village."

He wasn't going to stop.

"You also have your estate villages and planned villages and various other kinds of villages," he went on. "And finally, at the bottom end of it all, bringin' up the rear, as ya might say, is the hamlets. All a hamlet needs is a few houses, but no church nor a pub. Wouldn't catch me livin' in a hamlet! Nary a pub, can you imagine? Now Salisbury, ya see, where you're goin', now that's a fine cathedral city, is what that is."

I STASHED MY backpack at the local hostel, which was set on a grassy, tree-filled estate near the center of town (oops, city), and headed for Salisbury's main business district to get a feel for the place. The past could readily be recognized in the abundant Elizabethan-era houses and the huge cathedral, which boasted the highest church spire in all England, visible for miles outside the city limits. The interior, unfortunately, suffered from having plain, clear glass in its windows, the original stained glass having been smashed to bits by the anti-papist Cromwellians during the English Civil Wars. Considering the lack of stained glass and statuary and the general emptiness of the place, I almost asked for a refund of my fifteen pence entry fee. Besides, I wondered, when did churches start charging admission?!

I found it more enjoyable to lie on the grass on one side of the cathedral and stare up at the apex of the spire, watching the clouds glide swiftly past.

Later that evening, back at the hostel, a crowd of people were lounging on the lawn near a large storage shed that, for some reason, everyone called the Chalet. Someone was pouring wine. Somebody else handed me a joint, which I toked on and passed to someone else. The night was starry and warm and the grass next to the Chalet was soft and cool. The world was well represented among our little group: an Aussie couple, a drop-dead gorgeous

Dutch girl, a bearded Canadian with hair down to the middle of his back, a studious-looking young woman from New York, two New Zealanders, and Bert, the lone Englishman in our intimate crowd.

"And that's the problem with America," Bert said, following up on someone's disdainful comment.

I encountered such cognitive dissonance among so many of the people I met. They loved Americans. They would give anything to visit that country. They enjoyed American music, basketball, TV shows, and Frito-Lay Cheetos Sweet Chili Flamin' Hot Crunchos. And yet "the problem with America" was a popular topic among international young people, and especially common at youth hostels.

Such remarks made me defensive. In high school, I'd marched in antiwar protests. I insisted on spelling *Amerikkka* with three *k*'s, and I fervently hated Tricky Dick Nixon. I had thrown rocks at cops at rallies gone bad. But that didn't mean that *you*, Signor Italiano, or *you*, Fräulein Deutschland, or *you*, Lord English Bulldog, had any right to malign my country, especially not to my face.

"The problem with America," Bert repeated when he got everyone's attention, "is that you've got no King or Queen, no one who is the product of centuries of in-breeding, fratricide, patricide, empire-building, and other such admirable British traits. Y'see, that's why we allow you lot," here he indicated the Australians and Kiwis, then nodded at the Canadian hippie, "and you as well, to remain part of the Empire. See, you have the British monarch as your sovereign leader, even while we let you pretend to have your own governments. Rule, Britannia!"

Bert was drunk and bitterly sarcastic. I liked Bert.

THE TWO NEW Zealanders, Pat and Martin, joined me for breakfast in the hostel dining room. We all agreed the previous evening's gathering had been electric. Everybody had played off everybody else, the conversation bouncing like a wayward pinball marble. The weather, the weed, the wine, and the plentiful laughter had come together as if by design.

Pat, Martin, and I decided to visit Stonehenge that Sunday morning, and that we would walk the twelve miles there and take a bus back. Along the way, we passed through Old Sarum, the ancient capital of the region, but all that was left were some stone foundations and grassy earthworks. The rest of the walk was less than scenic. Hedgerows and thick forests edged both sides of the narrow road we followed, giving us views only of the sky directly overhead. Every time a car rounded a bend, we lurched into the bushes to avoid being smashed to bits.

Sometimes it pays to shell out for a round-trip bus ride.

Stonehenge itself, the stone circle, was both mundane and mysterious, staid yet strange. A bunch of really big rocks had been laid out in a circle on an unadorned flat stretch of land. But the magnetism of the site was undeniable. The stones themselves were massive—twice or three times the height of a man, each of them weighing as much as a dozen elephants. And the lintels, the upper stones that stretched between two standing stones—how in the world did they get up there? The technology to accomplish that task, back in good ol' 2500 B.C., didn't exist. That's where the tin-foil-hat boys start spouting their "chariots of the gods" rigmarole. And I could even see their point: Was this the work of man? So, yes, the stones had much to impress and perplex a modern-day biped.

The vastness of the surrounding plains made everything, including Stonehenge itself, seem magical, a scene out of science fiction. Like Volubilis in Morocco, the peculiar ruins were made even more bizarre by the remoteness of the setting.

Few tourists were milling about the monument that early afternoon. A bus group was just leaving the site as we entered, and maybe six or seven other people were still walking among and even climbing on the stones. (It wouldn't be for another year that Stonehenge was roped off to prevent visitors from climbing on the rocks.) The Kiwis and I were gobsmacked, as the Brits say, to be standing on this sacred spot more than four millennia old. I was not immune to its enchantment.

I didn't know it at the time, but I would return. In just a matter of weeks, I would be living in a tepee, stoned on acid, helping to create a rock festival from the ground up, and hanging out with one of the weirdest communal groups in England.

All in the shadows of mystical Stonehenge.

19

Jack and Jackie

I am rewarded for dressing 'respeckable' - English-to-English translation - Everything you wanted to know about the 1975 Ford Cortina 2000E - How to make a fortune in the trucking business - Advice from a successful businessman

I had seen plenty of Ford Cortinas on the English roads. They were the best-selling cars in Britain in those days—family-size cars, American in style. But I was about to learn far more about them than I cared to when a husband and wife stopped for me on the road out of Salisbury.

"Geddon, me bewty," said the man at the wheel. "Ya figgered da raisin we puller over furry, din 'ee?"

The driver was in his early forties, dressed in a disturbingly bright blue suit jacket over a shirt the color of pure Irish butter. He had a boxer's face, with a flattened nose and hammered cheeks. He wore a wide white tie under a gold chain with a medallion. On his hands gripping the wheel of the Cortina were two rings on his right, one of which held a diamond, and two more on his left. A gold bracelet with heavy links hung from his left wrist. The cologne he wore didn't just waft toward you; it attacked you. I think I know how the trench soldiers felt in WWI at their first whiff of mustard gas.

He looked at me in his rear-view mirror, awaiting my response. When he got none, he said again, "Ya figgered da raisin we puller over furry, din 'ee?"

His wife, about his age and wanting to be helpful, turned from her perch on the passenger side and draped her right arm over the seatback. She was attractive, despite wearing too much eye shadow and rouge. Her blonde hair had been clipped short, in a boyish but not unflattering way. Her smile was radiant, an eye-poppingly bright-white gleam, every tooth perfectly aligned, sized, and enameled. She wore even more jewelry than her husband: dangling gold hoop earrings, a rope-chain gold necklace with a diamond pendant, a brooch with some sort of semi-precious stones, assorted rings on her fingers, and a half-dozen bracelets that chimed like a carillon whenever she moved.

"He said," she explained, "'You figured the reason we pulled the car over for you, didn't you?'"

Her smile was ready to burst.

I told her that, no, I didn't know why they'd stopped for me, but I was grateful.

"I always appreciate it when people stop for me," I said. "Some people are just nice. Thank you."

The driver kept looking at me in the rear-view mirror.

"Oim Jack, oim," he croaked. "En thissis Jackie, moi missus."

The wife continued to smile at me. She hadn't stopped looking at me even while the driver was talking, as if she were gauging my reaction to his words.

"I'm Jackie," she said, interpreting for the driver. "He's Jack, my husband."

"My name's Mark," I offered, and told them I was

traveling to the West Country, no specific destination. Possibly Tavistock.

"Iss cuz ye dress respeckable," said Jack, his eyes darting between the road and my reflection in his mirror. "Ass wha i' is. We stopped cuzzy dress roi' noice. Ass roi', ass roi'."

Jackie didn't even hesitate to put it into English for my benefit.

"He says you dress respectable," she said. "We don't like the way most young people dress these days, do we, Jack?"

"Bleddy tossers!"

"Don't be teasy, Jack," Jackie said lightly, pushing her husband by the shoulder in playful remonstrance.

I was wearing my beat-up blue sneakers, jeans that hadn't been washed in over a week, and a smelly T-shirt with a picture of Frank Zappa on the chest, all embellished by my now-fraying djellaba from the souks of Fez.

"Ya loik da Too Fowzenee, moi 'ansum?" he asked, impenetrably. "Scot upgri'ed trim, i' 'as, one 'n' six mo'er, reckangle 'eadlamps, body strips, vinyl roof. Classes whudda is, ass roi'."

Jackie, her smile undimmed even a bit, said, "He wants to know if you like our car."

"Oh, very much," I said. "It's comfortable. Roomy."

"Ease fur execka'iff," Jack added to whatever he had been saying.

"The 'E' stands for executive," said Jackie, helpfully, though I wasn't sure what the letter *e* had to do with anything Jack had been saying.

The conversation went on like this for what seemed like weeks but was no more than an agonizing thirty minutes. Amazing what you can learn about an automobile in half an hour, whether you want to or not. The 1975 Cortina 2000E had a 1.6-liter engine and all the fancy trim available. Jack had already placed his order for a new 1976 Cortina Mark IV, which wouldn't be released for several months. The reason he could afford all these new cars, the diamond rings, and startlingly blue suit jackets was because of his trucking business, built from the ground up from a single lorry, which he had driven and repaired himself.

"Could still do, foize evar knee-dead."

Jackie, radiant as always, said, "He still could drive the lorries, if he was ever needed."

Strangely, I was beginning to not need Jackie's translations.

Jack and Jackie were naturally kind people. Jack, after hearing my uncertainty about my future in college—my future in *life*—was full of advice.

"Oil tellya uthcadoo, ol' son," he said, telling me what to do. "You desoid whucha loves tadoo, and then'ee maker plans to do it. Me, Oi allus loved me lorries, drivin' 'em, messin' about wiv da mo'ers. Wuz me passion, ya migh' call it. Right, luv?"

This last bit was aimed at Jackie, and his manner of speaking was sweet, touching even, full of nostalgia. In my mind I could picture a young Jack and Jackie—he coming home from a long run in his lone (but well-tuned) truck, she making him a hot dinner in their tiny flat, his arm about her shoulders while he drank a beer and she watched the telly, just happy to be together, mouths full of crooked yellow teeth and nary a gold bracelet to be found. For a moment I was overcome with an inexplicable fondness for these two people whom I hadn't even met an hour earlier.

"Jack loves his lorries," she said, grinning from ear to ear.

Jack looked adoringly at his wife and placed his right hand on her chin for just a second.

"Some maid, ain' her?" he said to me.

When their path finally diverged to the north, Jack pulled the 1.6-liter Cortina 2000E with vinyl roof and upgraded trim package to the side of the road, and I climbed out. Jackie rolled her window down and Jack reached across her, toward me. At first, I thought he wanted to shake hands. But then I noticed the currency he held. He saw my hesitation.

"'Ark at 'ee, Jackie. Him's loik I was as a lad, 'ee is," Jack said to his wife. "Won't take nothin' fur nothin'. Own bootstraps is what i' is, ass roi'." Then, to me, he said, "You're a loikly lad, is what you are. Wass marr widdy? Go ahead, take i'. Remember, you desoid what ta do, then'ee make i' 'appen. Ain' more to i' 'an tha'. Good luck, moi lover."

I gave a weak wave as they drove off, then I looked at the bill Jack had handed me. A twenty-pound bank note. I relished every detail of it—the glorious purple ink, the handsome visage of her Royal Majesty, Elizabeth, Queen of the Realm, and a mounted St. George spearing the shit out of a creepy dragon. Twenty pounds! Since arriving in England a week earlier, I'd been living on an average daily expenditure of less than three pounds (five dollars) for lodging and meals. Jack's unbelievable generosity would keep me in bunks and baked beans for a week.

Equally important, once I'd had a chance to calm down and think about it, was his advice. I'm afraid I've made Jack out to be a comical figure. And indeed, he was an almost music-hall version of a nouveau-riche, with the flashy clothes, the jewelry, the fancy new car, the wife with the shiny custom-made teeth, all failing to mask the man's humble background. But Christ, I thought, Jack had bought a single truck when he was young and had transformed it into a fortune twenty-odd years later, employed dozens of people, and gave out twenty-quid notes to wayward American boys who hadn't a clue what they wanted to do in life.

"Desoid what ta do," he had said.

Then make it happen.

20

Sign of the

Wounded Soldier

Footpath (oh, no!) to Moretonhampstead - Beware the dangers of the moors - Wild ponies - The sedate elegance of a Daimler - A down-at-heels public house - So this is what happens when the Big Boys go after you

A t the eight-hundred-year-old Three Crowns Inn in Chagford, where I stopped for a lager after Jack and Jackie dropped me off, I told the young man behind the bar that I planned to hike on Dartmoor the next day. His reaction was to give me a look that I might have expected from a Carpathian shepherd on hearing I was en route to Dracula's Castle.

"Cor, that's no place for a walk unless you're prepared," he said in a voice like Long John Silver's, setting the pint glass in front of me. I half-expected him to make the sign of the cross and hang more garlic over the doorways. "You've got your ordnance survey, I suppose. You've told your friends your route and what time you expect to arrive, I suppose. You've got Wellies and a mac, I suppose."

I don't suppose I knew what an ordnance survey was. I definitely didn't know what Wellies were. As for macs, I knew only that bankers didn't wear them in the pouring rain. I had no friends to whom I could tell my route and arrival time. I wasn't even sure of that myself.

"Oh yeah," I replied. "That's all sorted."

As he wiped the counter, he surreptitiously looked at my pitiful yellow backpack, stitched together as crudely as Frankenstein's Monster, and pursed his lips.

"People get lost out there all the time," he warned. "They get off on the wrong footpath and then you're readin' about them in the *Western Morning News.*"

I wasn't overly concerned. I had camped out frequently with friends as a teenager, although less to hike than to smoke pot and drink wine far from the prying eyes of adults. How hard could it be to follow a footpath, said the adventurer who had so recently been scraped, bloodied, and bowed by the man-eating Footpath to Goudhurst?

The next day broke clear and warm, a promising omen to begin a country ramble. In the hamlet of Great Weeke I connected to a footpath that took me through a pasture where I had to skirt cow patties at every step. Farther on were rugged hills with thick forests, meadows edged with tall thorny hedges, and more cattle pastures. At one point I found myself on a rise with a view in all directions. The hillock held patches of scrubby grass and a few granite boulders, but was otherwise bare. A cooling breeze had kicked in, a relief against the growing heat of the day.

And then I saw them.

Three wild ponies cantered up the far side of the hill I was on. Apparently, they didn't see me, because they began pawing at the ground and nibbling on the grass without concern. They were so natural, so unencumbered, so

. . .*free* that it took my breath away. I stopped breathing, both from astonishment and not wanting to scare them off. Their hide was a glistening auburn, their long manes dark brown. Their luxuriant tails swept nearly to the moorland floor. They were compact and sturdy, and looked hardy enough to withstand anything nature could throw at them. When one of them noticed me, the trio calmly turned away and walked down the hillside from where they had come, unperturbed.

By the time I reached Moretonhampstead some six miles on, without having been waylaid by highwaymen, phlebotomized by vampires, or mauled to death by an immense Baskerville hound, I felt that the publican at the Three Crowns would do better to save his footpath warnings for travelers to Goudhurst. My walk on the moors had been, apart from the exquisite scenery, uneventful. Only later did I learn of the sudden thick mists that descended on Dartmoor unexpectedly, leaving hikers disoriented and lost. I didn't know how quickly the rivers could rise, trapping a hiker or worse. I was unaware of the massive blanket bogs and valley mires that could drag down a full-grown man and drown him in seconds in a foul-smelling slough.

But that's how it is so often: The ill-prepared buffoon skates unawares past life's perils while the gent with the knee-high rubber boots, hiking stick, and ordnance survey map gets eaten alive by a Dartmoor feather bog.

In Moretonhampstead, on the eastern edge of Dartmoor, a Daimler stopped for me.

"Never been in a Daimler," I told the driver, a man in his mid-fifties with a full head of gray hair and the comfortable, self-satisfied look of an early retiree. "Very posh."

I was starting to talk like an Englishman. I sounded like a nincompoop.

"Excellent cars," said the man, whose name was Brian and who was indeed a youthful pensioner. "I bought this one new in 1962, last year they made 'em."

The 1962 Daimler Majestic Major was a beautiful automobile, made under the ownership of Jaguar Cars in Coventry, with long, swooping front fenders, a massive chrome grille resembling a shield, a large stylized wing for a hood ornament, and a 4.5-liter V8 engine that could reach 120 mph without breaking a sweat. The front and back seats were upholstered in a thick rich red leather that had gained an oh-so-English patina of handsome cracks over the previous fourteen years. The burled-wood dash with its funny round dials gleamed as if it had just been polished. And it probably had. Brian loved that car, as was obvious in how he drove it—carefully, carefully—and spoke about it.

At a place called Heathfield, we turned southwest, toward Plymouth. But instead of getting on the new Devon Expressway, Brian followed a two-lane country road that paralleled it.

"You don't mind, do you?" he said, noticing me looking at the road we were on and the one we hadn't taken. "I prefer the local roads mostly. Don't like to push the old girl too hard."

He smiled and patted the dash.

I didn't mind one way or the other. That was the beauty of hitchhiking and camping and staying in hostels: You didn't usually care all that much where you ended up on any given day, so long as you were moving more or less in the direction you wanted to go.

Brian was filling his retirement years with the purchase and management of a kennel, where he boarded dogs and bred English springer spaniels.

"Excellent shooting dogs," he assured me, to allay any unspoken doubts I might have had. "Very popular here."

The road carried on with no special interest, but when Brian spied an inn up on our left, at a wide spot in the road called Wrangaton, he slowed the Daimler.

"Fancy a pint, do you?" he asked, and I said yes.

The Wounded Soldier was a pub and hotel in what looked to be its declining years. Badly in need of paint outside, devoid of typical pubby charm within, the bar was just a place to get a drink. I wasn't surprised to find it empty. This was not the sort of charming pub to sell T-shirts saying, "I got a shot at the Wounded Soldier."

Brian called to the landlady behind the bar and ordered two pints of bitter, a generally low-alcohol English style of pale ale. The beer tasted especially good on that hot early afternoon.

The Wounded Soldier sat just at the southern edge of Dartmoor and had once been a busy passenger hotel when the Great Western Railway had a station nearby. But since the branch line that passed through the area had converted to freight only, the village had gone into an economic slump and the hotel had closed, leaving only the pub in business.

The woman behind the bar who told us all this reminded me of Marjorie Main, the stringy actress from the Golden Age of Hollywood who was best remembered for playing Ma in the Ma and Pa Kettle series of comedies with actor Percy Kilbride. She was in her sixties, sinewy, a tough old bird who looked like she wouldn't take guff from anyone. She wore a flower behind one ear and had on men's slacks and a button-down shirt.

"Plymouth?" she asked us, and we nodded. "I can tell. I've been here more than forty years. I can always tell."

Considering we were just off the main highway to Plymouth, I guessed she was right at least half the time.

"What do you call this village?" asked Brian, to be polite.

"Most people call it Wrangaton," she answered. "I call it *Wrong*-aton."

She was bitter about something.

"You probably drove in on that dual carriageway, I expect," she said, referring to the new Devon Expressway.

When Brian told her we'd driven on the local roads, she instantly felt a kinship with us. She saw we had nearly finished our beers, pumped two more from the tap, and huddled close to us.

"Then you know what they did," she said, as if sharing a secret handshake with us. "That bloody highway was put there for one reason and one reason only: to put us little folks out of business."

Brian nodded unconvincingly.

"Price of progress, I guess," he said.

Wrong answer, Brian.

"Progress?!" The woman was stunned. "Do you call it progress when a shopkeeper has to shutter his business because the big boys put in a fancy supermarket down the High Street? You find me a butcher anywhere about. You find me a baker. You find me a greengrocer. You can't. They've all gone! And now they're going after the pubs, they are. Walk into a supermarket with a tenner, if you can even stand all the bright lights inside, and walk out with a crate of bitter, and fare-the-well to the local public house. You know how much I made last week? Forty pounds!"

She was in a fury.

"Hard to make a living on forty quid a week," said Brian in sympathy.

"You tell me how someone can walk from the village to this pub with that dual carriageway standing in between them," she said. "Go ahead and tell me!"

I wanted to defuse the atmosphere, so I asked the lady how the pub got its name.

"Well, I named it after my Wallace, didn't I? He got it in both legs in the war. And you can't tell me he didn't. Walked with a limp and a cane the rest of his life, bless him."

By the time she'd finished telling us about Wallace's heroics on the beaches of Normandy, she had filled our pint glasses a third time.

"That's how the big boys do it," she said in a stage whisper, as if imparting some hidden knowledge that she wanted no one else to hear.

She held up her open right hand, stared hard at it, and slowly closed her fingers into a fist.

"They squeeze you."

21

Poor Mungo

Cornish identity - Pirate talk - Land's End - Searching for Dutchmen - The British diet circa 1976 - A fellow Californian - Cornwall with the top down - Mungo comes to a sad end

I n my travels over the past forty-plus years, I've been to many places that felt like the teacher had to go to an emergency faculty meeting and left the students in charge of themselves. Key West had that atmosphere. Perth and Fremantle on Australia's isolated west coast were two more. Cornwall, too, was such a place.

The county was considered to be one of the six historic Celtic Nations, along with Brittany, Wales, Scotland, the Isle of Man, and Ireland, and long resisted a cordial relationship with Her Majesty's government. It eventually became a member of the Celtic League to promote its Celtic identity. Many years after my visit to Cornwall, the European Union would recognize the Cornish as a minority ethnic group, distinct from the neighboring English. So remote was the region that a nationalist movement sprang up in the 1970s. A group calling itself the Cornish National Liberation Army was deemed potentially violent by law enforcement, but in the end, limited its actions to the equivalent of writing withering letters to *The Times.*

And then, of course, there was the accent. More specifically, a Cortina Jack accent, as I soon realized.

One of the more popular songs in England that summer was "The Combine Harvester," from a trio called The Wurzels. The song boldly knocked off a 1971 American hit, "Brand New Key (The Roller Skate Song)" by the singer Melanie. The lyrics were inane: "Oh, I've got a brand-new combine harvester / An' I'll give you the key." The only thing that made the song noteworthy was the singer's strong West Country accent, or what Americans call a "pirate" accent.

That way of speaking—and that song, immediately after its release in June 1976—could be heard everywhere in Cornwall. The farther west you traveled, the more you heard it (the retroflex rhotics *and* the song). Especially in the days when I was there, before time began to round off the edges from England's regional accents and grammatical peculiarities, a Cornishman's words were often unintelligible to an outsider like me. The Cornish routinely dropped their *h*'s, hardened their *r*'s, and left off the letter *t* at the ends of words.

None of the regional mannerisms of Cornish speech should come as a surprise, considering that English didn't fully penetrate the peninsula's population until the mid-1700s. Few Cornish people today still speak the old Brythonic language, which has more in common with Welsh than with Irish or Scots Gaelic. By the mid-1800s, the native lingo was, by any practical definition, dead. But a cultural revival at the turn of the nineteenth century kept it from becoming extinct.

By the time I arrived, many schools were teaching the old mother tongue again and, if not putting it back into daily use, at least renewing interest in preserving it.

Even when they were speaking actual English, though, the Cornish sometimes used expressions and pronunciations heard nowhere else in Britain.

'Ark at 'ee. Listen to him.

'Ee's gone up north. He's traveled outside Cornwall.

Wass marr widdy? What's the matter with you? Are you all right?

Dreckly. Directly, soon.

The first driver who picked me up in Cornwall opened the passenger door from inside and asked, "Whar be to?"

I was making my way from Tavistock, on the border of Devon and Cornwall, where I'd stayed in a hostel converted from a manor house that had been used for meetings between Eisenhower and Montgomery in the weeks leading up to D-Day. An out-of-tune piano dominated the parlor, and no one seemed to mind me playing old Beatles songs badly that evening.

On this day, I was traveling to the so-called Land's End Hostel. The hostel was actually in St. Just, on a hill overlooking the sea, about six miles north of the literal Land's End historical marker, which pointed in one direction to John o' Groats at the northern tip of the Scottish mainland and, in the other direction, to New York, 3,147 miles to the west across the sea.

By the time I reached the hostel I was hungry for dinner, so I heated some baked beans and opened a loaf of sliced white bread. My plan was to toast the bread and pour the beans on top, a popular dish in England in those days. Strangely, I was acquiring a taste for the death-by-carbs repast (not least because the price fit my meal budget). The pairing's innate lack of taste gave one the leeway, the motivation even, to flavor it with anything handy—salt and pepper, catsup, pickle slices, or dubious tuna salad discovered accidentally in the hard-to-reach back shadows of the communal hostel fridge.

England was not the culinary mecca in 1976 that it became in later decades. The English diet seemed to consist of little more than tinned biscuits, Heinz baked beans, over-cooked bacon, heated cheese sandwiches called toasties, dippy eggs and soldiers (soft-boiled, with toast cut into long strips for dipping), black pudding (the less-egregious name for fried blood sausage), fish and chips, shepherd's pie, and "jacket" potatoes (baked and stuffed, sometimes with beans and cheddar cheese). About the most exotic foods the Brits ate were chicken tikka masala from an Indian takeaway or spaghetti and meatballs at the local Italian red-sauce spot, complete with checkered tablecloth and burning candles jammed into straw-covered Chianti bottles.

Not judging. My own dietary history being composed largely in the names of Swanson, Chef Boyardee, Hamburger Helper, and Dinty Moore, I could be excused for thinking of baked beans on toast as a delicacy.

A man and woman in their mid-twenties came into the kitchen and seemed surprised to find me there, stirring beans on the stove. Robin and Dolores were a young English couple who had a private room at the Land's End hostel.

"Mind if we share the cooktop?" Robin asked cheerily as he set a bag of groceries on a nearby counter.

He and his partner were graduate students in aeronautical engineering ("We'll get a Brit on the moon one of these days," Robin said with a laugh), and they were the best of the British—cheerful and optimistic, ready to chat at a moment's notice, friendly to strangers, and with fiercely poor dentistry. Both Robin and Dolores could have frightened a small child with their smiles, which they used often.

"Is that all you're having, luv?" Dolores asked, staring into my pan of beans while she pulled out tomatoes, carrots, radishes, onions, lettuce, cheese, and a piece of steak from the paper sack Robin had set down.

"No," I said, defensively. "I've got toast, too."

Dolores, who had shoulder-length jet-black hair and couldn't have been taller than five-two, looked at the six-foot-tall Robin on the other side of me, raised her eyebrows slightly, and said to me, "C'mon then, have a decent meal for once. Here," she handed me a head of lettuce, "scrub this."

While the meat was sizzling, Dolores washed the other vegetables and cut them up for a salad. When the steak was done cooking a few minutes later, she cut that up as well and mixed it in with the vegetables. I had never in my life had meat in a salad, or even carrots or radishes for that matter. I thought of a salad only as flaps of chilled iceberg lettuce with chunks of under-ripe tomato covered in half a pint of Thousand Island dressing.

As we ate—and the meal was the healthiest, most delicious I'd eaten in weeks—two guys from Holland came into the kitchen and joined us. They had been at the hostel since the previous night and simply reheated their leftover meal from the day before. Timo and Gerrit stood out in a crowd—literally, as they were each close to six feet six inches and blond to a degree just shy of platinum. They could have been brothers, though they weren't.

They ate quickly, then Gerrit (or was it Timo; I never got them straight) said, "Hey, let's meet at the pub after you've finished your meal!"

Robin, Dolores, and I said sure, then watched them leave the kitchen, ducking slightly as they passed through the doorway.

St. Just was a small town, with fewer than five thousand residents, but large enough to have four public houses in its compact historic core. The King's Arms, from the fourteenth century, had a stone façade and a slate roof.

Inside was a fire blazing in the hearth, several dogs sleeping on the floor, a restaurant, and a convivial bar crowd on an otherwise quiet Wednesday evening. Robin and I each ordered a pint of the local bitter from St. Austell Brewery, and Dolores ordered a half. No Dutchmen.

The granite-face Wellington Hotel on Market Square had a bar popular mainly with tourists, it seemed. We had more pints of bitter, but no Dutchmen arrived.

Just off the square sat the Star Inn, a proper pub, as the Cornish might say, with no pretense of being anything other than a place to drink and socialize with one's mates. A rival to the King's Arms in age, it boasted a beamed ceiling, floors of both slate and bitumen-coated wood, and, draped across a wall, a large black flag with a white cross, St. Piran's Cross, the flag of Cornwall.

In the middle of our third round of pints that evening, Timo and Gerrit entered the pub and came straight for us, smiling. With them was a bearded American about my age who hailed from Orange, California, in the conservative heart of Orange County, just fourteen miles from La Mirada.

His unlikely name was Mungo, and he was a sweetheart, shy but friendly, quiet but talkative. And, as I would soon learn, he was a misfortunate son of Job over whom a black cloud rained continuously. On that night, though, as the six of us repaired to one of the pub's snugs for better conversation, I just wanted to talk about home.

"So, what's your beach?" I asked Mungo, since every Southern Californian had a favorite, whether because of its proximity or the quality of its surf.

"CDM," he said, meaning Corona del Mar, the small waterfront community just south of Newport Beach.

"Then you know the Wedge," I said.

"Broke my arm there."

"I go to Huntington," I said.

"Which side?" The state-run beach was to the south of the HB pier, the city-run side was to the north.

"State," I answered. "Lifeguard station number three."

"Shoot the pier, bra,'" he said, laughing and giving me the surfer greeting, a back-facing fist with outstretched thumb and baby finger.

THE NEXT DAY, Mungo, Timo, Gerrit, and I hiked along the rugged coastline, following the Southwest Coast Path, intending to go the six miles to Land's End. The Dutch-men carried full backpacks, having checked out of the hostel and planning to hike to Pendennis Castle, built by Henry VIII, some thirty-five miles away. The hardy Hol-landers figured they could get there in two days.

If you ever need a tall, happy, smart, and energetic hu-man being, grab the nearest Dutchman.

The coast along this stretch of Cornwall was dramatic, with high cliffs hundreds of feet above the crashing surf that sloped down to low draws from where you could walk right onto the shingled shoreline. Scores of seagulls seemed to follow us on our path past coves and inlets, up cliffsides, and down onto long straight stone-strewn beaches. Now and then we heard seals barking on the rocks below us, but we never managed to see them.

About four miles down the trail I saw something I never thought I'd see in England. I grabbed Mungo by the upper arm and pointed to the beach below us.

"Surf's up, dude!"

A half-dozen surfers were sitting astride their boards about forty yards from shore. The waves were small but, from where we stood, looked well-shaped.

Two out of the six surfers caught a four-footer, but did little more than maintain their balance all the way to shore. They didn't even kick out, but simply stepped off their boards when they skidded against the sandy bottom.

But still—surfers! In England!

I'd noticed that Mungo limped slightly; he had stopped several times along the way to rub his right hip, as if he were in some discomfort. But then he would charge up a ten-degree slope on the trail faster than I could, so I didn't give it any more thought at the time.

Land's End itself was disappointing. The car park was filled with trailers, buses, RVs, and estate cars (as the English called station wagons), and the isolated piece of coast, the westernmost point in all England, was filled with gawking tourists. A small shopping center selling tourist trinkets seemed to be the main attraction, along with a restaurant serving international tourist food like hamburgers, sausages, chips, and pie.

At least the complex had a pub, which appeared to be even more popular than the viewpoint at the famous Land's End signpost. Sitting alone at a table, as if placed there by Central Casting, was a squint-eyed old salt who looked like a sailing master circa 1850. His gray whiskers hadn't been cut in three or four days, and he was smoking a corncob pipe. He wore a captain's cap on his grizzled head and a navy pea coat draped across his shoulders, cape-style. Everyone else inside looked like weekenders from Frimley or West Wickham.

Outside the pub, we said goodbye to Timo and Gerrit, who marched off like soldiers to war. As Mungo and I walked away in the opposite direction, I noticed my companion's limp had grown more pronounced.

"How's your leg doing, Mungo?" I asked, nodding at the limb in question. "You're sorta dragging your heels a bit. You want to see if there's a bus back to St. Just? Or try hitching a ride?"

But he was game for hiking the six miles back to the hostel, so we set out. Since the subject of his limp had been broached, I guess he felt compelled to talk about it.

"I was in a car accident a couple of years ago and broke my hip and femur," he said. "Unfortunately, it didn't mend the right way and I had to have a couple more surgeries. Finally, they just decided to weld it back permanently. Basically, my femur is attached to my pelvis with a rod and metal plates."

I immediately felt queasy and my scrotum shrunk in horror.

"Open reduction and internal fixation, if you want to look it up sometime," he went on.

"Internal fixation," I repeated. "Isn't that something treated by a shrink, not an orthopedic surgeon?"

Mungo smiled politely, but I don't think he found it funny. I was about to tell him that I once had to see an orthopedic surgeon for water on the knee, but then thought better of it.

DESPITE ANY LIMITATIONS from his surgery, Mungo could still drive a stick, as I found out the next morning.

Immediately on his arrival in England in January, he had purchased an old Sunbeam, perhaps the coolest car I have ever ridden in. A basic description hardly does justice to that erotically alluring sapphire-blue 1954 Sunbeam Talbot MK IIA, a two-seater convertible with tan leather bucket seats. The beauty had the lines of a sporty roadster but the heft of a saloon, the English term for a sedan.

"You can hardly tell she was in an accident," Mungo said as we set out on an excursion to see some of Cornwall's highlights.

The top was down and the wind was up, blowing our hair as we followed the coast road north and east.

"I misjudged the traffic getting onto one of those roundabouts," he explained. "I probably should have bought an automatic, because shifting with your left hand

and driving on the left side of the road is hard to do."

I realized only then that the Sunbeam had no seat belts.

Fortunately, Mungo himself wasn't damaged in the accident. The car, not as fortunate, was put out of commission for a week, seven days during which Mungo was forced to kill time in Swindon, which, he assured me, was not easy to do.

Later he had driven north to Scotland to meet distant relatives.

"That's how I got my name," he said. "After Mungo Park."

I had no reaction.

"Mungo Park. The Scottish explorer."

"Oh, right," I said.

St. Ives, on the north coast of the peninsula, was an art colony filled with small independent galleries. The seaside village had been a popular resort for a hundred years, ever since a branch line of the Great Western Railway had arrived. The attractive, bustling village had been a holiday stop for so long that it had settled comfortably into the role, and didn't have the tacky boomtown flavor of some tourist meccas.

In St. Ives, Mungo told me he wasn't taking pictures of the photo-worthy streets and buildings because his camera had been stolen the day we met, just before he arrived at the hostel.

On the southern shore, just eight miles across the narrow Cornish peninsula, we parked the Sunbeam in the town of Marazion, then walked across a Belgian-block causeway to an offshore island that greatly resembled Mont Saint-Michel in France. This was St. Michael's Mount, topped by a 350-year-old castle and, like its French counterpart, could only be approached on foot during low tide. The first thing you saw when you walked across the mudflats to the island was a chalkboard sign informing visitors of that day's tidal schedule so they wouldn't get stranded.

Saint Michael's Mount, unlike its Gallic cousin, and despite a handsome medieval building crowning its apex, was not a village. Besides the fortress, it had only a café, a more formal restaurant, and a trinket shop.

On Saint Michael's Mount, Mungo told me he had been sick with a lung infection soon after arriving in England, six months earlier, and had to confine himself to his hotel room for nearly three weeks while the penicillin worked its wonders.

We followed a series of narrow roads around the bay, and stopped briefly in Penzance, famed in song thanks to the Gilbert & Sullivan comic opera, *The Pirates of Penzance*. The town was a lively commercial center, but held no appeal for us.

In Penzance, Mungo told me that he had brought too much stuff to England. He had a full-size backpack filled with clothing, a full-size suitcase filled with clothing, and a blue pinstripe suit in a garment bag.

Eventually, we came to the cutest little village anyone ever saw. Mousehole was its name, but the locals pronounced it *mau-zul*. The small, tidy commercial center was set so close to the shoreline that I wouldn't have been surprised if waves lapped at the shopfront doorways at high tide. The tiny houses and stores were mainly built of rough-hewn granite and brightly painted rubble. Cafés and boutiques and galleries crowded into the commercial buildings, and flowers filled the postage-stamp gardens of the residences on the adjoining lanes. I wanted to put the entire little village in my pocket and take it home with me.

In Mousehole Mungo told me that he had changed his entire bankroll into pounds sterling before landing at Heathrow. At that time, the previous December, he had paid U.S. $2.25 for a British pound. And then the decline kicked in. The pound sterling lost value against the dollar every month until, in June, you could buy a pound note for $1.70 American. He had lost more than fifty cents for every pound note he carried in his money belt. He estimated that he'd lost a thousand dollars by exchanging his money before his departure. I suspected he'd lost more than that.

Mungo was broke.

"I'm going back home next week," he said. "I already changed my ticket. I was originally going to stay through September. But I can't afford it."

He had made arrangements with a car dealer in London to take the Sunbeam on consignment and send Mungo the proceeds, minus commission, when the man eventually sold it.

Everything had gone wrong for Mungo. His poor investment in English pounds. His lung infection. His traffic mishap with the Sunbeam. His accident in which he broke his hip. His stolen camera. The way he had overpacked for the trip. God, even his fucking name.

Nothing worked out for Mungo.

Heel that I was, my first thought was not one of pity. Instead, I was disappointed because I had planned to ask Mungo if I could pal around with him in his cool car for the next month or so. Obviously, that was off the table.

Poor Mungo, I thought. *Some people shouldn't travel.*

22

A Devon Sort of Melancholy

An Irish hippie-comedian - Racism in England - Devon's best water - The steepest village in all the West Country - My lack of long-term plans - The death of a child

A truck squealed its brakes and a voice called out the window, "C'mon, I'll run ya over!"

Coming from a lorry driver, such words were enough to give a hitchhiker pause. But I inferred from his tone that he was offering me a lift, not threatening to kill me. I hoisted myself up to the high passenger door of the cab and clambered in. The driver had just dropped off a load in St. Just when he saw me with my thumb out.

He wasn't your typical trucker, or at least not in the mold of the Wally Thor Truckmaster School of Trucking, then famous in California for its local TV commercials. Truck drivers, in my experience, were fifty years old, with crewcuts and fat guts. Ciaran, on the other hand, from Waterford, Ireland, was no more than thirty and had long wavy hair well past his shoulders, a walrus mustache, and a dashiki. The only thing remotely trucker-like about him was the American country-western coming from his tape deck.

"We love country music," he said about his homeland. "Most of yer country music comes from Irish and Scottish choons, y'know."

When we'd first introduced ourselves, I thought he said his name was Karen, which made me wonder about his somewhat feminine appearance.

"Karen?" I repeated.

"Don't be an eejit, darlin'" he said good-naturedly. "It's Ciaran, not Karen." He spoke the feminine name in a nasally, exaggerated American accent. "Ciaran is Irish for the manliest of manly men. It's not a girl's name, mucker."

Ciaran's goal in life was not to drive long-distance lorries but to be a stand-up comedian. He regaled me with his impersonation of an Irish driving instructor. I couldn't understand all his words or cultural references, though, so the jokes went over my head, but his smile and delivery were so infectious I couldn't help but laugh.

Because Ciaran would be keeping to the major roads, and my destination was well off into the countryside, he wouldn't be able to take me far. But you expect that to happen when you're traveling by thumb.

We drove in silence for a few minutes, then Ciaran blurted out a frightening ambition he had.

"I'm planning to set the record for driving the longest period of time without stopping for sleep," he said in his musical brogue. "I'll just keep going until I'm ready to doze off."

"At the wheel?" I gasped, horrified.

He turned to me and smiled.

"Not a bit of it, darlin'," he said. "I'll stop just before I need a kip."

"And when are you going to do this?"

"Starting about twenty-six hours ago," he said. "And I'm near knackered as 'tis."

I wasn't sure if that was his sly Celtic humor or if he was deadly serious, but I wasn't unhappy when his route went one way, mine the other, and I began looking for a different ride. One came quickly enough.

From a racist.

"You've got problems with your Blacks in America," he stated after learning my nationality. "See, it's too late for you lot. But it's not too late for England. Do you see the Blackies in Scotland? Nope, nor in Wales. They won't 'ave 'em."

I was extremely uncomfortable. He hadn't said anything too revolting so far, apart from the disagreeable term "Blackies." His tone bothered me, though, as did the direction in which he was steering the conversation. I held no hope that we'd shortly begin discussing horticulture or the series finale of *Upstairs, Downstairs.*

"It's the same with them Pakis," he said. "'Ow come we're gettin' 'em but not Wales or Scotland?"

I had never heard the term "Paki," but I assumed he was referring to immigrants from Pakistan.

"Maybe England has more opportunities for immigrants to find work," I suggested, not realizing I had just shortened the fuse on the time bomb driving the car.

"Work?!" he almost shouted. "I'll say it's work. It's a lot of work standing in line to collect your pay packet for bein' a lazy bastard. You know what they get? A single man on the dole gets fourteen pounds a week. Fourteen pounds! He lets a bedsit for five quid a week and the rest he spends on lamb curry. Then he writes to his family back home, stuffs a tenner in the envelope to prove what a toff he is now, and tells 'em about the land o' milk 'n' 'oney where they're so 'appy to 'ave 'im that they give 'im a nice packet o' the ready every Monday morning."

I learned later that a decent unskilled job in England paid about forty pounds a week, nearly three times a single man's unemployment payment. Fourteen pounds a week on the dole sounded like starvation wages, not a disincentive to look for full-time work.

Throughout England, I was to hear similar racist views, though most such comments were couched in less direct terms. People used phrases like "the Black problem" and "the Pakistani situation." Or they'd say, "We need to limit immigration because the current welfare system is unsustainable." I was in no position, as a foreigner myself, an outsider, to comment on England's economic and social woes, but the latent (and sometimes not so latent) racism was the single trait that I found most objectionable among many of the English I met.

THE HOSTEL IN Elmscott (which took eight hours of hitching to reach) was much farther in the boondocks of north Devon than I'd realized. The building had once been a schoolhouse, but with the exodus of so many rural people to the cities, nobody needed it for education anymore. The building was converted into a youth hostel in 1948. A spaced-out hippie couple who lived upstairs ran the place, probably high as shit, from what I could tell. When I asked them for a bunk, they smiled as if I'd just revealed the path to satori.

"The best thing about staying here is the water," the young woman said.

"The best in Devon," said the young man. "Miss Ironside, I believe it was, was a diviner, and she found the spot, only ninety-five feet down."

The nearby hamlet up the road consisted of three or four houses and some farm outbuildings—no shops, restaurants, or pubs. But that was all right. The remote quarters would be a good place to hunker down for the weekend, when most of England's offices and shops in the larger towns were closed anyway and hitchhiking was harder than during the week. I could read, write in my journal, maybe look around some of the area villages.

Saturday broke softly, with a heavy mist hanging over the coast. I walked along the little roads to Hartland, a proper town with pubs and restaurants and people on the streets. The houses were plain-fronted, stuccoed, and painted white or pale yellow, all so unlike the medieval rough-stone buildings of Cornwall.

From there I thumbed to Clovelly, five miles farther on, perhaps the most photographed village in the West Country. You could not find a more up-and-down settlement in all England than Clovelly. The main street dropped four hundred feet in elevation in just half a mile. You might look out your window to see the rooftop of a neighbor's house on one side and a basement window of a house on the other side. The stone-paved High Street was so steep that cars weren't allowed. You either walked or took one of the tourist donkeys lodged at the stables at the top of the village. A handful of quaint shops, snack bars, and historic houses, their window boxes bursting with fuchsias and geraniums, lined the main road and the few short stair-streets that branched off from the High Street. At the bottom of the road lay the sweetest little harbor on the planet. The entire complex looked as if it might spill into Bristol Channel at any minute.

I followed two donkeys pulling a sledge full of ale casks to the street-level bar of the seventeenth-century New Inn. Inside, I ordered a pint and considered what I would be doing in the next few weeks. Based on recommendations in my guidebooks, I had a rough plan to travel through Somerset, specifically Cheddar and Bath. My money was holding up as well as expected; I was on a budget of £2.50 a day, or about U.S. $4.50. The budget wasn't princely, but apparently more than a man on the dole earned, though not by much. Two pounds fifty was enough to pay for my nightly bunk, buy food to prepare for breakfast and supper in the hostels' communal kitchens, and have a few pints with a toastie or meat pie for lunch at a pub. Those were all the basics I needed. And if I saved a bit on one day, I could splurge the next.

Occasionally I had to shell out for laundry. And I probably should have done so more often. My clothes were filthy, but they still passed the smell test, so I felt no urgency on that score.

On the road back to Elmscott, a quiet young man, no more than thirty, picked me up and confided that he had just lost his five-year-old daughter to disease.

"It was meningitis," he said in a hollow voice. "She was happy. A happy little girl. Just so…so normal."

The mist I'd walked through that morning had returned, heavier now, leaving drops of moisture on the windscreen.

"You know, it takes you like that," he said of the disease, making a snapping motion without actually snapping his fingers. "She was playing with her friends one day, she was in hospital the next, and we buried her three days after that."

He turned to me with a forlorn look that broke my heart a thousand times.

"I haven't reconciled to it yet," he went on. "I don't suppose I will. Or that I even want to. I mean, how can you?"

He lived with his wife in a council house in Bude, he said, on the other side of the Devon-Cornwall border. Even though my hostel was slightly out of his way, he said he would drive me there.

"This weather, this late, not so good for walking," he said.

"What's a council house?" I asked, imagining some sort of a period mansion or an architectural style unique to England.

He looked at me curiously, as if I might be pulling his leg.

"You don't have council houses in America? Cor, you must! What it is, see, the town council provides low-income flats or a little house to people who are on the dole or don't earn big wages. So what you've got to do, see, is get a cash-in-hand job. Otherwise, the council says you're earning too much and you can't stay in council housing any longer."

When the underpaid bereaved young father dropped me off at the gate to the hostel, I was grateful I had no gun. I believe I might have shot myself from sheer depression over his story.

Sympathetic suicide, however, would have been a misuse of my time, because the next few days would prove to be some of the most memorable of the entire journey.

23

This Is Not a

Rehearsal

Strawberry fields for a day - Amsterdam advice - No hippies allowed - Steve - Life's too short to waste on substandard ale - Tandem hitchhiking - Falling in love with Mrs. Stone - We make plans for the hippie fest

A handwritten three-by-five index card next to the Cheddar bunkhouse door caught my attention.

Labourers Wanted! Pick strawberries. 75p p/hr. Hard work. Cash in hand. Apply to Warden.

The warden, as the head of the hostel was called, was a taciturn man of middle age who sized me up.

"'Ave ya ever picked strawberries a'fore?" he asked in a Somerset accent that was similar to that of Devon and Cornwall.

"Yes," I lied. "In California, where I'm from."

He looked at me dubiously.

"Wha' sor' o' strawberries d'ye grow in California?" he asked.

Different kinds of strawberries?! I knew only one—red, juicy, and sweet.

"We grow only one sort," I said, amazing myself. "The best ones on the planet. Have you ever had a ripe California strawberry?"

The warden smiled and relaxed.

"Oim just 'avin' a bit of fun wiv ye, lad," he said with a wink. "The farm is just a moil down the road, and ye'll be needed there at seven, no later. Work 'ard and ye'll be rewarded, as i' 'tis in loif."

In those days, a pint of beer at a pub cost between 25p and 40p, depending on the location and the specific beer, so I figured every hour I worked picking strawberries was worth about three pints down the pub, as the locals said. Hell, if I put in eight hours, my bar bills would be covered for the next week or ten days.

From the hostel, our picking crew consisted of a small, quiet, older man from Liverpool, two Irish girls, and me. We followed the warden's directions to the edge of town and found the field.

A man approached us and said, "From the 'ostel, loik?" We nodded, and he indicated we should follow him. Already several pickers were combing through the neat rows of low-growing fruit. The farmer stopped by a large shed and handed each of us a white plastic bucket.

"Nah ye pick the froo' and pu' i' in 'ere, en there's no more to i' 'en tha'," he said, giving each of us a container. "If i' 'as green on the top or the bottom, leave i' on the vine. If i's red, you pu' i' in the container. Nah then, your names for the record, if ye please."

Ten minutes later, each of us had been assigned our own row, perhaps a hundred yards long. I was nothing if not an eager beaver. Wanting to prove my worth to the farmer, I filled my first bucket within twenty minutes. He failed to be impressed.

Back in my row, I realized that bending over at a ninety-degree angle was not a sustainable method of picking the berries. My lower back muscles were on fire. For a while I was on my knees, going from plant to plant like a man mimicking a little person. I could feel the moist earth grinding into the knees of my jeans, and began mentally subtracting the cost of laundry from the price of beers in a pub. I tried waddling, my ass inches above the dirt as I attempted to duck walk up the row. But my knees rebelled, sizzling in anguish only fifteen minutes later.

Fifty minutes after starting, I brought up my second full bucket for drop-off and picked up an empty container.

The Irish girls were nearly halfway up their adjacent row. I hadn't gone thirty feet, and was in agony. I looked at the other pickers. Most of them, I assumed, were locals. The men wore American-style baseball caps or wide-brimmed straw hats, with gloves and sunglasses. They all picked from the ninety-degree stoop, with a slight, bouncy bend in their knees, and their picking progress was obvious.

I walked over to the Irish girls.

"Why are these people picking their rows so quickly?" I asked, not expecting an answer. "We get seventy-five pence an hour no matter how many we pick, right?"

The lassies had already looked into the matter.

"They're gettin' paid by the poond," said the taller, prettier one, in what I can only describe as the sexiest accent I'd ever heard.

"That's the way to make the best money," said the other. "If ya know whatcher doon."

That summer, the summer of 1976, would prove to be England's hottest on record up to that year. Daytime highs of ninety degrees and worse were commonplace that June, July, and August. And to this day, nearly half a century later, the people of England still speak of that dreadful summer with a mix of terror and pride.

And I had no hat.

I'd just filled my fourth bucket when someone told me the time. I had been there for only an hour and a half but was already sweating like a fat man in a sauna.

Every time I leaned over to grab another strawberry, my lower back screamed in agony. The packed earth under my fingernails was so thick and compacted that it would never come out unless I could find a small shovel. The knees of my jeans were so dirty and wet that the mud had penetrated through to my skin. My shirt was wringing wet with perspiration, and nine a.m. was still a way off. My neck hurt. My arms were sore. Everything ached. For some reason, the cuticle of my right middle finger was bleeding vigorously, making a red muck of the dirt caked there.

I just wanted to leave.

But I vowed to continue through to the end of the second hour. The man across from me, when I asked, said it was 8:40. Then, an hour later, he told me it was 8:48. He stopped answering me after that. When I finally carried my last bucket up to the loading dock, the farmer stuck his hand into the fruit I'd collected.

"Won' be able to use tha'un," he said, throwing a green strawberry into a waste pile. "Nor tha'un, neither. Nor most of 'em, by the looks."

"That's all for me today," I said, "I'll just put in the two hours and call it quits."

The farmer looked at his wristwatch, and countered, "Two hours is in five minutes."

He made me stand there, feeling foolish, for the next five minutes, then handed me one pound fifty.

"Maybe I'll come back and work some more tomorrow," I said.

"Oi dou' i'," he said, looking me squarely in the eyes.

ANYTHING IS POSSIBLE after taking a long hot shower, which is what I did as soon as I returned to the hostel. I put on my (only slightly filthy) second pair of jeans and felt refreshed, ready to take Somerset around the waist and dance. Then I crawled back into my bunk and slept for three more hours.

We had a pub crawl after dinner with the two Irish strawberry girls, a girl from New York, another girl from Colorado, a couple from Bristol, the older man from Liverpool, and myself. Somehow, I found myself attached to Rita, one of the Irish women, for the evening. Our night ended at the King's Head, a seventeenth-century pub whose stone interior, cozy wood stove, mismatched furniture, and various nooks fulfilled my every dream of a typical British country pub.

The barman at the King's Head, on learning that I was thumbing through Europe, couldn't lavish enough praise on the glories of Amsterdam.

"As much weed as you want," he said. "And a red-light district like nothin' you ever saw. The biggest in Europe."

"What about the museums?" I asked.

The bartender suddenly stopped pulling the draft beer he was working on and stared at me. But he was perceptive enough to realize, a second later, that I was kidding.

And then threw his bar towel at me.

I SPENT SEVERAL days in Cheddar, on one of which I hitchhiked nine miles south to visit Wells Cathedral and nearby Vicar's Close, a street of perfectly symmetrical stone row houses from the 1500s. The day after that I hitched a ride to Glastonbury for a look at the famous abbey ruins and laughed at all the "No Hippies Allowed" signs atop Glastonbury Tor.

A handsome, sturdy young man about my age stood

next to me atop the conical hill. The roofless ruin of St. Michael's Tower was just behind us.

"Ya kin see Dorset there," he said, pointing south, "and the Channel's just beyond. Over there's the Somerset Levels," he said, referring to the flat lowlands stretching out to the Bristol Channel. "To the north, those hills are the Mendips, far off on the horizon. To the left is Wales. And that, behind us…" he paused for a few seconds. "That's Wiltshire, where you'll find Stonehenge. Aye, 'tis a canny view from here."

His accent wasn't like the West Country voices I'd been hearing for the past week or so. It sounded to me almost Scottish, even though I'd never met a Scot in my life.

His name was Steve Hobson. He described himself as "a right pit-yacker" from County Durham, which was indeed almost to the Scottish border, and so accounted for his accent. He was a rough lad, with tattoos up and down both his arms, a thick bristly beard, and a habit of looking at you with a sideways squint, as if checking to see whether you were trying to lift his wallet. I liked him straight off.

After we scampered down the steep hill, we passed a pub called the Rifleman's Arms.

"Fancy a pint?" I asked, and immediately felt like a complete dummy once again, though I didn't know what I'd said wrong.

He gave me the sideways squint with which I would become so familiar, snorted, and nodded his head in the direction of the city center.

"Haddaway, man, 'at's not a proper poob," he said.

In the heart of the old town, at a building that looked more like a prince's palace than a place to gulp a brew, he turned into the doorway and I followed.

The George & Pilgrims Inn, on the Glastonbury High

Street close by the abbey ruins, had been refreshing customers since 1475, by some accounts. Its stone floors and
coffered ceilings didn't look five hundred years old, but
the pub was plenty old enough.

"Life is too short to waste on substandard poobs," Steve
said. He ordered us two pints of Miner's Arms Brewery
Own Ale, brewed in the nearby Mendip Hills. "Life is
also too short to waste on substandard ale," he said, clink-
ing his Imperial pint glass with my own. "I've been ad-
dicted to it ever since I got here."

He had been in Glastonbury for two days.

Steve wanted to know all the places I'd been to. He had
plans of his own to travel abroad one day but was waiting
until he could afford a motorcycle.

"I'll ride from the tip of Denmark to the toe of Italy's
boot," he said, almost dreamily. "Then I'll ride from Portugal to the Iron Curtain, and if they'll let me in I'll just
keep going to Red China."

For now, he was just spending a week off from his job
as a mechanic's assistant, touring the country's more
mystical sites.

"Goin' to Stonehenge tomorrow," he said.

When I mentioned that I'd recently been there, he suggested I return with him, for the Solstice Festival.

"It's a rock concert and a gathering of the tribes," he
said. "There'll be Druids and hippies and lots of girls and
drugs."

Weed and women were always an attraction, but I disliked the idea of revisiting a place. I was in Europe to see
something new every day. After several hours with Steve
at the George & Pilgrims, however, and several more
pints of Miner's Arms Own, I began to change my mind.
I missed live music. In high school and after, I'd attended
hundreds of rock concerts. I'd played gigs in my own
band. And I'd been disappointed in the lack of

opportunities to hear live music since arriving in Europe. A rock festival? Yeah, sure, why not?

"Aye, that's belta, marra," he said, incomprehensibly. "Now let's go to the curry place 'roond the corner. I'm clammin'."

HITCHHIKING IS DIFFICULT enough when you're on your own. Hitchhiking with two people is more than twice as difficult. It's no longer a question of whether a driver wants conversation and has enough room; with a pair of hitchhikers, he also has to consider whether he can fend off two potential murderers bent on stealing his money and car and leaving him in a roadside ditch.

Steve and I weren't exactly angelic in appearance, either, which couldn't have elevated our prospects. Steve looked like a motorcycle hood, with his stocky muscular physique and his week-old set of thick whiskers. I looked like some kind of long-haired, wispy-bearded brigand myself, in my djellaba and scarred dirty yellow backpack. Think about it: If you were driving past Sherwood Forest, would you, in your jaunting cart, give a ride to Little John and Alan-A-Dale, trying to appear cherubic on the roadside? I'm not sure I would.

Enough drivers either were carrying hidden weapons to prevent us from causing mayhem or were planning a hitchhiker-assisted suicide, because we made our way south to Salisbury in good time, despite there being two of us.

"There's a youth hostel nearby," I said when we were dropped off in the downtown shopping district.

Steve was dealing with the same sort of budgetary limitations as I was. He did some quick mental arithmetic.

"Let's go down to the TIC and see what they might have in the way of a B&B," he suggested. "If we share a room, it won't cost much more than a hostel bunk."

At the Tourist Information Center, on a photogenic pe-
destrianized street called Fish Row ("Bonny!" Steve
said), a woman at the counter gave us a list of private bed
and breakfasts to choose from. We selected one at random
from the least expensive on the list, and the woman placed
a phone call for us. After confirming our reservation, she
gave us directions to a house on Folkestone Road, a
twenty-minute walk on the far side of the River Avon.

We were greeted by a smiling, pleasantly pudgy
woman of around sixty who seemed thrilled to welcome
two smelly, unshaven nomads into her beautiful brick
home in a handsome residential section of the city. She
directed us to the parlor and asked us to sit.

"I knew you'd be here momentarily when I heard from
the TIC," she said, "so I've put tea on."

She left for the kitchen and returned with a steaming
teapot, three cups, and a plate of sugary biscuits. She was
Mrs. Stone, she said, and ran her home as a B&B with her
husband. The house had been built in 1913 and was as
ornate as that date implies. The wooden ceiling moldings
and medallions were elaborate. The woodwork around
the doorways was equally stunning. The carpeting was
rich, and the furniture was old-fashioned but looked brand
new. The house smelled of fresh-cut lemons. A crystal
chandelier glowed dully over a shining mahogany table
in the dining room. I had always thought a B&B was run
by an elderly widow trying to eke out a meager income in
her declining years. From the looks of things, Mr. and
Mrs. Stone were far from having to eke.

Steve gave me a look and pulled his wallet from his
pants pocket, so I did the same. But Mrs. Stone shook her
head.

"Tomorrow after breakfast will be just fine," she said.
"Speaking of, I generally do a fry-up, if that's okay with
you. There'll be ham, eggs, sausage, bacon, cereal

with milk, toast with butter and jam, orange juice, and coffee or tea, as you prefer."

I believe my stomach growled loudly at that point.

"I can make the eggs dippy or scrambled, but you can tell me in the morning how you want them."

Steve's stomach, too, began to growl.

"Oh!" she said in mock surprise. "We've eaten all the biscuits. Let me bring out some more."

The guest room we were to share was on the second floor, at the top of a wide staircase. A demilune table in the hall held a vase with fresh flowers. Our room was immense and easily could have been used as a studio apartment but for the lack of a stove and refrigerator. It even had an en-suite bath.

"Now, let's see," she said after we'd set down our packs on the floor so as not to stain the pristine decorative spreads on the twin beds. "What time would you like to be up in the morning so I can have your breakfast nice and hot?"

Steve and I agreed we'd rise fairly early, at seven, to get started on the road to the Summer Solstice Festival at Stonehenge.

"And I expect you'll be going out to the pub tonight," she said. "We have a very nice one just around the corner a bit, the Rose and Crown. Two young men like you will probably find our little neighborhood boring and you'll want to go into town. But you'll know where that is. If you're not back by eleven, I'll leave the front door key under the mat."

I'm pretty certain that both Steve and I fell in love with Mrs. Stone at about the same time.

MRS. STONE WAS thoughtful to advise us on a nearby pub. Steve and I agreed to make it our last stop of the night, so in case we were too drunk we wouldn't be far from

Folkestone Road. Our first stop, though, was in the heart of the city, at the similarly named Bell & Crown, in a building from the mid-1300s.

Steve seemed to have good taste in beer, so when he suggested a couple of pints of Butcombe Original, I concurred, despite its name.

"They love this quaff in Bristol," he said.

The Haunch of Venison, circa 1320, was an even older pub, with paneled walls that belonged in a palace and a slate tile floor that held the ghosts of centuries. Steve ordered us two pints of Courage Directors.

"They named it that way," Steve explained, "because it was originally made exclusively for the directors of the brewery. Life's too short to drink a beer that's just average."

After several more stops along the way, we finally made it to the Rose and Crown.

"Two of the local," Steve said to the barkeep, who pulled two pints of something called Wadworth 6X ale. Turning to me, Steve said, "When you're unsure what to ask for, order a pint of the local."

We took our drinks to a beer garden in the back. A broad lawn ran down to the River Avon, which was flowing fast and deep. Geese and ducks lined the banks, squawking and settling in for the night beneath weeping willow trees. The stirring spire of Salisbury Cathedral was lit up in the distance. I can't remember ever having been in a more serene setting.

Steve told me frankly that he didn't have long to live.

"My da and my granda both kicked it before they were forty," he said. "It's a congenital weakness of the heart."

I was aghast at his matter-of-factness.

"Was it diagnosed by doctors?" I asked.

I couldn't believe that someone as vibrant as he was could be doomed to an early death, even though he appeared to take it philosophically.

"Maybe it skips a generation," I offered, having no clue what I was talking about.

Inside the pub, a bell rang for a few seconds, and a man's voice called loudly to the drinkers, "Time! Time, gentlemen, please."

"All I know is," Steve said, sipping his ale, "ya can't wait around to have some adventures, a good time. If ya want to try something new, do it now, because you might not get another chance. This is not a rehearsal. This is the one life ya get."

He took another, longer drink from his pint glass.

"Life is not a rehearsal."

24

Henge '76: Invasion of the Wallies

Morning fry-up - In the tepee circle - I am put to work at the festival - A naked girl, shivering - Respite at the hostel - The police arrive in force - We build a lean-to next to Stonehenge - The ashes of Wally Hope

"One should not ignore the fact that the festival is illegal. Nor should one overlook the sordidness of the circumstances on the site."—Chief Superintendent Frank Lockyer, Wiltshire Constabulary

"A group of drop-outs set up a sordid encampment near the monument... All the trespassers claimed the same name: Wally." —Mr. Kenneth Marks, Under Secretary of State for the Environment, to Parliament

"In other words, and not to put too fine a point on it, for some days Stonehenge was hijacked and held hostage. This must never happen again." —Mr. Michael Hamilton, M.P. for Salisbury, in remarks to the House of Commons

T he transit van was a bust on four wheels. Strange symbols and rainbows of every color decorated the vehicle's exterior, as if challenging the police to not pull it over and search it. Thoroughly. But when it stopped at the side of the road for Steve and me, we didn't think twice but ran straight for it.

Someone threw open the rear doors and we scrambled inside. The interior was dark, but I could make out six or seven other people, some resting on a jerry-rigged settee along one side of the van, the rest sitting Indian-style on shag carpeting that lined the van's cargo hold. The smell of weed was strong, and someone put a joint in my hand no more than thirty seconds after the doors closed. I was pretty sure these guys were going to Henge '76, the Summer Solstice Festival.

That morning, Mrs. Stone had rapped on our door at the B&B and stuck her head primly inside.

"I can bring you some tea and toast," she chirped, "and you can have a proper breakfast downstairs when you're ready."

"Yes, please," Steve croaked from under the covers.

I didn't object.

Breakfast in the dining room was as I'd imagined it would be from Mrs. Stone's description the day before. She had even cut up the toast into soldier strips so we could soak them in the dippy eggs.

Our bill for the night, including breakfast, was four pounds sterling, split between us. We gathered our gear upstairs, came back to the living room, and said our good-byes to Mrs. Stone. We hadn't even met Mr. Stone, who-ever he was, but we considered him a lucky man indeed.

She said something quietly to Steve at the door. He smiled and turned toward the street. As I stood in the doorway, she placed her hands on my forearms, leaned in close, and said, "Now don't you go and forget all about us back in your USA."

The ride from the traffic circle near Folkestone Road to Stonehenge took only twenty minutes. When we arrived, the rear panel doors opened to intense sunlight. Everyone stumbled out the back to a scene I will never forget.

Hippies were everywhere. Small groups of them were coming up the A303 from the west, others from the east. I saw hippies cresting a rise to the north. In the distance, hippies were climbing over the stones of the monument. They were setting up tents and tepees and makeshift shelters that resembled the sort of lean-tos a desperate mountaineer might construct at the last minute in bad weather. Scattered about the field one could find hogans, hovels, wickiups, and homemade sun shades. Pennants, flags, and brightly colored strips of cloth flapped and snapped from tree-branch poles next to the rude lodgings. The growing colony on the grassland looked like a cross between a medieval fair and an Arapaho village.

And the cars! The vehicles filling up the grounds marked the strangest, motliest collection of transports I'd ever seen. Morris Minors with peace symbols on the doors. VW Beetles in psychedelic colors. More transit vans like the one that had picked us up. Renault Dauphins. Deux Chevaux. Motorcycles with sidecars. We even saw several gypsy wagons that, for all I knew, could have been pulled there by donkeys.

Some of the campers had already set up tape decks and speakers. Rock music blasted from the main camping area, just a few hundred yards from Stonehenge itself (or "the stones," as everyone called the monument).

Steve and I walked among the other new arrivals, marveling at the energy, the smiles, the good vibes that radiated from every corner.

The cosmic center of the gathering was a dozen tepees

that formed a circle, about fifty feet in diameter. At the focus of the circle, a firepit was blazing, even though the outdoor temperature was already in the seventies.

Steve was nothing if not bold, and said we should go into one of the tepees.

"Let's see what they're about," he said, squinting at me over his shoulder as he lifted the flap and went inside.

We were the only people in there wearing clothes. The other dozen men and women were almost or entirely nude, and the smoke from the pot was thick enough to hurt your eyes. We threw our packs down against the inner walls, trying to look casual, as if we belonged there, and sat down among the others.

Someone played a hand drum, and others began chanting. Soon a kind of semi-organized incantation with a bouncy rhythm wafted through the group, completely out of nowhere, and everyone in the tepee began to sway as they sang.

Honestly, I found it phony, as if people were playing hippie because they thought that's the way hippies were *supposed* to act. The five or six girls in the tepee, all shirtless, were small-breasted and unhealthy-looking. A few of the men in the enclosure looked to be over thirty, even over forty, and their paunches hung out over their genitals. No one would have considered the nudity erotic.

Steve and I left our packs in the tepee; we had nothing worth stealing, so we weren't worried. We spent the rest of the afternoon scampering about the stones with the hippies and dropping in on other small groups of dope smokers to partake of their weed.

Yet amid the counter-cultural, hippie vibe, capitalism reared its profitable head. On the windshield of one car, someone had painted in whitewash, "Opium." Another had a hand-painted sign in the window that said, "Hash." One of the gypsy wagons was dispensing bottles of ale for 50p each. No one that I saw was selling food, though, and I considered how we would fill our bellies. That's probably why I was never a committed, full-time hippie: I occasionally wondered how I would eat.

Around six that evening, a general call went up for volunteers to help finish building the main music stage.

"We should lend a hand," I said to Steve. "Heck, you're a mechanic. You probably know more about tools than all these people combined."

He gave me the squint-eye.

"Once they learn you can twist a spanner, they lock onto ya like a dog on a bone," he said.

But he relented, and we joined the stage crew.

The plan, as I gathered, was to have several stages, all of which seemed to be half-built and awaiting completion. Steve and I remained on the main stage. By that time, the blue skies were covered in threatening cumulonimbus clouds, which soon began to piss rain on us.

A hippie-in-charge told Steve and me to collect the two-by-fours, sheets of plywood, and metal poles from a lorry parked at the side of the road, and for an hour or so that's what we did. Back and forth, back and forth, the two of us carried wood and poles from the truck to the stage, from the truck to the stage, from the truck to the stage.

"Hey, Steve," I said at one point, "are we the only ones carrying this stuff?"

But whoever had remained behind was also working, because every time we dropped off another sheet of plywood, the stage was in better shape than before. The stage wasn't tall, only about four feet above the ground, but it looked sturdy to me. It covered an area of some sixteen by sixteen feet, sizable but not huge.

Around eight or nine, Steve said he'd had enough.

"It looks bloody well finished to me," he said.

We sat down in front of one of the tepees that had a pot cooking over a small fire ring and hoped to be fed. We hadn't eaten since Mrs. Stone's fry-up at seven that morning. We were tired, achy from our labors, and starving.

"Here ya go, Wally," someone said and passed me a plastic bowl of stew.

The stew was bland. I believe it had potatoes and carrots. The ingredients were difficult to discern because of the brown sauce that covered everything. The Brits loved their brown sauce, which is similar to Worcestershire sauce. At any rate, whatever was in the pot was undercooked. The stew smelled more like boiling water than actual food. And the temperature was so hot I could have scalded my lips.

It was the most delicious meal I'd ever eaten.

Everyone in the tepee circle called everyone else Wally. I gathered there had been a chief hippie named Wally, who had died recently, and his ashes had been brought to the festival. People kept referring to "Wally's ashes." I began to feel like I was into something way over my head. Nude people cooking tasteless stew, discussing cremains disposal on the site of a mystical stone circle.

This wasn't what I signed up for.

"We should go back, I s'pose, see the job's finished proper," said Steve, referring to the stage. He'd been refreshed by the stew.

Good thing we went, too, because the rain had bogged down the volunteer construction effort. A tent-like tarpaulin roof had been mounted above the performance area, but one side of the main stage sagged a little and needed shimming to make it level. The rear half of the stage still lacked plywood flooring. Someone said the generators were operating, and a band brought out their amps and guitars, despite the stage's incompleteness.

People were aware of our efforts. Bottles of wine were

passed around. A jug of West Country cider called scrumpy, rough and dry, landed in my hands. Smoldering joints and pipes were passed among the workers. Occasionally someone would bring us an ear of boiled corn or some crackers.

"Here ya go, Wally," they would say, handing us a treat.

Meantime, though, Steve and I and the rest of the stage crew were getting drenched. The skies had opened up and the rain was pouring down—not the light mist of earlier but a full-on gully washer, as we used to say where I grew up. The bands kept playing despite the weather, which concerned me. Only four years earlier, guitarist Leslie Harvey of the Scottish band Stone the Crows had been electrocuted onstage when he grabbed an ungrounded microphone. I was worried about the bands playing in the rain, and hated to think of someone dying a horrible death on the stage I was building.

Steve and I had nowhere to sleep that night. The tepee where we had left our backpacks was overflowing with bodies, so we took our packs and sleeping bags and returned to the semi-dry ground beneath the stage.

"Should be all right here," Steve said, without a trace of certainty in his voice.

"Yeah, this should be great," I said weakly.

Once the sun had set, the temperature dipped twenty or thirty degrees and was still dropping sharply. At least the rain wasn't penetrating the stage above our heads. We unrolled our bags to sleep, but before I could crawl inside, a naked girl sat down across from us.

She was shivering so fiercely that I thought she might hurt herself. Her teeth clicked like castanets. She lay down and embraced herself to keep the cold at bay. Then she sat upright, her knees tucked under her chin and her arms around her legs.

"Where are your clothes?" I asked her, but she gave no answer.

"She's mortal," Steve said, implying she was wasted.

I looked around at the ten or twelve other people stretched out beneath the stage, but no one seemed to have taken an interest in the girl. I crawled out from our nook and found a roll of large plastic garbage bags I'd seen on the stage earlier that night. I removed two of them and returned to Steve and the naked girl. She had toppled onto her side, her knees still tucked up under her chin, still quaking like an aspen leaf.

In one of the garbage bags, I poked two holes at the bottom outer edges. In the other, I tore a hole in the middle of the bottom seam and two holes on either side of the bag. I touched the girl on the shoulder.

"Sit up," I said. "Put your feet in here."

She slid into the first bag and put her feet through the holes at the bottom. Then she put the second bag over her head, through the hole I'd torn. Her arms fit through the holes on the sides.

"Now lie down and let's smooth it all out," I said.

I took as much slack as I could out of the first bag and held it in my fist, then did the same with the other one. I tied the two pieces of slack plastic into a knot at the girl's waist, hoping they would stay together to form a kind of cocoon.

"Brilliant, marra," said Steve, watching the whole process with interest. "But why don't you open up the bottom piece so she wears it like a skirt instead of just having her feet poke out?

"Because the wind and cold would get inside, I think. And it would probably get all bunched up around her knees. This way she can pull her feet inside to sleep or poke them out if she needs to get up and walk around."

I closed my eyes to rest, but a new band had come

onstage directly above us, playing even louder than the previous one. I found out later the group was called the L.S.D. Band. Don't bother looking them up on Spotify: Henge '76 may have been their first and only performance. At least, I like to think so. They were absurdly awful. I'm not sure they were playing any songs that they had rehearsed; they sounded like five guys bashing away at their instruments without any sense that four other musicians shared the stage.

I couldn't sleep because of the noise and was getting a headache from the day's labor, the cold, the wine, and the wet. Steve was snoring about five feet away from me. The girl was on the far side of him; she had ripped off the garbage bags and was naked again, shivering worse than before, if that were possible.

I got out of my sleeping bag and dragged it over to her.

"Here, you can use this for a while, then I'll use it for a while," I said.

The girl didn't seem so incoherent now. She quickly climbed into the bag without thanking me.

From my pack, I pulled out another shirt to put on top of the one I was wearing, and unfolded my djellaba. The latter garment was only long enough to cover me from shoulder to mid-thigh, so I decided to sit like the girl had been sitting, with my knees tucked up under my chin, and pull the djellaba around my whole body. It mostly worked, but every time I fell asleep I toppled over and awoke.

I pulled a smoke from my shirt pocket, but my matches were wet. I crawled on my hands and knees to someone else who was awake and smoking and got a light. Two barefoot young men were fast asleep in the dirt, without covers.

Despite the cold and the wind and the aural horrors of the L.S.D. Band, I managed to get a solid twenty or thirty minutes of sleep before dawn. At sunrise, the girl in my sleeping bag awoke and somehow knew I was the one who had lent it to her.

"I'm going to look for my friends," she said. "I couldn't find them last night, but they have a tepee. You and your friend can come."

I woke Steve. The girl draped the remnants of the plastic garbage bags around herself out of a newfound modesty. We found her friends quickly; their shelter wasn't more than twenty yards from the stage. They were one of the bands scheduled to perform. We sat in the body-heat warmth of the tepee until around seven, then said our goodbyes, promising the band we'd watch their act that night.

"I've got an idea," Steve said. "Let's go to that hostel you mentioned back in Salisbury."

"You don't want to be at the festival anymore?"

He gave me the squint-eye.

"Yeah, I do," he said. "But what about this as a plan? We go back to the hostel and check in. We use the launderette, take a long hot shower, and get a wee kip in a nice soft scratcha before the afternoon lock-out. Then we'll come back to the festival. We can liberate some hostel blankets for a lean-to. And we can always go back and sleep at the hostel tonight if we want."

The plan made sense, I thought, despite the intended thievery, so that's how we proceeded. The warden, though, was reluctant to let us check in so early, relenting only after we told him a slightly embellished version of the miserable night we'd just spent. We may have added details about "bloodshed" and "robbery at knifepoint." The hostel was closed to all guests from noon to four, so we showered, did our laundry, used the toilet ("a proper netty," Steve called it), and even managed to get an hour-long nap before twelve. As we readied to leave—whether permanently or temporarily, we weren't sure—we each jammed a horsehair hostel blanket into our rucksacks.

Before leaving Salisbury to return to the festival, Steve wisely suggested we buy some heavyweight plastic sheeting and a length of cord for building our intended shelter. We also bought two jugs of cheap wine. We walked to the Stonehenge road, where we quickly got a ride from some other festival-goers. When we arrived at the site, I saw far more cars parked along the road than there had been the day before, and I could also see the flashing blue lights of red-and-white police wagons near the festival site.

Someone was speaking through an electric megaphone.

"Can you hear what they're saying?" I asked, but Steve couldn't make it out either.

We arrived at the gate that opened onto the makeshift festival grounds and saw at least a hundred policemen. One of them put his hand up and said directly to me, "There is no festival. It's an illegal gathering. Anyone entering will be arrested for trespass."

But scores of longhairs were simply walking past the cordon of cops and going to the festival despite the warnings. And the police didn't seem to be enforcing the ban. I looked at Steve, he looked back at me, we both shrugged, and walked by the officers.

The crowd had swelled since we had left that morning. Their numbers had grown into the thousands, with more tents and tepees and gypsy wagons spread across the field adjacent to the giant stones. Unlike on the first day, when the hippies had romped among the standing rocks of Stonehenge, a barbed wire barricade now surrounded the monument, with a heavy police presence at the tourist entrance.

The festival had become even more festive than it had been the day before. Dogs ran among the tents and tepees.

Men in loincloths flew kites. Bare-breasted women in billowing ankle-length skirts blew soap bubbles. Frisbees and beach balls sailed through the air. Ten men and women had formed a drum circle, and in turn were encircled by several dozen onlookers, who clapped to the beat and danced to the rhythms.

As on the day before, the early afternoon was rich with blue sky and sunshine, but by three the weather had turned dark and windy again. Steve and I were too busy trying to meet naked girls and smoke reefer to erect the lean-to.

"We don't need to set it up yet," he said. "Won't take but five or ten minutes. Besides, if we do it now someone might cop it. Let's see if we can find something to eat. I'm clammin'."

Finding food at the festival wasn't difficult. A campfire seemed to burn in front of every tent and tepee, and many had crude cooking grates on which stew steamed and tea-kettles hissed. (The Wallies may have been dirty, smelly, naked, drugged-out hippies, but they were still tea-drinking Englishmen at heart.) If you wanted something, all you had to do was squat by the fire and say, "How do, Wally?"

Around six p.m., we decided to put up our lean-to. We chose a spot against a rickety picket-and-wire fence close to the monument. We cut a couple of small holes at one end of our two blankets, threaded our thin rope through the holes, and tied the rope to the pickets to hold the top in place. We found a few heavy stones to hold the bottoms of the blankets taut at a forty-five-degree angle, so we could stretch out our sleeping bags underneath. Then we did more or less the same with the plastic sheeting, laying it on top of the blankets and letting it dangle over each outer edge, in case the weather turned wet again.

By the time we had everything done, and had laid out

some of the plastic as a ground sheet, the wind had kicked up so strongly that it blew the blankets and plastic out from under the rocks that held them in place.

"We're going to need more stones," Steve said, and we went off in search of some.

That's when the rain began to fall even more heavily and the wind stirred even more than before. When we returned to our campsite, the top layer of plastic sheeting had torn off and blown away, as had our ground cover. The blankets, still tied to the picket fence, were flapping in the rain and wind like a flag, making a *thwomp-thwomp* sound as they danced. Our backpacks were getting as saturated as Steve and I.

We brought out the two jugs of wine we'd bought in Salisbury and went in search of someone with a half-empty tepee who might be interested in drinking some of it with us. And if we happened to fall asleep in the process, in the warmth of their canvas shelter, so be it. Three spaced-out acid heads in the tepee we invaded were amazed by my American accent, and kept saying things like, "Say, 'hello'" and "Say, 'My feet are sore.'" My djellaba freaked them out as much as my way of speaking. They laughed for no reason and kept waving their hands in front of their faces. I'm pretty sure one of them dosed the wine, because I started peaking about forty-five minutes after we'd entered the tent.

Fortunately, the acid trip was a mild one. I was able to fall asleep not too long after midnight and had pleasantly psychedelic dreams until dawn.

THEY BURIED WALLY Hope on the morning of the Solstice. His real name was Philip Russell, and he founded the Stonehenge Free Festival in 1974. He was a wanderer, a hippie philosopher, and had taken the name Wally after a dog by that name had gotten lost at the Glastonbury festival a few years earlier. The entire crowd had picked up on the owner's cries for his dog, and thousands of people were soon chanting, "Wally! Wally! Wally!"

After the first Stonehenge festival, Wally Hope and others had remained behind in a hippie encampment. When they were arrested for trespassing, each gave his name as Wally. The press had a field day, with headlines like "Wallies Give Judge the Willies." Soon the Wallies were a communal tribe, bouncing among England's free festivals, a sort of English version of the Dead Heads.

Wally Hope was arrested on a trumped-up drug charge in London a year later, thrown into prison without bail, and branded a schizophrenic, a diagnosis that resulted in so many prescribed drugs that his mental and physical health deteriorated. He committed suicide later that year, 1975.

He was cremated, and a friend brought the box containing his ashes to Henge '76. On the top of the box were carved the words:

Wally Hope
Died 1975
Aged 28
A victim of ignorance

The police allowed the hippies inside Stonehenge that morning. Following a ceremony by a dozen or so white-robed Druids, the ashes of Wally Hope were ceremoniously scattered among the stones that symbolized the gathering, and the community, that he had started.

The festival was over.

25

At the Windmill with Harry Luck Twelvetrees

Letters from home - Abandonment on the roadside - A good walk spoiled by Andy - Fiddle tunes in a country pub - Beers for Harry - Did Gordon kill any Jerries at Ypres? - Enough snuff

I was relieved to find three letters waiting for me in London in care of general delivery.

One was from my grandma, telling me what all the relatives had been up to. One was from my Dad, telling me all about the Dodgers' line-up that season. And one was from my Mom, telling me to be careful. My Mom had also stapled a five-dollar bill to her letter. She *stapled* it, fearing, I'm certain, that it would accidentally flutter onto the floor unnoticed as I pulled the letter from the envelope.

Fat chance.

I'd just arrived in the city from Southampton, where I'd gone with Steve after the festival. We'd walked around the docks to look at all the ships, and we'd drunk beer in a couple of sleazy waterfront dives. But I found the huge port city uninteresting and wanted to move on.

Steve decided to go with me to London, even though he would have to return to his job up north in a day or two. At the onramp to the motorway, where we stuck out our thumbs for a lift, the first car that came by was a two-seat sportster.

"I can take one of you," said the driver, a well-dressed man in his forties. "If you like."

I looked at Steve, shook him by the hand, and placed my backpack in the small storage space behind the passenger seat.

"Let's meet up at the hostel in Earl's Court," I said.

Steve looked stunned. We'd become fast friends almost overnight and had shared some wild times. The doomed lad hadn't expected me to abandon him.

"But if we don't manage to connect, all the best, Steve," I said. "Good luck with everything." As the driver pulled onto the roadway, I turned my head and called to him one last time. "We had a blast, right?"

I half expected that he would shout, in parting, "And don't forget! This is not a rehearsal!" But he simply stood there, mouth half-open, bewildered by my unexpected departure.

And rightly so.

To this day, decades gone by, I can't explain why I left him there, so suddenly, without explanation. I don't *know* why. I know only that I still have nauseating guilt over it. I feel worse yet when I recall that I didn't even book into the Earl's Court hostel.

My main reason for wanting to stop in London was to check for mail. Once I had my letters in hand, I decided to move on north. I boarded a commuter train that same afternoon from St. Pancras station for the twenty-five-mile ride to the entirely forgettable St. Albans City, where I stayed at a brick youth hostel in the former Memorial Hall ("For those who gave their lives in the Great War").

The next day I hitched to a small village, in Northamp-
tonshire, called Badby. If I'd been a painter, I would have
been charmed by the seventeenth- and eighteenth-century
buildings, the thatched roofs, the handsome Anglican
church, and the crooked headstones in the churchyard
cemetery. But what could a non-artist do? I spent most of
the afternoon and evening two miles away in the larger
town of Daventry, which at least had ten or twelve pubs
to prevent the locals (and the odd hitchhiker) from shooting themselves out of boredom.

In the morning, I started on a walk through the countryside with a fellow hosteler, a thirty-two-year-old engineer from London named Andy, who had recently lost his
job because of circumstances "that have absolutely nothing to do with me whatsoever," he said emphatically. Not
that I had asked. His lack of self-worth was apparent in
his constant boasting. He told me about his "fab flat,"
about his "gorgeous girlfriend," and about his engineering degree from Cambridge ("very, very difficult to ob-
tain"). Andy's constant chattering, mainly about himself,
put a damper on my twelve-mile hike through the surrounding woods, wheatfields, meadows, and country
lanes.

That night three of us from the hostel (*not* including
Andy) went to Badby's pub, the Windmill, a seventeenth-
century thatched-roof brick inn whose small, homey interior looked like grandma's house, if grandma were a character out of Dickens with a penchant for cheery log fires
in the hearth, mismatched upholstered couches and
chairs, flagstone floors, rough-timber-beamed ceilings,
and a small wooden bar full of beer and whisky. Some
grandma.

The people who came and went that evening were a
picture of English village life, with farmers in boots,
proto-punks in leather jackets and spiky haircuts, retirees

in knitted vests and tweed jackets playing chess, a minister smoking a pipe contemplatively and clasping a half pint of beer at a table, and a middle-aged couple holding hands while sitting in side-by-side lounge chairs. I felt as if I'd walked uninvited into a neighborhood party.

We'd been there long enough to drink a couple of pints when a middle-aged man near the small bar called to a lanky elderly gentleman on the far side of the pub who had just entered with a smaller, pudgier man.

"Harry!" he said in a loud voice. "Harry Luck Twelvetrees. D'ja bring yer fiddle?"

Several other patrons began to encourage Harry.

"That's right, Harry," said one. "Give us a tune."

The codger named Harry must have been in his eighties from his appearance. But he was tall and erect, with a military bearing and a lavish white mustache. He wore a cloth cap (which he removed to reveal a full head of hair as white as an angel's wing), a tweed jacket over a rough, plaid shirt open at the neck, and gray slacks with bicycle clips still clasped above the ankles. On the table where he was planning to sit was, indeed, a violin case, which he had just placed there.

"I'll just get something to wet my insides first, if you please," he said.

The bartender didn't wait for Harry's order, but had already pulled a pint of beer and even carried it over to the old man's seat, something I hadn't seen him do for anyone else that night. When he returned to the bar, he turned off some of the overhead lights, which made the fire in the hearth seem to glow even more fiercely.

"Well, I know only two or three tunes," Harry said, which was obviously untrue because everyone in the pub laughed when he said it. "So you may recognize this one."

I was unfamiliar with traditional Celtic music—which wasn't normally found in pubs in the English Midlands—

and was delighted by Harry's interpretation of the lively, complex melodies. He played jigs and reels, bouncy numbers that compelled the crowd to clap in time or sway from side to side. Harry himself moved only his right forearm and the fingers of his left hand, but was otherwise still, concentrating on the sound.

"That deserves a drink," he said when he stopped, and everyone laughed as he lifted his pint glass and took an especially long swallow.

He played one more "set," three different tunes linked together without a break in between, then placed the fiddle back in its case.

I was so moved by what I'd heard that, despite my constant poverty, I told the bartender that I wanted to buy Harry a beer.

"That's not necessary, younker," he said, using a back-country phrase for *young man.* "But if you want to carry over another pint on me, I'd be obliged."

I took the glass of lager he'd pulled and walked across the room to where Harry Luck Twelvetrees sat with the other old man. They both looked up at me as I stood there.

"I told the bartender I'd bring this to you," I said, setting down the pint.

Harry reached across the table and placed his hand on the other man's arm.

"He means barman, Gordon," Harry said. "I do believe he's a Yank. They call them bartenders over there."

Gordon irritably withdrew his arm from Harry's grasp.

"I know what a bartender is, Twelvetrees!"

Gordon looked to be as old as Harry, and they were obviously longtime if slightly crotchety pals. They had both been born in Badby, as they later told me, had gone to school together, and had enlisted at the same time in the First World War.

"Now that was a *real* war," said Gordon, directing his

full attention to me, as if I'd argued otherwise. "Not like this jungle shooting you have today. *Bah!* Never even *see* the enemy. When you killed a man back in our day, you had to look him in the eye, face-to-face. That's the kind of war *we* had to fight, Sonny Jim."

I was Sonny Jim, from the looks of things, and I don't think Gordon meant it nicely.

Whereas Harry had the physique of a former athlete, Gordon was short and squat. He wore a necktie that seemed to be choking him and making his face crimson. Like Harry, he wore a tweed coat and had bicycle clips still attached to his pants legs. I imagined Harry pedaling over to Gordon's farmhouse, whistling at the door, and the two of them riding through the dark lanes they'd known since boyhood to the Windmill Inn.

"You never killed anyone, Gordon," said Harry, gently. "I was attached to your elbow the whole time, now, wasn't I?"

Gordon ignored his friend and looked at me, almost angrily, as if I was the one who had accused him of making up war stories.

"Did I not! I left two Jerries at peace with my bayonet at the third Battle of Wipers," he said, mispronouncing the Belgian city of Ypres. "I shall never forget that day, the third of September, nineteen-seventeen, a Thursday."

He turned back to Harry and continued, mockingly.

"And where was you, Harry? As I recall, you was in a RAMC field hospital with a particularly debilitatin' case of the skitters."

"They were afraid I would become dehydrated, Gordon," Harry replied.

Gordon turned back to me and said, "Codswallop. Irritable Bowel Syndrome is what it was. Ask him if he's still got it. Go ahead and ask him. Irritable Bowel Syndrome. He'll be bustin' for the bog any time now."

"I also have Irritable *Gordon* Syndrome, which is much worse," Harry said, calm as ever.

We were interrupted by a man from a nearby table who held out a small rectangular tin container.

"Harry?" he said, offering the tin. "Gordon?"

The two elderly gentlemen reached into the canister with a thumb and forefinger and plucked out a small amount of the contents. Then the man held the container in front of me. I looked at him questioningly, as I had no idea what he was offering.

"Snuff," he said. "Just a pinch, no more."

Harry Luck Twelvetrees put his pinch up to one nostril and sniffed it in with a quick, violent snort. Then Gordon did the same. I followed suit but inhaled too much. As soon as I snorted the powdery tobacco, I knew I had made a terrible mistake. My head raged, my face was on fire, and I was dizzy.

Gordon began to laugh hard and slapped the table with his fat hand. Harry tried to hide a slight smile.

"Dip your finger in your beer, lad," he said, "and let a drop run down your nostril. You'll be right as rain in a trice."

I did as Harry recommended, tilting my head back to inhale a bit of beer, which only made Gordon laugh all the harder.

"I guess that'll be the last time you challenge *my* war record, Sonny Jim," the old coot said between outbursts of laughter. "I guess no more of that from you!"

26

The Sex Lives of
Hitchers and Hikers

*Kneecapping, at best - To the Lakelands - The fearsome
Lady Dowager - In Keswick, 'touristy' can be a compli-
ment - Laughed at by louts at the Dog & Gun - A hidden
swimming hole - Seven angels in underwear - I fall in love
again*

I an feared he could never go home. The Belfast native lived now in England and worked for the British Army in a civilian capacity.

"That's why I won't go see the family," he said. "Anyone finds out I'm tied up with the British Army, it won't
just be me they go after but me ma and da, as well. I won't
stand a feckin' chance. I go back and the UVF will kill
me for being Catholic or the Provos'll kill me for working
with the British Army. The best I could hope for is a knee-
cappin' from one side or t'other."

We were headed toward the cathedral city of Lincoln,
about an hour north. Ian pulled off the motorway and
bought an ice cream bar for each of us at a roadside kiosk.

He was only in his mid-thirties but was nearly bald. To hide it he had let the hair on one side of his head grow long and combed it over the bald spot. We sat on an outdoor bench to eat our ice cream bars; whenever a breeze came up, he reactively placed the palm of one hand on top of his head to hold the comb-over in place.

"I reckon livin' in the States, you don't have to worry about such things as the Troubles," he said. "Although I hear your people in Boston, Pennsylvania, are grand supporters of the IRA."

He was referring to NORAID, the Irish Northern Aid Committee, an Irish-American fundraising group that was frequently accused of diverting money to the Provisional Irish Republican Army.

"If I could raise the cash," Ian said, "I'd bring me whole family over here, just be done with all that shite."

The violence wasn't limited to Northern Ireland. The previous August, the IRA had set off a time bomb in a Surrey pub that injured thirty-three patrons. The next day another IRA time bomb was discovered and disarmed in the busy London shopping area of Oxford Street. The day after *that,* an explosive-ordnance specialist was killed trying to defuse an IRA booby-trap bomb on a crowded avenue just steps from Kensington Palace, home to various members of Britain's royal family.

Ian's safety concerns were not idle.

I'd gotten past my fairy-tale views of Britain. When I arrived, I had expected a made-up land of red-coated gentry drinking sherry on horseback as they prepared to ride to hounds, peasant farmers tugging a forelock as they passed the country squire at the gate to his stately manor, old curiosity shops, half-timbered houses tilting picturesquely over cobbled streets, pretty girls in short-short miniskirts in Carnaby Street, and grandmotherly widows selling bird seed to feed the pigeons in Trafalgar Square.

But too many boring towns, examples of latent racism, and news of sectarian violence had dulled my naïve expectations.

After having seen London, I figured England's other large cities held little that could compare. I had originally planned to carry on the next day to York, but when a ride came along from someone going all the way to the storied Lake District, nearly four hours away in mountainous Cumbria, I took it.

"Yep," I said, "that's where I'm headed."

Cockermouth, where I stopped for the night, was an active market town with plenty of restaurants, pubs, and shops in the central business district and enough listed buildings to keep a history buff busy for days. Among the sites I hoped to see were the birthplace of the poet William Wordsworth and Cockermouth Castle.

The Wordsworth home, a large but plain Georgian townhouse in the business district, disappointed me. It displayed few of the poet's possessions. The docents gave as much attention to the garden as to the house's interior furnishings. But I had to take some responsibility too: Despite being an English major, I knew virtually nothing about Wordsworth, neither the man nor his poetry.

From there, Cockermouth Castle was an easy half-mile stroll away. The iron gate and the thick foliage alongside it obscured any view of the castle itself. I finally came to the gate, along the aptly named Castlegate Road, but found it locked, with no signs indicating opening and closing hours. Cockermouth, I knew, wasn't interesting enough for me to spend two nights, so if I wanted to see the castle, it was now or never. A skinny guy like me could worm through a section of the fence, which is what I did.

What a charmer, I thought—a homey sort of castle, with some crumbling parapets, a sturdy keep, and an air of domesticity. The castle had just enough mixture of bold and old to make it intriguing, as if it had plenty of stories it could tell. The twelfth-century structure played significant roles in the Wars of the Roses and the English Civil Wars, after which Parliament ordered the castle dismantled. Much of it had since been restored, but parts of it were still in ruins as I explored the exterior and grounds. I placed a hand on the castle walls and marveled at their age.

I continued skirting the castle's perimeter when I saw someone trotting toward me. He was a middle-aged man wearing a long leather apron, gloves that ended above his wrists, and a blue cotton work shirt whose rolled-up sleeves revealed hairy forearms. In one hand he held a pair of pruning shears and in the other a spade.

"Who are you?" he demanded. He seemed frightened, but not of me. "What are you doing here? How did you get *in* here?"

I told him that I'd just come through the fence because I didn't see any keep-out signs.

"Oh," he moaned. "Lady Egremont is going to have my head if she catches you here." He looked worriedly behind him, then back at me. "Come on, come with me. Lively, if you please."

At the main entrance, he unlocked the bolt and pulled the gate open barely enough for me to squeeze through.

"Come for the festival in July," he said, hurriedly, inviting me back and shooing me away at the same time. "The Dowager usually opens the grounds to visitors during the festival."

The Dowager, Lady Egremont. I had trespassed on the Dowager's estate. I was pleased with myself. I wanted to meet her, have some tea and crumpets with her, sit by the fire with her, stroke her hump, and gently wake her when she dozed off in the midst of our polite conversation.

Maybe I *would* return in July, as the gardener had suggested.

THE ENGLISH LAKE District, which included Cocker-mouth, was a large region in northwest England. Wedged between Wales and Scotland, it contained what many believed to be the most beautiful landscapes in the British Isles. The tallest mountain and the deepest lake in all of England were there. The villages were like nineteenth-century paintings, so pretty they cried out to be captured in art, and could be found at every turn, on the mountain-sides, in the deep dales, alongside sparkly lakes. The Lakelands, as the district was often called, had some of the best fishing in the nation. A national park, not surprisingly the most popular one in England, lay within its borders.

I thought I might spend another day or two in that rugged, eye-pleasing countryside, but somewhere other than in Cockermouth. The next morning, I set out for Keswick, another Lake District market town, which the people there pronounced *KEZ-ick*, as if the letter *w* were too much to deal with. The town claimed Samuel Taylor Coleridge as a former resident, but like my penetrating knowledge of Wordsworth, I knew Coleridge by name only and, apart from a single reading of "The Rime of the Ancient Mariner," not by his poetry.

The River Greta ran along the edge of Keswick. The hostel, in an old watermill (like the one in Cockermouth), sat right at its edge. But by the time I arrived, the hostel had locked everyone out and wouldn't reopen until four. I stashed my backpack under a bridge by the Greta where no one would bother to look for it, then wandered around the agreeable little settlement.

I've always had a fondness for tourist towns. When people complain that this place or that is "too touristy," I almost always respond, "Well, why do you think people go there if not for the fact that it's historic or picturesque or full of activities or has lots of good restaurants?!" There's a *reason* that some destinations are "touristy." They're usually *interesting*.

Keswick, a touristy town, no doubt, attracted visitors primarily because of the utter beauty of its surroundings. Steep, stunning volcanic and slate mountains rose from all sides of Derwentwater, the sprawling glacial lake on whose northern shore the town stood. Stately spruce trees stippled the landscape, and emerald grass covered the meadows and the mountain slopes.

Keswick was full of visitors on that hot, sunny day, thronging the pubs, cafés, coffee bars, gelaterias, pizzerias, and shops selling Cornish pasties, crafts made of Lakelands slate, outdoor gear, candy, suitable-for-framing posters of Lake District scenes, and gift boxes of locally brewed ales and ciders. The market square had competing pubs facing one another on either side and, at the far end, an old clock tower rising above something called the Moot Hall. In July, the town would celebrate the seven-hundredth anniversary of the market charter granted to Thomas de Derwentewatere (after whom the lake was named and misspelled) and his heirs by Edward I. All the tourists I saw that day were happy—and why wouldn't they be, in such a place as Keswick?

A barman at the three-hundred-year-old George Hotel, seeing my red face and perspiration, suggested I try a shandy, which is a fifty-fifty mix of lager and lemon soda (similar to 7 Up). When he saw how much I enjoyed that refreshing drink on the hot afternoon, he recommended an equally restorative beverage, but one that didn't dilute the beer as much. In a lager and lime, as he called it, the bartender added just enough lime juice, an ounce or two, to give the beer a citrusy kick. I couldn't imagine a more ideal drink on a bright, eighty-degree afternoon.

Later, at the nearby Dog & Gun, everyone in the pub laughed when I conspicuously ordered a lime and lager. The only one who didn't laugh was the bartender, an older gent in a white shirt and black tie with an apron tied at his waist.

"Are you sure that's what you want, sir?" he asked.

I looked over my shoulder to see a half-dozen locals watching me order a drink like I was playing a scene in a silly TV sitcom.

"I just had one at the George a little while ago," I said to the other patrons, somewhat defensively.

"I suppose they *would* serve a lime and lager at the George," one man said, cracking up his mates. "You'd think they'd've got it right after all these years!"

The bartender, still unsmiling, told me that what I wanted was a lager and lime, but he could see that I didn't understand his meaning.

"Y'see, if you want your beer flavored by the lime, you ask for a lager and lime," he explained. "If you want a glass of lime juice flavored with some beer, you might ask for a lime and lager. But I wouldn't suggest it."

The funny boys behind me, on hearing this, laughed even harder. I decided not to storm out in a huff. Instead, I turned again to my appreciative audience, smiled sheepishly, and shrugged my shoulders.

"What can I say?" I said. "I'm a bloody Yank."

I FELL IN love again, but only after an exhausting day of hitchhiking. Since coming to the Lake District, I had wanted to see Lake Windermere, the largest natural lake in England. The park near my family home in La Mirada was named after Windermere because of its own body of water, a one-acre reservoir. But I had no luck getting a ride on the winding mountain road, so instead walked to the A66 motorway, heading east. I eventually made my way to Kirkby Stephen, another ancient market town in the Lakelands, but much smaller than Keswick. My map showed a river flowing through it, and I immediately set off in search of a swimming hole.

A slot canyon near the Stenkrith Bridge, a mile south of the market square, offered just the place for a dip. The water flowed faster and deeper there, rushing among limestone boulders, creating small falls and cascades. Hidden by some bushes, I changed into my cut-off jeans, then tip-toed into the icy waters. I stayed there most of the afternoon, switching between reading a sci-fi novel called *Wild Card* and taking more dips in the swimming hole.

That night I stayed at a spartan, stone-fronted hostel on the village's High Street that had no live-in warden, just a list of chores from which each guest was obliged to choose one. I was the only guest.

I returned to the swimming hole the next afternoon and was astounded to see seven nubile nymphs splashing in the water in their underwear. I was already wearing cut-offs, still damp from the previous day, and called to them from the shingle river bank.

"Mind if I join you?"

They could hardly say no, and were all smiles and waves indicating I could come in as I pleased. The healthy young women had just finished their first year at the University of Bristol and were now spending part of the summer walking the Coast to Coast Trail, which had been completed only four years earlier. Their trek had begun in St. Bees on the Irish Sea. Over two weeks they planned to walk 182 miles through the Lake District and across the Yorkshire Dales to Robin Hood Bay on the North Sea. They stayed at a different hostel every night. Kirkby Stephen marked the end of their first week, though the town was shy of the halfway mark. The young women would make up the difference on the Dales, where the walking was easier and they could make better time across longer distances.

We swam, lay out in the sun, and swam some more. One of the girls was especially cute, with reddish blonde hair, creamy skin, and a band of light freckles across her cheeks and the bridge of her nose.

"I bet your name is Colleen," I said. "Either that or Eileen."

She saw I was joking about her Irish looks, and just shook her head and smiled. She had beautiful teeth. *No way is she English,* I thought.

"Doreen? Maureen? Noreen? Kathleen? Irene?"

Now she was outright giggling and turning red. She was embarrassed! I knew I could go on with more names, because I had once tried to write a silly St. Patrick's Day-type of song about a man who can't decide which of seven Irish dancing sisters he wants to marry, and I had used all those names in the lyrics. Now I had to come up with a punchline.

"Is it Mabel?" I asked.

At this point, she burst into loud laughter and splashed water at me. I knew that she liked me, but, being the first-class chowderhead that I was, my initial thought was not if I could make a move on her later on but if the Mabel line could be the kicker to the song I had never finished writing.

He jigged with Maureen and Kathleen and Eileen
But none of them won an award
He reeled with Doreen and Noreen and Irene
But all of them left him quite bored
All of the sisters just gave his feet blisters
So he laid his cards on the table

To their father he said, none of them will I wed
For my heart belongs to Mabel

Well, it could still use some work.

"It's Ruth," she said. "Let's go back into the sun. It's cold in here."

"You go," I said. "I think I'll swim a little longer."

As she left for the river bank, I watched her body emerge from the shoulder-deep water. She was tall and slender, and I couldn't take my eyes off her.

The girls and I were the only hostelers that Thursday evening. A hawk-faced woman who acted as a part-time nonresident warden checked the girls in while we were all at the communal table eating the meals we'd prepared. The unsmiling warden—she looked like she should more properly be the warden of a women's prison—gave me a "don't even think about it" glare as she left for the night.

Following dinner, the girls and I went to the village pub, the Black Bull, the only bar in town with a jukebox. A few of us stood near the pub's TV set and watched "Top of the Pops." The show struck me as trite, even amateurish, as a handful of second-rate bands made poor attempts at lip-synching songs I'd never heard of. British viewers had made TOTP one of the most popular shows of the television week. "Tot pee" was an apt acronym, I thought.

After five pints over three hours (the Bristol girls did a fine job of keeping up with me), I was feeling loose and happy. Too soon, the barman called, "Time, gentlemen, please!" Outside the pub, walking back to the hostel, one of the girls noticed Ruth wasn't with us.

"She's just like this on the walk," said one of her companions. "Always lagging behind. Mark, go and fetch her, will you?"

Ruth was still at our table, staring moodily into her empty pint glass. As Steve might have said back at

Stonehenge, she looked mortal. But when I tapped her shoulder, she looked at me as clear-eyed as a school-teacher.

"Time to go home, Mabel," I said, wanting to make her laugh.

Outside again, I saw that the rest of the girls had gone on and were about a hundred yards down the High Street. Ruth held me lightly by my upper left arm and leaned against my shoulder.

"Can you make it all the way to the hostel, Eileen? Or is it Noreen?"

She made a pouty-lipped face and looked at me accusingly.

"We've known each for eight hours and already you've forgotten my name is Mabel," she said in mock indignation. "I don't think I like you anymore."

Inside the hostel's communal kitchen a tea kettle was already whistling by the time we walked in. Six young women peered out the kitchen doorway at Ruth and me, and, as if in a bad TV comedy, turned quickly away and scattered when I caught them staring.

Ruth was not plastered, as I first thought, but just a little drunk and silly. We all were.

One of the walkers poured the tea. During the past four weeks, since arriving in England, I had learned to enjoy "a nice cuppa," as the Brits would say, despite my having been a diehard coffee drinker since age twelve. I was even learning to distinguish between some types of tea, prefer-ring robust black blends like English Breakfast and loath-ing teas that had any foreign additives, like the oil of bergamot that defiled Earl Grey. I learned that you should swirl boiling water in a teapot and empty the water *before* steeping a full pot of tea. Heck, with my greatly enhanced knowledge of pubs and teas, I probably qualified for a British passport.

Several of the young women finished their tea and tod-dled off to their bunks in the girls' sleeping quarters. The rest of us chatted quietly in the common room until nearly midnight. I couldn't imagine how these seven young women were managing to hike an average of thirteen miles a day over fairly rough terrain if they were drinking four or five pints of lager and staying up until twelve every night. I never could have done it.

Ruth sat on a sofa next to me, her right arm pressing against my left, her head lolling onto my shoulder. When she began to snore, I told the other girls someone should take her to bed, at which point they all began giggling or nudging one another or rolling their eyes.

"I guess I'll see you before you leave in the morning," I said to the last few hold-outs as I rose from the couch and let Ruth slowly slump onto the cushions. "G'night."

In my lonely quarters, with just me and eleven empty bunks, I stripped down to my skivvies and climbed into bed. The day had been enjoyable, what with the swim-ming and the evening at the pub and the chit-chat over a pot of tea. Just a simple, pleasant, uncomplicated day. No hitchhiking required. I had nearly dropped off to dream-land when the door opened narrowly and someone slipped inside.

"Who's that?" I asked. The room was too dark to make anything out.

"It's me," said a sweet voice from the shadows. "Mabel."

27

An English Farewell

Unhorsed by the rigors of constant hitchhiking - The warden is a bitch - The spookiest hostel in all Britain - The most boring towns - "Sorry, all full" - Dover again - Bernard - The rich boy

Hitching had taken its toll. I began to hate it, but I didn't have enough money for buses or trains.

The long waits by empty roads. The vagaries of the weather. The uncertainty of ever reaching a given destination by day's end. Scenery that passed too swiftly. Packing and unpacking and packing again. Rising early to "get a good start," only to stand by a roadside for hours. Worse was arriving in a town on your list to find nothing worth visiting in the first place—West Covina with cobblestones. Instead of lingering in a single spot with a bevy of beauties, as in Kirkby Stephen, I engaged in a series of one-night stands (not that kind), looking for something that might make me want to stick around for a few days.

Consider my itinerary in the first week of July.

Thursday: Maeshafn, North Wales, was barely a village. The middle of nowhere would have been an improvement on Maeshafn's location. The hostel, a purpose-built wooden structure from the 1930s, lacked any charm. Worst of all was the warden, a flat-out gorgon, a bullying harridan. The moment I'd checked in she told me my "chores" were to wash communal pots and pans and dishes left behind by other hostelers from their morning's breakfast and to sweep the floors of the kitchen and common room.

"And I'll need it done now, thank you," she said without even looking at me.

Friday: I knew I couldn't stand another day with that ugly grimalkin at the Maeshafn hostel, so I traveled seventeen miles south to Llangollen, which could hardly have failed to be an improvement. Ty'n Dwr Hall, the local hostel, was a falling-down wreck of a once grand mock-Elizabethan manor house from the reign of Victoria. Inside, it fulfilled every notion of a haunted mansion or the scene of an Agatha Christie murder mystery. If there had been other travelers, it might have been amusing to explore the old pile, but the place was too large and spooky to investigate on my own. The nonresident warden left for the night at seven, and I was the only living person in the manor house. The wide oak staircase creaked like someone moaning. A large dining room echoed even when no one spoke and had atmospheric cobwebs hanging from its dusty glass chandelier. Eerie passageways went either to nowhere or to somewhere I probably didn't want to go, at least not by myself. A noisy lightning-and-thunder storm raged through the night. Because of the horrible weather, I couldn't even walk into town, so I stayed in my bunk, reading and trying not to notice any wandering wraiths.

Saturday: Despite a wealth of Elizabethan-era houses and listed buildings, Shrewsbury bored me. To show you how blasé I was, I spent the afternoon in a movie theater watching *Death Race 2000,* a contender for the worst film ever made (unless you are a huge fan of Sylvester Stallone driving over unsuspecting pedestrians to win a cross-country race against David Carradine).

Sunday: I hitched for eight hours to St. David's, Wales, but the hostel was full. I had to take a room at a B&B in town for three pounds, which I could ill afford. Sited on the tip of a peninsula in the far west, St. David's was the sort of place whose highlighted activities in a guidebook were having a picnic and going on a hike. My mind was growing numb. The most fun I had was removing my load from the laundromat dryer to find the milky residue of powdered laundry soap stuck in the folds of my clothes. A calendar pinned to the laundromat wall showed the date to be July fourth. The Fourth of July. The Bicentennial. The two-hundredth anniversary of the USA's birth. I tore it off the wall and used one of the pages to scrape the detergent from my still-damp Levi's.

Monday: Someone would have to tell me why I ever went to Crickhowell, because other than the fact that it had a hostel, I am at a loss to explain my thinking. Situated in the Usk Valley of Wales, the town made St. David's look like Times Square on New Year's Eve. The exception was The Bear, a five-hundred-year-old coaching inn with a cobbled courtyard, ancient stables, smoke-stained oak beams in the ceilings, and a kind woman at the bar who gave me a behind-the-scenes tour.

Tuesday: I had hoped to stay in historic Bath, but its hostel was full, so I continued hitching to the next nearest hostel, in Newbury. I checked in, exhausted, after eight that night. My journal notes about Newbury are trenchant: "A nothing town."

Wednesday: I wanted to see the historic monuments of Winchester, home to a famous cathedral of that name. But a fierce rainstorm descended on the town, drenching me as I went in search of the local hostel. I could have saved myself the trouble because—and I apologize in advance for the repetition—the hostel was full.

In seven days, I had hitchhiked some five hundred miles, failed to book a bunk at three hostels, stayed in at least four towns where the most exciting thing to do was go on a hike away from the town, scared myself to death in a lonely haunted mansion in the remote Welsh mountains, and gotten drenched in a storm, along with everything in my backpack, and all for what?

To end up in Chichester.

Chichester had a cathedral, which technically granted it city status. But Chichester's most ardent defenders could hardly raise an argument why anyone would consider the place more than a town with a really big church in the middle.

I spent all day at the movies, where I saw *All the President's Men*. I had read the book by Carl Bernstein and David Woodward and enjoyed it immensely. The movie, as movies tend to do, failed to be as interesting as its source material. But the film, nonetheless, was tense, thrilling, and full of mystery. What a life it must be to work for a newspaper, I thought.

At this stage, anyone reading my tale could be forgiven for thinking of me as an uninquisitive, restive, ungrateful lout whose special life skills were poor planning and a lack of appreciation for the wonders in front of him.

The problem with such an assessment?

It was accurate.

I had to leave England. I had to make plans. I would go back to Paris, perhaps work a few days at Shakespeare and Company in exchange for a bed. I would go north, to Holland, and see if the weed scene in Amsterdam was everything people made it out to be.

Chichester lay near the English Channel, a hundred miles from Dover. And so to Dover I went.

I was mildly surprised to find the hostel there had room for me, and I immediately felt better about myself and my plans. The next day I would cross the Strait of Dover to Calais and find bold new adventures on the Continent. I was ready to meet people, to go places, to *do things.*

The Dover hostel was interesting in that nearly every guest had either just arrived in England or was just leaving. Two arrivals from Calais that day were a French-Canadian couple, she sullen and plain, he with flaming red hair in a ponytail and an urge to tell anyone who would listen why the French were rude jerks.

"'Oh-ho, you have such a funny accent,' they say to me," he complained. "'You must be a farmer in Canada if you speak that way.' The French stink, they are stupid, and no one would ever go there if not for the food."

A sixteen-year-old boy from France was resting on his bunk nearby and came over to me after the Canadians had left.

"I don't think they had a very good time in France," he said with a laugh. His name was Bernard, and he looked like a young version of John Lennon, with shoulder-length hair and round wire-rims.

"I 'ave learned English from my records," he said. "So I tell my mother and father I must come to England to improve my language."

If what he said was true, he'd done a good job of it. For some reason, I'd always thought only Russians learned English from rock 'n' roll albums. When I told him he looked like John Lennon, he immediately ran to a mirror above a wash basin in the bunk room. He examined his face from all sides, then came back to where I was sitting.

"The Beatles are gods to me," he said. "And John Lennon is the best of them all. The best!"

Bernard wasn't old enough to go to the pubs, so that night I made the rounds with a mid-twenties single guy from the San Francisco Bay Area. He had been in England for a month but had no plans to cross the Channel to France. His name was Lawrence, he said.

"Do your buddies call you Larry?" I asked.

"No," he said. "Nobody calls me that. It's Lawrence."

At the White Horse, a three-hundred-year-old pub in a six-hundred-year-old building, Lawrence said he traveled only by train and, occasionally, in a pinch, by bus.

"Dad says it pays to travel comfortably," he pronounced, "because you're able to get much more work in after you've arrived."

At the Elephant and Hind, which had been pulling pints for two hundred and fifty years, Lawrence told me that he would be joining his father's investment firm after his sojourn in the United Kingdom.

"Dad says I won't make vice president probably until I'm thirty," he said, "but that's so I can learn the business from the ground up, which he says is very important."

At the Lord Nelson, a pub that dated to 1805, we had another pint, and Lawrence told me about the problems with swimming-pool plumbing.

"Dad says it will take months to repair," he said. "But I've been able to use Francis's pool in the meantime. Do you know Francis Ford Coppola?"

I was beginning to hate Lawrence

At the Cinque Port Arms on the waterfront, a pub that had been getting sailors drunk since the 1700s and probably had been the scene of more than one shanghai by smugglers and pirates, Lawrence complained about the difficulties of cashing travelers cheques. I began to wish the smugglers might return and shanghai Lawrence.

"I tried to convince Dad to just give me cash," he said, "which would have been much easier to deal with. But he said if you have cash, you're just a target. I guess you can't argue with that."

Lawrence, not to put too fine a point on it, was a rich, clueless chucklehead.

"Larry, let me ask you a question," I said. I was a little drunk. "We've been to five pubs tonight. I've picked up the tab at four of them, Larry. You're rich. I'm not. I'm poor, Larry. I'm nearly broke. Why aren't *you,* Larry, buying *me* drinks?"

Flabbergasted is the only word that comes to mind to describe his reaction.

"You don't seem like you needed anyone to buy you drinks," he said.

In his favor, he did seem a little abashed.

I was wearing the tattered Moroccan djellaba that I had used as a ground cloth for sleeping in ditches. My clothes still had the residue of laundry soap. A hole above the big toe in the canvas of my blue sneakers had recently presented itself, along with my sock-encased big toe. I hadn't shaved for more than a week. I was the last person on earth who looked like he could pay for drinks.

"Okay," I said. "I see. But let me ask you another question, Larry. Why the hell are you staying at youth hostels? From the looks of it, you could be staying at nice B&Bs or hotels."

Lawrence took another sip of the pint I'd paid for.

"Dad thought it would be a good idea," he replied. "He said it would be a way to make friends while I was here."

WHEN WE RETURNED to the hostel, Bernard, the teenage French boy, was waiting for me.

"I 'ave a great idea," he said. "You should come with me to my 'ome in Hesdin. You can meet my parents and my sister and stay at our 'ouse. Then we can go to Paris."

It would prove to be a painful way to begin my last weeks of travel. But it would also lead to a revelation that would change my life.

28

The Epiphany

Bernard's family - Like fattening a goose - The bomb craters remain - A worried mother - Paris again - My Italian flower-selling neighbors - Bernard the bore - A revelation

B ernard and I walked to the ferry building the next morning, a Sunday, and bought passage to Boulogne, which was closer than Calais to his family home in Hesdin. His mother met us at the docks and drove us to their small but well-kept modern suburban-style house on the village outskirts.

They kept giving me food. It seemed like we ate every two hours. We ate hearty soups and freshly baked bread dipped in red-wine vinegar and olive oil. We ate stews that had been cooked for hours in a crock pot. We had baked chicken with a side of steamed broccoli and cauliflower. We ate savory crepes stuffed with mushrooms and béchamel sauce. The parents poured wine with each serving. I marveled at the fact that they dispensed as much wine to sixteen-year-old Bernard as to twenty-two-year-old me. After every meal, Bernard's sweet mother would bring out cakes, palmiers, tarts, and galettes. But the meal

wasn't finished unless everyone consumed a quart of robust, bitter black coffee.

The older sister was away, so Bernard slept in her room
and I slept in his. I went to bed that night with a swollen
stomach. My abdomen was literally distended. You could
have bounced a quarter off my belly. It hurt—not from
having eaten anything in particular, but from sheer
volume.

In the morning the family insisted that I accept their
hospitality for another night. Bernard and I went hiking
in the woods surrounding Hesdin, which had been
bombed severely in World War II by the Allies when the
Germans controlled it. Thirty years later, shell craters
could still be seen in the meadows and forests.

"Sometimes they 'ave found live bombs," Bernard
said.

Most of the afternoon we spent listening to Beatles records in Bernard's room while he attempted to sing like
John Lennon. Bernard began to annoy me.

The food kept coming. At various times throughout the
day I found myself up against plates of rich spinach-and-
cheese quiche, beef bourguignon, and ratatouille, accompanied by potato dauphinoise, olive tapenade on small
slices of sourdough bread, baked brie, and glazed carrots.
Several bottles of wine were poured. Finally came the
profiteroles, crème brûlée, and macarons, followed by
endless cups of black coffee.

That night my stomach was not simply distended but
painfully bloated. I lay in my bed but could sleep only on
my back. Lying face down was impossible, and even lying on either side hurt too much. I slept for a bit, and
dreamed that someone was force-feeding me, pouring
great gobs of food into my gullet through a funnel
jammed into my throat. I awoke at around two in the
morning, terribly uncomfortable. I made my way to the

bathroom and, like a Roman voluptuary, forced myself to vomit the surfeit of foodstuffs loitering in my gut.

The next day, along with Bernard's mother and a cute little neighbor girl whom she babysat, we went for a walk and a picnic among the same woods and rolling hills that Bernard and I had explored the day before. Over chèvre, crusty bread, apple slices, and wine, Bernard asked his mother if he could go to Paris with me. The problem with that, in my view, was that I had never invited him to go anywhere. Bernard was a sixteen-year-old kid. But I did feel an obligation. He had invited me to his family home, after all, and they had been exceptionally welcoming. I hadn't had to spend any money on food, drink, or lodging. I would have been rude to tell Bernard he couldn't come with me.

Bernard's mother didn't like the idea at all. I was silently relieved.

"What if you can't find a campground?" she said in halting English.

"There are a million campgrounds in Paris," said Bernard. "It's impossible not to find one."

"Bern, don't forget," I interjected, "it *is* your national holiday in a couple of days. The campgrounds might be booked up."

July the Fourteenth marked the storming of the Bastille during the French Revolution, and was the French equivalent of America's Fourth of July.

Bernard's mother munched on her picnic sandwich and looked worried. Then an idea sneaked up on her and she raised her face to Bernard.

"What if someone steals your pack?"

Aha! Mother logic!

Bernard, to his credit, reached across the picnic basket on the blanket the four of us shared and took hold of his mother's forearm.

"It will be fine," he said and smiled at her. "Everything will be good. Mark will be in charge. 'E 'as been everywhere."

But I hadn't been everywhere. I didn't want to be in charge. And, as it turned out, it wouldn't be fine.

BERNARD'S FATHER WAS a harmless, funny little man whom I suspected was drunk most of the time. His passion was comic books; piles of them, all in French, were stacked around the little living room, in corners, atop cabinets, on chairs near his own. He sat in a recliner, always with a little glass of something beside him, and chuckled contentedly over the comics. He spoke no English whatsoever but had taken a liking to me. At each of our endless meals, he invariably offered me an aperitif before we sat at the dining table. During the meals, he would pour me an especially generous amount of wine and make sure my glass was never empty. At the end of each meal, he would offer me a digestif, handing me the bottle for inspection. He certainly knew how to use alcohol.

On that last night of my stay with Bernard's family, we went to a sedate festival in the village square. Strings of lights had been hung every which way above the plaza. A four-piece band played French rock songs I'd never heard before. Elderly couples danced in an old-fashioned way, children chased each other across the square and between the dancers, and the few teenagers in attendance hung out on the square's perimeter, aggressively bored. The band kept looking at their watches, as if they had another gig later that night.

THE NINE-FIFTY A.M. train to Paris left on time, as we, in turn, left Bernard's mother, father, and neighbor girl waving to us from the Hesdin station platform. Bernard's mother was crying.

After arriving at the Gare du Nord, we took the Metro to the George V station and the tourist office. I wasn't particularly hopeful of what we would find in the way of accommodations there. Just as I had arrived at a peak vacation time on my first visit to Paris, our arrival now coincided not just with Bastille Day but with the finish of the Tour de France, the world's most popular bicycle race, four days later.

Leaving the Metro, we found ourselves in the middle of a rainstorm. Not a good time to be setting up camp. Besides, as the lady at the tourist office told me, they don't book campsites.

"Then is it possible for us to get a hotel room for two for less than forty francs?"

Forty francs was around eight U.S. dollars.

The woman shrugged, looked askance, and said in perfect English, "No way."

She did give us a brochure, however, of campgrounds on Paris' outskirts.

Bernard and I hitched a ride in the rain to the Bois du Boulogne, where at a campground we booked five nights for forty francs total.

We set up Bernard's two-man tent, then spent the rest of the afternoon and early evening walking around the Boul'Mich in a light mist, the residue of the storm. Bernard had been to Paris only once before, when he was a child, so everything was new to him. But instead of reviving any sort of childlike sense of wonder in me, his constant exclamations of "Oh! Oh! Oh!" perturbed me. His enthusiasm was less endearing than unendurable.

I bought two bottles of wine and we returned to our camp. On our right were two friendly young Dutchmen, Joris and Martin, and on our left were two even friendlier Italians, Claudio and Mario. Earlier, the Hollanders and the Italians had come over to watch and help us set up our tent, introduce themselves, and tell us how disappointed they were that we weren't girls.

"I was hoping Sophia Loren would take this campsite," said Claudio, the more outgoing of the Italians. "Instead, what do I get?"

The rain had dissipated, leaving behind a pleasant night with a sky full of stars. Someone lit some logs in a fire pit, and the younger campers brought out guitars, harmonicas, and even a jews harp. The wine flowed and the pot reeked, and our playing and singing got louder and louder. Eventually, sometime after midnight, we all got tired of the constant complaining of the older campers with their families nearby, and we went to bed.

The next day, I showed Bernard some more of the sights of Paris. He said, "Oh! Oh! Oh!" at the Sacré-Cœur. He said it again at the Eiffel Tower, and again at Notre-Dame. I felt like a combination tour guide and babysitter. We stopped so I could buy another pack of Gitanes because Bernard had smoked half the pack I'd bought the day before.

"We should return now to the camp," he said around mid-afternoon, "to check on our stuff."

I told him we had no need; the campsite was secure. Moreover, we knew the campers on either side of us. They wouldn't let strangers rifle through our belongings. Not that he or I had anything worth stealing anyway. But Bernard insisted.

Back at camp, we made even better friends with our neighbors, all of whom had a fine sense of humor.

"Hello, Los Angeles," shouted Claudio when Bernard and I walked up. "We were just about to steal all your money from the tent. Now we have been disappointed."

"I guess they'll have to kick you out of the Cosa Nostra," I shot back. I sat in someone's camp chair and stretched my tired legs. "Hey, Mario, what do you guys do for a living back in…. Where did you say you're from?"

"Teramo!" Mario and Claudio both answered at once.

"The most beautiful place on earth," Claudio added. "We sell flowers from Teramo."

"They must be beautiful," I said.

"The most beautiful flowers in the world," Mario said.

"Teramo, very famous place," Claudio said. "Da Vinci, Michelangelo, Enrico Caruso, Mario Lanza. You know these people?"

I nodded.

"All from Teramo! My father was Christoph Colon and my mother was Claudia Cardinale!"

The day after that we did the guidebook routine again, with Bernard making his "oh-oh-oh" noise at Pere-Lachaise, the Arc de Triomphe, and the Louvre.

At the campsite, our new friends, Bernard, and I smoked cigarettes and drank wine. A German girl and a few other younger campers somehow ended up sitting around our fire ring and joining in the chatter. Joints were passed around and more wine was poured. I noticed that Claudio and the German girl were getting sexy-cozy with one another.

"Hey, Mussolini," I called to him from across the low blaze between us. "Are you reforming the Pact of Steel?"

Unexpectedly, he knew precisely what I meant.

"Tonight," he replied, with a big smile, "we will resurrect the Axis!"

Apparently, we managed to stay a little more subdued than the previous evening, because we got no complaints about the noise.

Bernard sidled up to me and said in a stage whisper that could be heard by almost everyone around us, "I think Claudio wants to fuck her."

He sounded like a twelve-year-old boy who had just

learned about sex. I stood, pulled Bernard up by the shoulder of his shirt, and led him several feet away from the fire, into the darkness.

"Hey, man, that's not cool to talk like that," I chastised. "Especially when everyone can hear you. Now knock it off."

I left him there and returned to my seat by the fire. The last I saw of Bernard that night was when he was walking shirtless among the party-goers, his skinny pigeon chest an embarrassment. He was holding his arms in a parody of a circus strongman.

"I am a 'e-man," he said loudly to the group in general, though no one but me seemed to be listening. "I am a 'e-man. I am a 'e-man!"

In the morning, Bernard wasn't in the tent. I crawled out into the dawn and saw Claudio and the German girl sound asleep, cuddled together near the ashes of last night's fire. No more than three feet from them in his sleeping bag was Bernard. He just couldn't leave them alone. Did he want to watch them have sex? Was he jealous and wanted to prevent it? I kicked him in the bag, but it took several more kicks to wake him.

"Are you an idiot?" I whispered angrily when he finally stood up. I pulled him ten feet away from the sleeping couple. "What were you thinking? You knew Claudio and that girl liked each other. But you had to sleep right next to them all night! You couldn't give them any privacy? You're like a child, Bern. You have to grow up."

If it weren't for the fact that I had no tent of my own, I might have left Bernard then and there. But our time in Paris was coming to a close. Bernard would go back to his family, and I would leave for more adventures.

Without Bernard.

I SPENT THAT Saturday alone. I told Bernard that he was

on his own that day, and I went into the city without him. I walked mostly around the Left Bank, my favorite part of Paris. I retraced my Hemingway journey, passing by his early apartment, his writing studio, and the former site of Sylvia Beach's Shakespeare and Company. I passed La Closeries des Lilas, Hemingway's favorite café when he wanted to both drink and work. Too rich for my budget, though. I kept walking.

The Rotonde and the Dôme had become so famous that only wealthy tourists could drink there. La Coupole struck me as too modern, too slick. The Select, however, was just right for someone like me. I wanted to be alone with other people. It had a reputation for letting customers linger a long time over a drink. The decor was in an attractive Art Deco style. At its tables once sat Picasso, Fitzgerald, Cocteau, Henry Miller, Matisse, Man Ray, Isadora Duncan, Samuel Beckett, and, of course, Ernest Hemingway.

What a life Hemingway had led, I thought as I sat at one of the Select's sidewalk tables and drank a beer. And not just his mature adventures in Cuba, Africa, the Spanish Civil War, and the rest. As a young man, almost exactly my age, he had worked as a reporter for the Kansas City *Star,* then the Toronto *Star,* then as a special correspondent based in Paris, of all places. He traveled, he wrote newspaper articles about his travels, he interviewed intriguing people (including Mussolini), and he found time to write fiction.

The Epiphany occurred right then and there, on July 17, 1976, at four in the afternoon, at a sidewalk table at the Café Select, while drinking a dark and foamy bock.

I would become a journalist.

The choice had been right in front of my nose. A journalist. But of course!

I liked to write and was good at it. I liked talking to

people. I was organized. I kept good notes in my journal, recalling events and conversations accurately. I was enormously interested in politics and current events and history. As a boy, I would rise at six every morning with my father and have coffee with him. When he finished a section of the Los Angeles *Times,* he would hand it to me across the table so I could read it. I even had my favorite columnists, especially Jack Smith and, in the sports pages, Jim Murray. We subscribed to *Reader's Digest, Sports Illustrated, The Saturday Evening Post,* and *Boy's Life,* and I would devour them when they arrived in our mailbox every month.

I was so excited at that moment that I wanted to rush down Boulevard Montparnasse and tell everyone about the revelation. How could I have been so dumb, so blind, not to have realized years ago that journalism was the path I needed to follow?

But I had to consider some practical complications—at least, in terms of college. I would have to write to my mother to ask that she make the phone calls and file the paperwork necessary for changing my major from English to Journalism. There wouldn't be sufficient time after my return home to do it myself before the beginning of the fall semester. I would have to restart my junior year to meet all the criteria for a bachelor's degree in journalism. I was already on the five-year plan; now it would be a five-and-a-half-year plan. I wouldn't graduate until after I'd turned twenty-four. So what? Who cares? I would be a journalist.

I would be a journalist.

29

An End,

and a New Start

Cigarette standoff - Tour de France - Bye, Bern - No Vicki - A free apartment stay - Amsterdam - The most charming town in Europe - Kindness on the road to Heidelberg - I lose my hostel I.D. - Pfennig-pincher - A traveler for life

I didn't have to get rid of Bernard, because, in the end, he walked out on me.

When I got back to the campground after my moment of self-discovery at the Select, another party was going on. Our little corner of the campground had become a social magnet for other young campers. I even met a German girl of my own, Sabrine. Later that night, before the party died away, I told Bernard to get his sleeping bag because I would be needing the tent.

"And I also need you to go to the camp store and buy me some cigarettes," I said. "You smoked all mine."

He looked as if I'd just slapped me hard across the face.

"I do not 'ave to buy you cigarettes," he said in a confused and hurt voice. "I bring you to my family's 'ouse. I let you sleep in my tent."

He had a point, of course, but I didn't care. I had grown to actively dislike him. So too had Joris and Martin, who pointedly asked why I was traveling with him.

"I sort of got roped into it," I explained.

The next day the Dutchmen, Mario, and I went to the Place de la Concorde to watch the finish of the Tour de France. Claudio was spending the day alone with his German girlfriend. We left the camp without telling Bernard.

I knew nothing about bicycle races, but the Tour de France caused a lot of excitement among the Parisians. The crowds were dozens deep along the entire length of the Champs-Élysées. Every five minutes or so a cluster of multi-colored racing caps flew past the heads of the onlookers to great roars of approval. Fights almost broke out among the various competing groups of supporters.

That evening, at exactly six, I stood below the Arc de Triomphe. My sister Vicki, who was acting as a tour guide for a student-travel company, was supposed to have been in Paris on that day. We'd made plans months ago to meet at the arch on that date.

While I waited, I watched a ceremony of some sort in which fifteen bent, elderly men with a great many glittering medals pinned to their jackets put flowers on the grave of the Unknown Soldier. By seven I had given up any hope of meeting my sister and returned to camp.

Bernard was gone.

"He was very angry," said Claudio, who had remained at the campground with his new girlfriend. "He packed up the tent, threw your things into the fire pit, and left."

My pack! My sleeping bag!

"I have your things," Claudio said. "I wiped off the ash and put them in my tent."

I slept that night outdoors.

A HITCHHIKER'S WORST enemy isn't a lack of traffic. It's another hitchhiker. I walked five miles out of Paris, passing at least twenty hitchhikers heading in the same direction I was. Eventually, I got three rides that took me across the border into Belgium. A young Dutch couple picked me up about an hour later. They were going all the way to Utrecht and beyond, to the east. They seemed pleased that I would join them most of the way.

They dropped me off with smiles and waves about six miles south of the city. The lateness of the hour, nearly eleven, made it impossible to walk to the hostel in town; besides, the lodgings would have been locked for the night by the time I arrived. I figured I'd have to find a clump of soft earth where I could lay down my sleeping bag. I came to an all-night convenience store before I found a decent place to sleep, so I bought a 7-Up and drank it as I walked.

A car stopped on the street after it passed me, then tooted its horn. The guy and girl inside wanted to give me a ride. She was French, he was Dutch.

"We have a place for you to stay tonight," the young woman said. "If you want."

Her flat was up a narrow, steep, almost-ladderlike flight of stairs. Inside we smoked cigarettes, listened to Miles Davis, and drank beer. Then she showed me to a small studio apartment like her own on the opposite side of the building.

"This belongs to my friend," she said, "so please leave everything in the morning as you found it."

And with that, she shook my hand firmly, as Northern Europeans tend to do, and turned back to her own room.

The friendliness, the kindness of people, is a thing of heartbreaking beauty to me. How many times did a stranger, without being asked, buy me a coffee, bring me home for a meal, give me a place to stay, take me where I needed to go because the directions were too complex, help me exchange strange currency into other strange currency, make sure I found a hotel room, buy me a beer, and much more besides? Such favors could never be repaid to those generous people. They treated me like family without knowing anything about me. Some will say their trusting nature marks them as dupes and fall guys. I say it makes them almost godly.

The only way those favors could ever be repaid was for me to pay them forward, something I have tried to do ever since, whenever I can.

THE NEXT MORNING was drizzly and cold. But a hitchhiker can't be dependent on good weather. Straight off I got a lift from two English rock 'n' rollers with shag haircuts, leather jackets, tight pants, and platform shoes. They looked like Rod Stewart's backup band. They said they knew a good cheap hostel for me, and dropped me off at a place called Sleep-in.

This hostel was a different animal from the official YHA ones I'd been staying in. No stern wardens. No lists of chores to do. The first thing I noticed was a long guitar solo from Pink Floyd's psychedelic album *Atom Heart Mother* blasting from the hostel's stereo. I was assigned a bunk in the dorm for five guilders (two dollars), so the price was right.

Everything about Sleep-in was loosey-goosey, as if the whole enterprise was being run by Ken Kesey and the Merry Pranksters. No one bothered to separate facilities by gender. After tossing my gear on my bed, I went to the washroom to clean up a bit only to find a girl stripping down to take a shower. Later that night, a couple were getting it on in a bunk right across from mine.

Outside, I went to see what Amsterdam was all about. I walked to Dam Square, dominated by hippies playing guitars and harmonicas, panhandling, and casually puffing on weed. I strolled the shopping streets along the curving tree-lined canals edged with houseboats.

Bikes outnumbered cars, and the bikers were aggressive; I was nearly run down four or five times that afternoon.

While making my dinner in the communal kitchen, I met two Canadian young men who said they knew a coffee shop where we could buy hash. A coffee shop, in Amsterdam and elsewhere in the Netherlands, usually referred to a café that openly sold weed and hash, which, while not legal, were tolerated by the authorities. Because people often smoked their purchases right there, the wags called these establishments "cough shops."

In the coffee house, customers were drinking tea and coffee from the coffee bar, but they were also toking up right at their tables. In the back of the shop, a super-hippie with hair down to the middle of his back, beads and bracelets everywhere, and a serious expression stood at a counter with a bright overhead light. Three or four people had formed a line on the opposite side of the counter, and each in turn spoke softly to the dealer, who would then weigh some dope on a scale and take the customers' money.

I bought three grams of dark green Moroccan hash, which looked remarkably similar to the camel poop I'd fallen into on the road to Volubilis.

The next day, the Canadians and I smoked hash and went to the Van Gogh Museum, where we all agreed that a guy who painted that way was certain to kill himself sooner or later. The brilliant but disturbing paintings were the work of a madman, no denying. We smoked hash in Vondelpark, then went to the movies and saw *Taxi Driver*. Afterward, we smoked a little more hash and ate a late lunch at an Indonesian deli. That night, we smoked more hash and played chess.

In the morning I said my goodbyes to the handful of people I'd met and thumbed a ride to Osnabrück, then onward to Kassel and Wurzburg, in Bavaria.

I had no idea where I was, where I was going, or what I wanted to do.

ROTHENBURG OB DER Tauber could well have been the most charming, intact, medieval walled city in all of Europe. One could circle the entire town by walking along its crenelated battlements. The block-paved streets swirled and curved and sloped, passed under five-hundred-year-old archways, and intersected at unexpected angles. The homes and the shops slanted to various degrees, their high-pitched roofs stippled with tiny windows and their window boxes bright with flowers. The people of Rothenburg ob der Tauber were perfectly aware of just how agreeable and good-looking their small city was.

Dinkelsbühl, to the south, where I stopped briefly the next day, could hardly compare with Rothenburg. It had an abundance of gaily painted medieval houses, handsome towers, and gatehouses in the city walls, but its streets seemed too wide, its churches too cold and offputting, its emotional vibe lacking the joy that seemed to imbue its northern neighbor.

No matter. I hadn't planned to stay overnight in Dinkelsbühl, anyway. I was heading to another classic walled city, Heidelberg. Getting there, though, had proved to be a problem. Rain had been coming down since I left Rothenburg. Few people wanted to pick up a sopping-wet hitchhiker.

A few cars passed me from behind, but I didn't even stop walking or turn around to face them; I just stuck out my thumb as I continued trudging toward Heidelberg.

Left-hand thumbing, I called it. A sign that you'd given up. Another car came up from behind and slowed as it came alongside me. The driver beeped the horn and I climbed in. He was an American Army major stationed nearby. He wrote down his name and phone number, told me to call if I wanted to have dinner with his family one evening, then dropped me off at the hostel doorway.

Who were all these wonderful, generous people, and why weren't they running the world instead of the warlike megalomaniacs then in charge?

Heidelberg was a lively university town, famous for the traditional sword fights among its competitive students, which left many of them with a dubious badge of honor, a Heidelberg dueling scar. The next day, I roamed through the old town perched on the side of a hill, over-looked by a castle above and, on the opposite side, under-pinned by the broad Neckar flowing below. But I could work up no excitement. In four days I would be flying home from Frankfurt. Despite the beautiful surroundings of the ancient city, I was more enthusiastic about the up-coming change in my course of study to Journalism.

"WELCOME," SAID THE warden at the Frankfurt hostel the next day. "Your papers, please."

He meant my I.D. card—the one, it seems, that I'd left at the front desk in Heidelberg. The responsibility of col-lecting a hosteler's I.D. card upon checking out belonged to the hosteler. I had screwed up. Despite having spent the night in more than fifty hostels (when I wasn't sleep-ing in bookstores, cheap hotels, or farm-field ditches), and never having forgotten to collect my I.D. card even once, I had lost it on checking into the second-to-last hos-tel of my months-long journey.

The air expelled from my lungs and I felt ready to crumple.

"I left it behind at Heidelberg," I explained to the no-nonsense man at the desk. "Could you possibly call the Heidelberg warden and verify that they have my card so that you can let me check in?"

He snorted, turned away for a moment, then completed the check-in paperwork.

"There will be a penalty fee assessed of one Deutsch-mark," he said.

A Deutschmark was worth forty cents. The total nightly cost was 10.80 DM, which left me with slightly less than four dollars for meals and drinks and anything else that came up in the next forty-eight hours. I would be flat broke when I got on that homebound plane.

At the hostel again, I showered, then lay on my bunk, where I re-read large portions of my journal from the past months. I was staggered to realize, thanks to my oversized map, that I had traveled more than seven thousand miles, mostly by hitchhiking, through Morocco, Spain, France, Luxembourg, Germany, Belgium, the Netherlands, England, and Wales. No wonder I was tired of the road.

And yet I knew I had become a traveler for life.

30

The People You Meet...

I recollect their faces, their voices, and even, in some cases, what they wore or the gestures they made. I remember them more than I recall the stained-glass windows of a church, the shopfronts of the quaint towns, the highways I traveled, or the bunks I slept in.

Peta, the Australian girl, and Mahboob, the Pakistani traveling scissors salesman, the first two people I met and talked to in a youth hostel.

Udo Kortz, the German army lieutenant who very well may, to this day, have my jacket. I would still like it back, Udo.

Jürgen, Martin, and Andreas, the Cochem Brain Trust, who were so proud to show me their town's local whorehouse and dutifully take up the mantle of Tic-Tac-Toe-ism.

Dashing Tom Starr, the expatriate English tutor from Minnesota, preparing to ride his motorcycle along the Stasi-sentineled highway back to Berlin.

Madame Defarge, otherwise known as Daniela, the owner of the bleak Daniela's Hotel in Paris.

Everyone at Shakespeare and Company: noble bookseller George Whitman, Linsey Lee and her *Edible*

Wild Plants of Martha's Vineyard, the Beat poet Ted Joans, and all the other literary lodgers.

Tony in Dijon, who cooked me a steak.

All the pretty girls at the street protest in Avignon.

The guy whose name I never knew who took me into Barcelona, bought me a coffee, and found a place where I could change francs into pesetas on a Friday evening, then disappeared into the gloaming.

The Spanish hippies who were giddy at the mere thought that I'd been to the Haight and Golden Gate Park.

Mal and Geoff, the budding architects who so kindly let me join them for a trip around Morocco, taught me about architecture, and shared with me the tragedy of the Great Seville Robbery.

Gwyn and Jane, the two foxy Welsh girls who insisted on a single room for the three of us in Madrid, and the radio-taxi drivers who helped us get out of town.

Gini and Tío Tom in Pamplona, who took me on an epic pub crawl, showed me where I was likely to get gored at the running of the bulls, and taught me to eat snails and mussels.

The stunning blonde German who spoke English and her boyfriend who spoke Spanish in their Mercedes, and our language three-way en route to Poitiers.

Brian, his Daimler, and the bitter publican serving bitter at the Wounded Soldier.

Mungo, my fellow Californian in Land's End, with his good English car and bad karma.

The seven angelic coast-to-coast hikers in Kirkby Stephen, and "Mabel" most of all.

Steve from Newton Aycliffe, County Durham, my Stonehenge concert buddy, whose sad eyes, when I took an offered ride and left him behind at the side of the road, will haunt me forever.

Gordon and fiddler Harry Luck Twelvetrees, vets of the

Great War, arguing and taking snuff at the Windmill in Badby.

Lawrence, the rich kid from San Francisco, who swam in Francis Ford Coppola's pool and would make vice president by the time he was thirty in Dad's investment firm.

Bernard, "I am a 'e-man," the immature teen whose sweet family was so kind to me at their home in Hesdin.

Martin and Joris, the Dutch boys, and Claudio and Mario, the Italian flower sellers, our campsite neighbors in Paris.

The Dutch couple in Utrecht who picked me up near midnight, treated me like a friend, and gave me, a stranger, my own studio to sleep in.

The good hippies who ran the Sleep-In hostel in Amsterdam (cough, cough, got a match?).

The faces and names of many others have slipped into oblivion. But these are the ones I will never forget, the ones who made things worthwhile. People are the authentic reasons to travel, far more than monuments and palaces, grand boulevards and gracious plazas. Give me the choice between having a conversation with an eighty-year-old war vet or shopping in a luxury boutique, and I come down on the side of the vet—hard of hearing and cranky though he may be—every time. Even the people who made me angry, like Bernard, or the ones with a perpetual gray cloud above their heads, like Mungo, still hold a special place in my memories.

I had taken some time to realize it, but here was another lesson learned on the road: People, not places, are the reason to travel.

31

...And the

Things You Learn

No one cares how you dress. But given the option, dress discreetly.

Arriving in a new town, go first to the train station, where you're likely to find a tourist information center or at least a wall rack of helpful brochures. (Or, I guess, just use the Internet.)

The Germans, according to Pakistani scissors salesmen, appreciate fine quality like no one else.

Despite what people may tell you, not everyone in Europe speaks English.

Phrasebooks, pidgin English, elaborate gestures, and humility will get you much further in a foreign land than you might imagine.

Those who travel light may have more to lose than those who carry a lot.

Ersatz coffee causes bad breath.

Tic-tac-toe isn't universally known. Weird, right?

Trier, in case you were wondering, is the oldest city in Germany.

You'd be surprised how even moderate Frisbee skills can be considered impressive overseas.

Cheap meal options: Wurst in Germany, croque monsieur in France, *bocadillo de jamon* in Spain, couscous in Morocco, cheese toastie in England.

Inspect the hotel room before you accept the key.

Paris is a funhouse. And a madhouse.

Men, leave the bidet alone. Just pretend it's not there. It's not for you anyway.

Wine is cheaper than beer in France.

Straitlaced people, Right Bank. Cool people, Left Bank.

Homesickness is a ruthless mistress, able to transform Paris into a Colorado chicken ranch.

For a certain type of woman, bookstores are an aphrodisiac.

Don't sweat train travel. It's easy. You'll be fine.

Trains can bypass a station. They have to stop at a terminal.

When you can smell your own pits, self-neglect has gone too far.

Agreeable tablemates and potluck frequently make for the most memorable meals, even when canned ravioli is involved.

Try not to prejudge different nationalities by their clichés. They're rarely accurate—including those about Americans.

Travel plans have a habit of going south unexpectedly. Always have a fallback strategy.

Don't be deceived by cuteness: Citroën Deux Chevaux are slow, noisy, and uncomfortably small—and I would give anything to own one.

Call a Basque a Spaniard at your peril.

When trouble is brewing, walk the other way.

Buildings   are   designed   from   a   collection   of components to meet an overarching aesthetic. They're not just "cool buildings."

When someone knows what he's talking about, just shut up and listen.

Bureaucracy often strives to do little more than extend its own existence.

Camels have any number of disagreeable qualities. Shun them.

Wabi-sabi is a Japanese aesthetic that finds beauty in imperfection.

Backroads destinations sometimes provide an opportunity to experience discrimination firsthand.

No matter where you are, no one is allowed to grab you and pull you into his shop. Narrow your eyes, pull away from the person, and tell him to fuck off.

In cooking, use the finest spices—or why bother?

Do not stare at Muslim women. Or anyone else, actually.

Dirt and sanitation aren't the same. A butcher with a dusty shop coat at an outdoor market may still wave the flies off a baby goat hanging from a hook.

Bargain in the marketplace, but only if you're serious. Don't be afraid to walk away from a bad deal.

When you don't have a clue, politeness and decorum go a long way.

Islamic architecture versus Mudejar? Place your bet on Islamic, every time.

To know a people, wander among their public street markets.

Thieves are ingenious. You can't be too careful in guarding your valuables.

One large measure of a man is how well he reacts to disaster.

You can't have everything, but you can have a wife.

Old men were once young.

If you ask a taxi driver for directions, be careful he doesn't flip the flag on his meter.

Canned meat with a foreign-language label is a crapshoot.

It's good to have a waiter be a little afraid of you, but you must always leave him a tip.

Weird food? Try it! Nothing tastes as terrible as you were afraid it might. And you can boast about it later on.

Visit Mont Saint-Michel. You will thank me in your prayers.

I will never be persuaded that individual humans, at their core, are anything other than kind and generous. It's the human race as a whole that worries me.

An English footpath is sometimes more a wish than a reality.

Cities require a cathedral. Towns, a good-size population. Villages, a church, a pub, and a couple dozen houses. Hamlets? You don't want to live in a hamlet.

Oxford University is a collection of discrete, separately administered colleges. Who knew?

Cromwell and the Puritans despised stained-glass church windows, and I've never forgiven them.

Sometimes it pays to shell out for a round-trip bus ride.

Decide what to do, then make it happen.

People get lost on the moor all the time. Next thing you know you're reading about them in the *Western Morning News.*

That's how the Big Boys do it: They *squeeze* you.

The English language wasn't common throughout Cornwall until two hundred and fifty years ago.

"The Combine Harvester" is an earworm worth avoiding. Otherwise, it stays with you for the rest of your life, possibly longer.

England was once a culinary desert in which baked beans over toast was considered a decent meal.

If you ever need a tall, happy, smart, and energetic human being, grab the nearest Dutchman.

Don't convert all your money into foreign currency before leaving home. The exchange rate can come back to bite you in the ass later on.

Nothing is more tragic than the death of a child.

You wouldn't think so, but picking strawberries is back-breaking labor.

A pint in an English pub in 1976 cost between twenty-five and forty pence, or forty and sixty-five cents U.S.

Anything is possible after a long hot shower.

Life is too short to waste on substandard pubs.

Hitchhiking with two people is more than twice as hard as hitchhiking solo.

Consider value, not price. The cost of a shared room at a B&B may be the same as or not much more than a single bunk at a hostel, and far more comfortable.

Nothing on earth is as filling and delicious as an English fry-up breakfast.

Dippy eggs are soft-boiled and served in the shell, often alongside strips of toast called soldiers.

Life is too short to drink beer that's just average.

When you're unsure what beer to ask for, order a pint of the local.

Life is not a rehearsal.

Nudity, per se, is rarely erotic.

Once they learn you can twist a spanner, they lock onto you like a dog on a bone.

When you have nothing worth stealing, it matters little where you stash your gear.

The larger the appetite, the tastier the meal.

Even in extreme circumstances, plastic garbage bags will never compensate for a lack of clothing.

Drinking anything offered by three stoned hippies is probably a mistake.

Gallantry, though rarely acknowledged, is its own reward.

Guilt never dies within a thoughtful man. It can't be expiated.

Shed the company of annoying people.

A fine fiddle performance deserves a drink.

Cranky old English soldiers pronounce the Belgian city of Ypres as *Wipers*.

Beware of snuff.

Never order lime and lager when you want lager and lime.

Humor might just be the most effective aphrodisiac.

Nothing warms your insides, and your state of mind, as much as a nice cuppa.

When sleeping overnight in a haunted mansion, stay in bed, hide under the covers, and hope for the best.

Death Race 2000 may be the worst film ever made.

Many young people in foreign countries really do learn English from rock 'n' roll records.

If your name is Lawrence, encourage people to call you Larry.

Always pay for drinks when it's your turn.

Aperitif before dinner, wine with dinner, digestif after dinner.

There are campgrounds in the Bois du Boulogne, the Central Park of Paris.

The Tour de France is an acquired taste.

Europe is a ceaseless banquet of the senses.

The warmth and generosity of strangers is a never-ending wonder.

Epilogue

O n the morning of my flight home, I left the hostel on
foot and walked through Sachsenhausen, Frankfurt's nightlife neighborhood with all the apple-wine
pubs. I wasn't sure exactly how far away the airport was
(it turned out to be just over seven miles), but I had plenty
of time before my late-night flight so I decided to hoof it.
Turning off the main road I found myself on a country
lane that rambled through thick woods.

The sounds of the airport, still miles away, echoed
among the trees. The reverb of the jet engines led me to
think that I was about to come upon the airport at every
new bend in the path. I finally arrived some three hours
later and found a comfortable seat in the terminal waiting
area. I was thirsty, but the terminal had no water foun-
tains. None at all. I would have gotten water from a wash
basin in the men's room, but that would have cost twenty
pfennigs, or about eight cents, just to enter. I didn't have
twenty pfennigs. I had planned to conserve my remaining
funds so that by the time I stepped into the airport I would
have exactly no money in my pocket.

Unfortunately, my plan worked.

I staked out one of the men's toilets. A woman was sitting on a stool just inside the entrance. Her job was to
keep the bathroom tidy and clean and to collect the admission fee from anyone who entered. I figured she
would have to take a break sooner or later. How long can

someone just sit on a stool in a men's toilet without shooting themselves?

Then I saw her standing in the doorway. She fumbled into her purse, pulled out a cigarette, lit it, and took a long puff. She ambled down the terminal corridor, stretching her legs and the small of her back as she walked. Without hesitating, I dashed into the men's room, used the toilet, washed my hands, and gulped down enough water to last me hours. When I left, my stomach sloshed.

Around five p.m., I heard my name being called over the airport loudspeakers. By the time I reached the information desk, whoever had paged me was gone. Two hours later, I got another loudspeaker page requesting my presence at the information desk. This time I didn't walk; I trotted. Again, no one was there. *Who the hell was paging me?*

Then I heard a voice behind me.

"Mark?"

The voice belonged to my sister, Vicki. We hugged and laughed and talked for the next three hours. She lent me money so I could buy a cookie and a cup of coffee. I kept the change in case I needed to use the toilet again. I joined her gang, which included the head of her tour company, who was my former high school history teacher, and a fun group of high school kids on their first trip to Europe. Their schedule had changed, and they were now on the same flight I was on. I had given Vicki my air-travel itinerary before leaving, and she managed to put two and two together at the last minute.

The tedious flight (in-seat entertainment units hadn't yet been invented) stopped in Chicago, where we went through Customs, then continued to LAX, where my Dad was waiting for us. He looked healthy and tanned and handsome and was glad to see us both. Vicki got her bags right away and went home with two of her friends who had come to meet her on arrival. As I waited for my back-pack at the conveyor belt, my Dad nodded at some people standing directly opposite, also waiting for their luggage. Frank Zappa, looking bored and smoking a cigarette, waited for his bags along with the rest of his iconoclastic rock band. They had been on my flight home and I hadn't realized it.

God damn. I was back in Los Angeles, California, USA!

When we arrived in La Mirada, I said goodbye to my Dad and promised I'd come to see him in Downey in the next day or two. Then I went inside and saw my Mom. She was stunningly beautiful, movie-star beautiful, and always had been, but never more so than at that moment. She grasped me around the shoulders, pulled me close, and squeezed until it almost hurt. She poured me a cup of coffee. Even though the foul-smelling brew was Folgers Instant, it may well have been the single best cup of coffee I'd have ever had, to this day. It's certainly the one I remember more than any other.

I was home at last. I sat back on the living room sofa and closed my eyes. But I didn't have too much time to waste.

I had a career to begin.

The End

Oops! Postscript

A lmost forgot," my Mom said the next morning. "This came for you a few days ago."

She handed me a postcard. On one side was a tourist photo of the Rialto Bridge in Venice, complete with a row of gondolas in the foreground. On the opposite side, next to my name and address, was a message:

Dear Mark,

Thought it was about time to get in touch with you. We are now in Venice, definitely one of the best cities in the world. We now have 20 countries behind us and everything is going really well. Our girlfriends from Switzerland met us in Paris. We head down to Greece and Turkey now via Yugoslavia. The USA is not on for us this winter—no money or time to plan things. Maybe next winter or summer would work, though. We have jobs lined up in Zermatt running a hotel ski shop, giving lessons, and acting as guides. Here are some poste restantes: Crete, 5 Oct.; Athens, 21 Oct; Istanbul, 2-15 Nov. Let's hear your news and what's doing. Regards from your Morocco companions,

Geoff & Mal

Acknowledgments

MY WIFE, KATHY FOX, was extraordinarily supportive of me writing this book, mainly by letting me hide out in my treetop writing studio for hours and hours daily when I probably should have been training our bordoodle Penny, running errands, taking care of the lawn, and handling the many other quotidian responsibilities of married life and home ownership. Thank you, Kat. I love you.

Paul Ehrlich, a keen reader and brilliant editor, kept me on the straight and narrow path with his trenchant comments.

I'd be remiss not to thank Michele and her team at the Black Cow in Pleasantville, New York, where much of this book was written. To provide a friendly place where anyone, whether stranger or regular, can work, hang out, chat, laugh, plan, or just zone out on a blue-sky morning over a large Genetha's Cabin is a gift to the community in general and to this writer in particular.

About the Author

MARK ORWOLL WENT on to earn a Bachelor of Arts in Journalism at San Diego State University and a Master of Arts in Creative Writing at San Francisco State University. He has had a long career as a journalist, starting in newspapers in California and ending up in magazines in New York City. He was on the staff of *Travel + Leisure* for thirty years, where he had more than two thousand by-lines and held an assortment of titles, including Managing Editor and International Editor.

He is now a freelance writer specializing in adventure, food and wine, and offbeat travel for such outlets as the *Los Angeles Times, Slate Magazine, The Saturday Evening Post, Condé Nast Traveler,* the *Sydney* (Australia) *Morning Herald, Frommer's Travel,* and the Travel Channel, as well as his alma mater T+L. He is the author of three previous books: *John Wayne Speaks, e-Travel,* and *Cross Purposes.*

And all because of that long, strange trip to Europe.

www.ingramcontent.com/pod-product-compliance
Lightning Source LLC
Chambersburg PA
CBHW030359130626
46549CB00004B/1553